D0576149

Eunice Boardman Meske
Professor of Music and Education
University of Wisconsin—Madison
Madison, Wisconsin

Mary P. Pautz
Assistant Professor of Music Education
University of Wisconsin—Milwaukee
Milwaukee, Wisconsin

Barbara Andress
Professor of Music Education
Arizona State University
Tempe, Arizona

Fred Willman
Professor of Music and Education
University of Missouri—St. Louis
St. Louis, Missouri

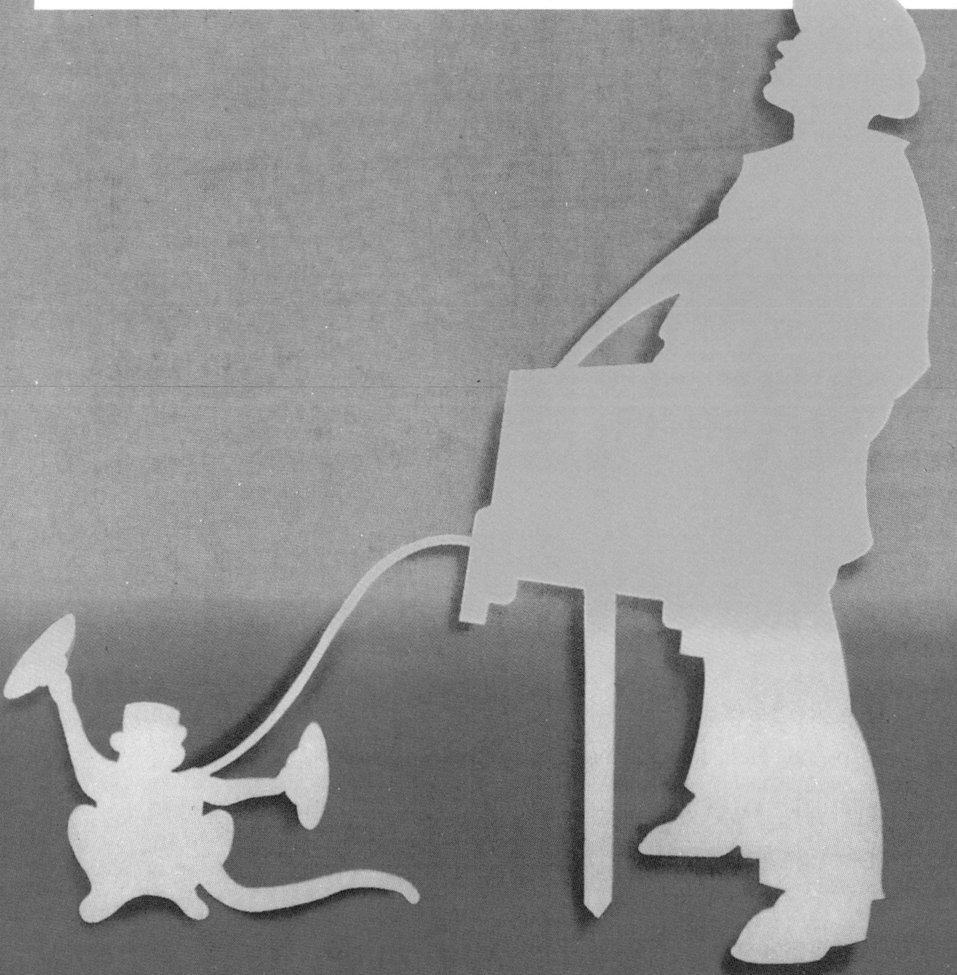

Holt, Rinehart and Winston, Publishers
New York, Toronto, Mexico City, London, Sydney, Tokyo

Special Consultants

Nancy Archer
Forest Park Elementary School
Fort Wayne, Indiana

Joan Z. Fyfe
Jericho Public Schools
Jericho, New York

Jeanne Hook
Albuquerque Public Schools
Albuquerque, New Mexico

Danette Littleton
University of Tennessee at Chattanooga
Chattanooga, Tennessee

Barbara Reeder Lundquist
University of Washington
Seattle, Washington

Ollie McFarland
Detroit Public Schools
Detroit, Michigan

Faith Norwood
Harnett County School District
North Carolina

Linda K. Price
Richardson Independent School District
Richardson, Texas

Dawn L. Reynolds
District of Columbia Public Schools
Washington, D.C.

Morris Stevens
A.N. McCallum High School
Austin, Texas

Jack Noble White
Texas Boys Choir
Fort Worth, Texas

Printed in the United States of America

ISBN 0-03-005293-9
890 041 9876543

Acknowledgments for previously copyrighted material and credits for photographs and art start on page 237

Table of Contents

Unit 1

Music To Explore

The First Quarter

HARMONY

melody

Merry Are the Bells

English Round

1.
D C D

Mer - ry are the bells and mer - ry would they ring;
Gai - ly o'er the house - tops, gai - ly through the streets

2.
C D

mer - ry is my - self and mer - ry would I sing.
sound the ring - ing bells as mer - ry friends do meet.

D C D

With a mer - ry ding, dong, hap - py, strong, and free and a

C D

mer - ry, mer - ry sing song, hap - py let us be!

How Di Do

Words and Music by
Woody Guthrie

Brisk talking blues

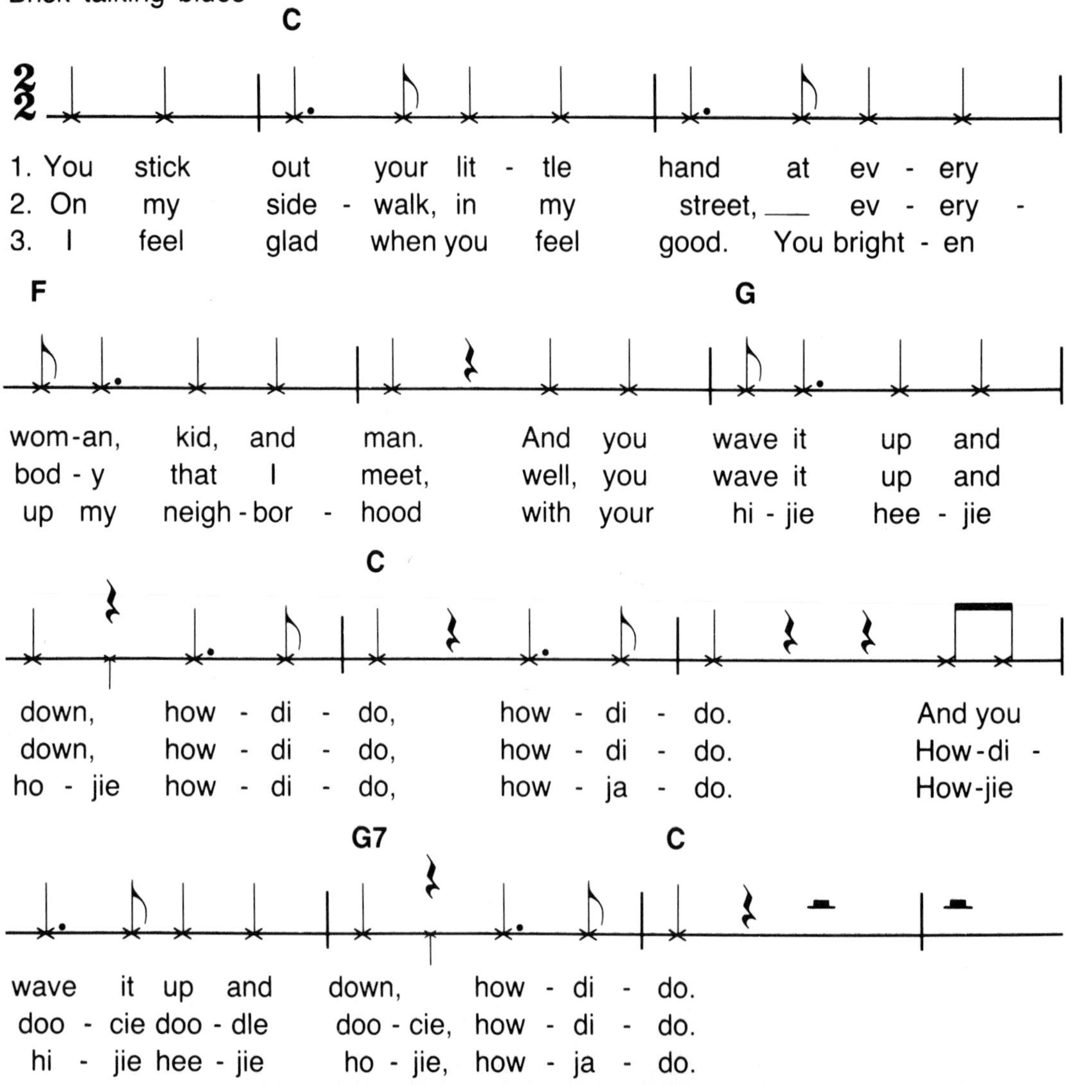

C

1. You stick out your lit - tle hand at ev - ery
2. On my side - walk, in my street, ___ ev - ery -
3. I feel glad when you feel good. You bright - en

F G

wom-an, kid, and man. And you wave it up and
bod - y that I meet, well, you wave it up and
up my neigh-bor - hood with your hi - jie hee - jie

C

down, how - di - do, how - di - do. And you
down, how - di - do, how - di - do. How-di -
ho - jie how - di - do, how - ja - do. How-jie

G7 C

wave it up and down, how - di - do.
doo - cie doo - dle doo - cie, how - di - do.
hi - jie hee - jie ho - jie, how - ja - do.

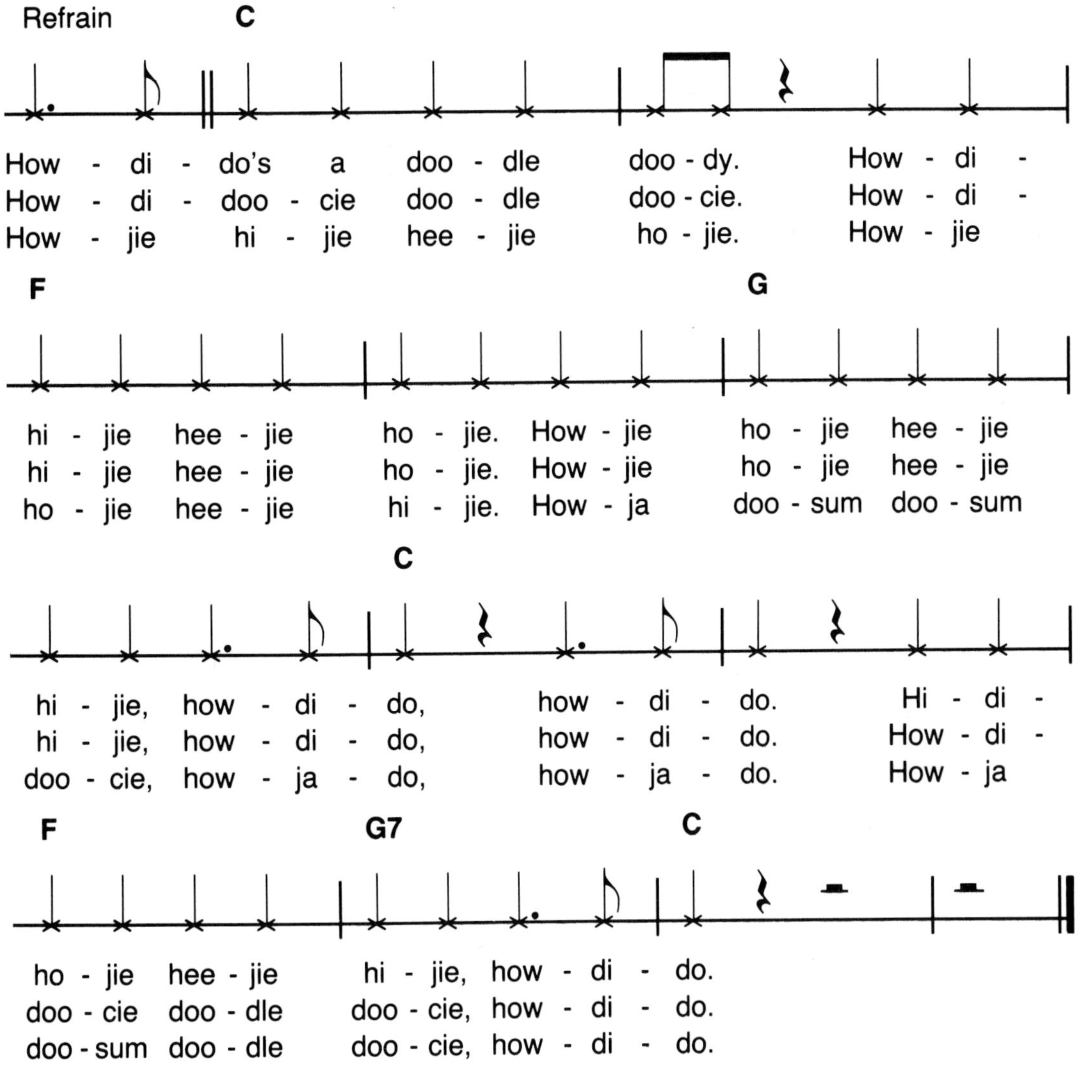
Refrain
C
How - di - do's a doo - dle doo - dy. How - di -
How - di - doo - cie doo - dle doo - cie. How - di -
How - jie hi - jie hee - jie ho - jie. How - jie
F
G
hi - jie hee - jie ho - jie. How - jie ho - jie hee - jie
hi - jie hee - jie ho - jie. How - jie ho - jie hee - jie
ho - jie hee - jie hi - jie. How - ja doo - sum doo - sum
C
hi - jie, how - di - do, how - di - do. Hi - di -
hi - jie, how - di - do, how - di - do. How - di -
doo - cie, how - ja - do, how - ja - do. How - ja
F
G7
C
ho - jie hee - jie hi - jie, how - di - do.
doo - cie doo - dle doo - cie, how - di - do.
doo - sum doo - dle doo - cie, how - di - do.

LISTENING

Tennessee Wig Walk

Words by Larry Coleman
Music by Norman Gimbel

Dance the following musical arrangement:

Introduction

A A
Instrumental
Coda

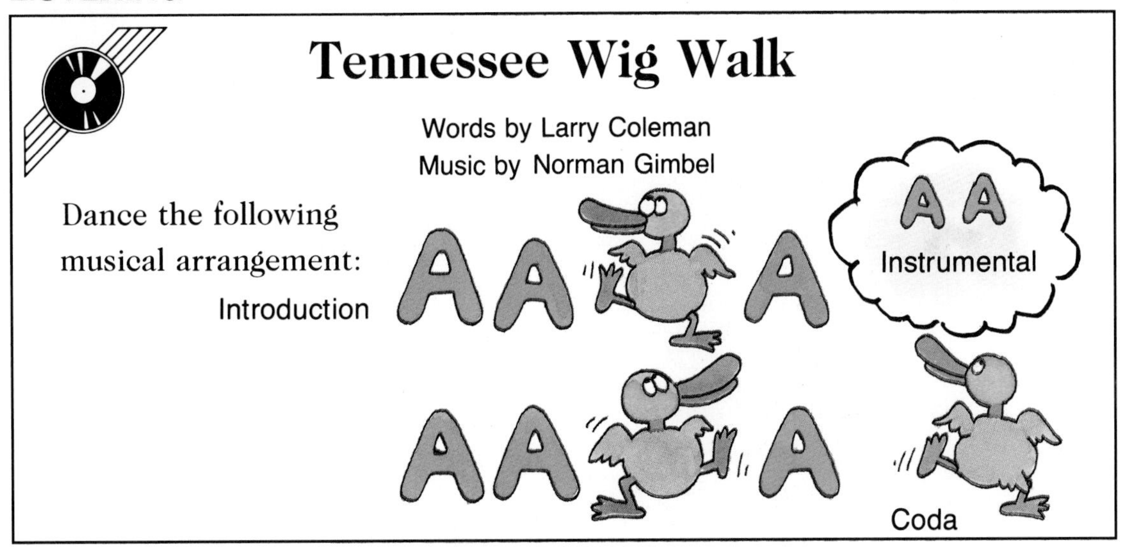

Table

by Wassily Kandinsky

Once there was a long table. Oh, a long,
long table. Right and left at this table
sat many, many, many
people.
people,
people,
people.
Oh, a long, long time at this
long, long table sat people.

Narrator: (Solo Voice) Once there was a lo----ng table

Accompaniment: ah ooh eee

Oh, a long, long table. Right and left at this table

ah eee ooh

Sat many, many people people people people. Oh, a long, long time

ah ooh people people

At this long, long table sat people.

ah ooh

Weave Me the Sunshine

Words and Music by
Peter Yarrow

Peace Like a River

Old Southern Hymn

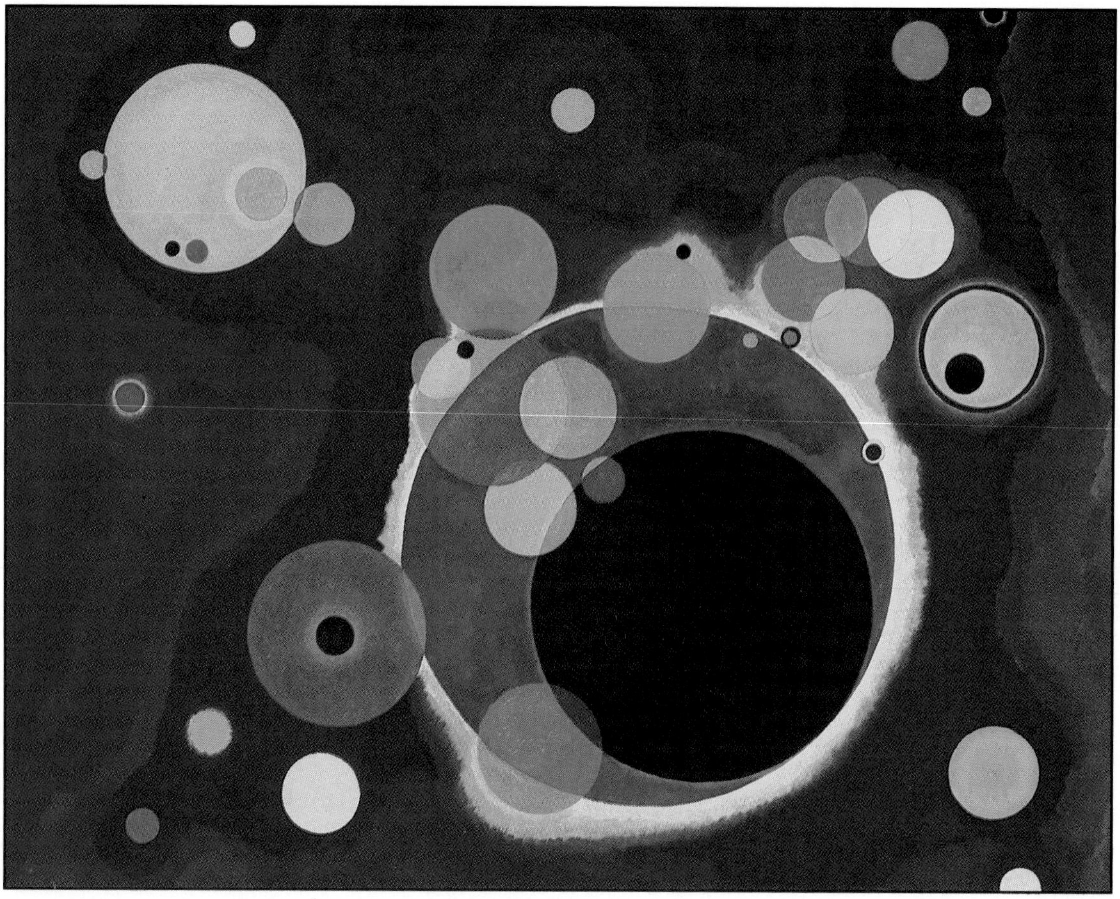

Several Circles by Kandinsky, Collection, Solomon R. Guggenheim Museum, New York.

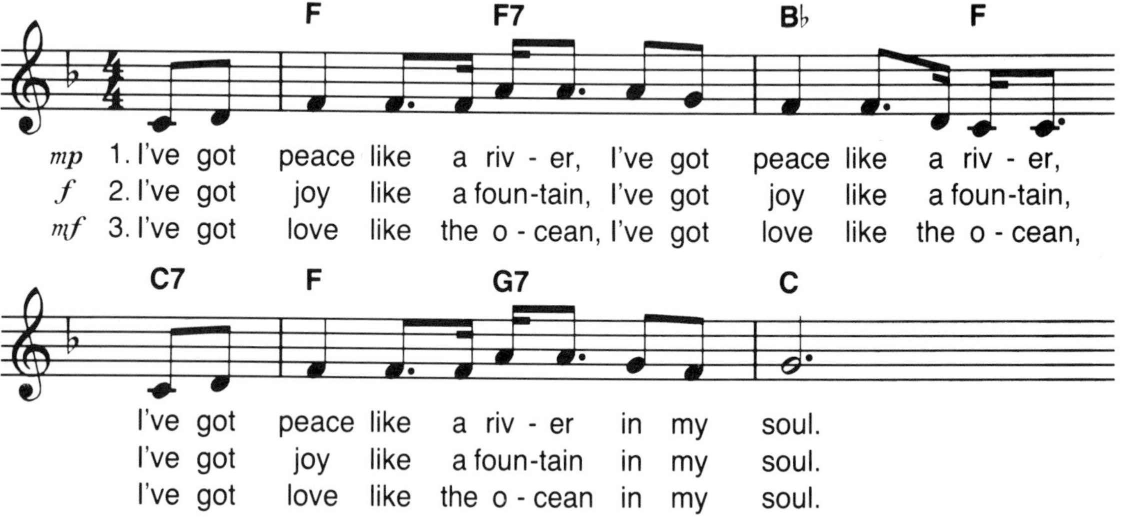

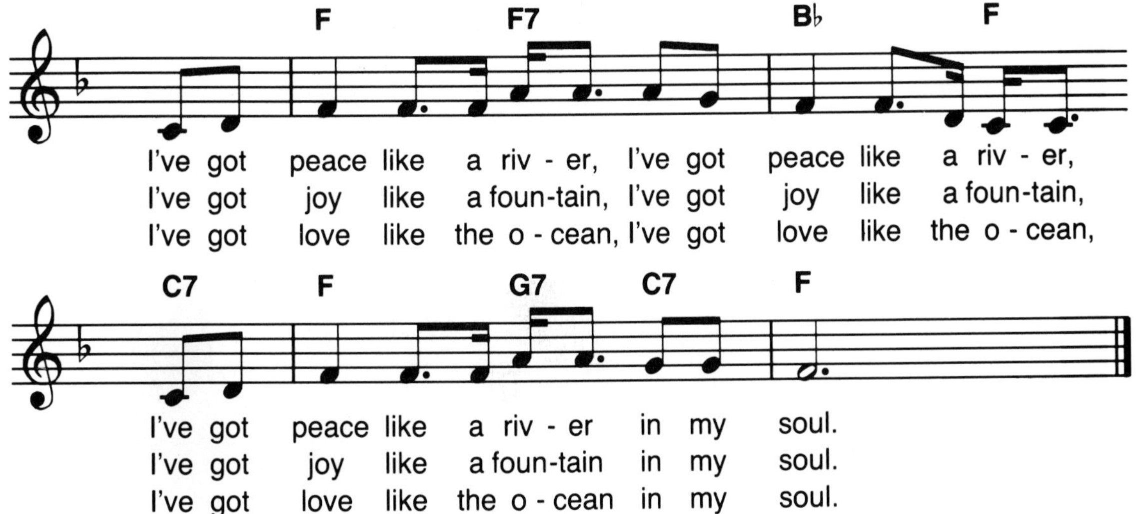

LISTENING

String Quartet in C Major, ("Emperor")

Second Movement

by Franz Joseph Haydn

Listen to the music. The **form is theme and variations**. The main idea, played by the violin, is followed by:

Variation I – violin duet
Variation II – cello plays the melody
Variation III – viola plays the melody
Variation IV – melody played an octave higher by 1st violin

Would the mood of this music be the same if it were played by a quartet of woodwind instruments?

"Measure" a Rhythm

What do these things measure?

Here is a rhythm ruler.
What do you think it will measure?

Can you measure the sounds in the rhythm pattern?

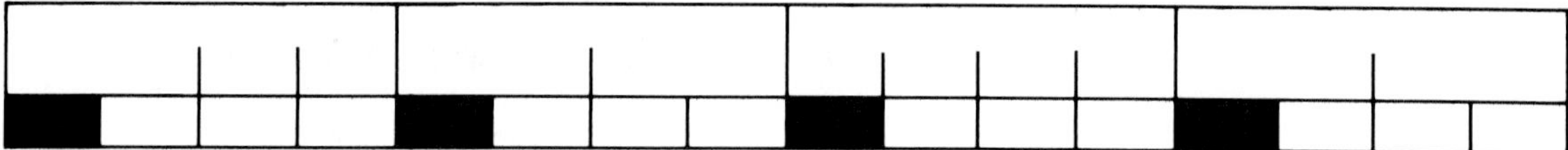

Can you measure the length of each **note**?

Why Shouldn't My Goose?

Traditional Round

Sweetly Sings the Donkey

Old English Round

Kookaburra
Australian Round
D G D
1. Kook-a - bur - ra sits in the old gum tree.
2. Kook-a - bur - ra sits in the old gum tree,
D G D
Mer - ry mer - ry king of the bush is he.
Eat - ing all the gum - drops he can see.
D G D
Laugh, kook - a - bur - ra, laugh, kook - a - bur - ra.
Laugh, kook - a - bur - ra, laugh, kook - a - bur - ra.
D G D
Gay your life must be.
Leave some there for me.

Alto Xylophone I
1.
D
Alto Xylophone II
2.
A
F♯
Soprano Xylophone
3.
A
Bass Xylophone
4.
D
Alto Metallophone
5.
A
F♯
Soprano Glockenspiel
6.
A
Alto Glockenspiel
7.
A

Symphony No. 4

Fourth Movement

by Peter Ilyich Tchaikovsky

People plan trips.

Composers plan musical trips.

Can you map Tchaikovsky's musical trip?

The Silver Birch

Words adapted by
Marcella Bannon

Russian Folk Tune

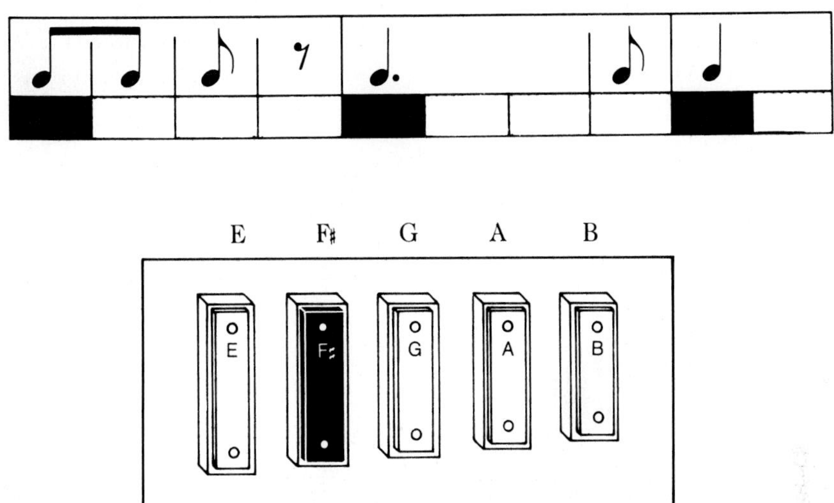

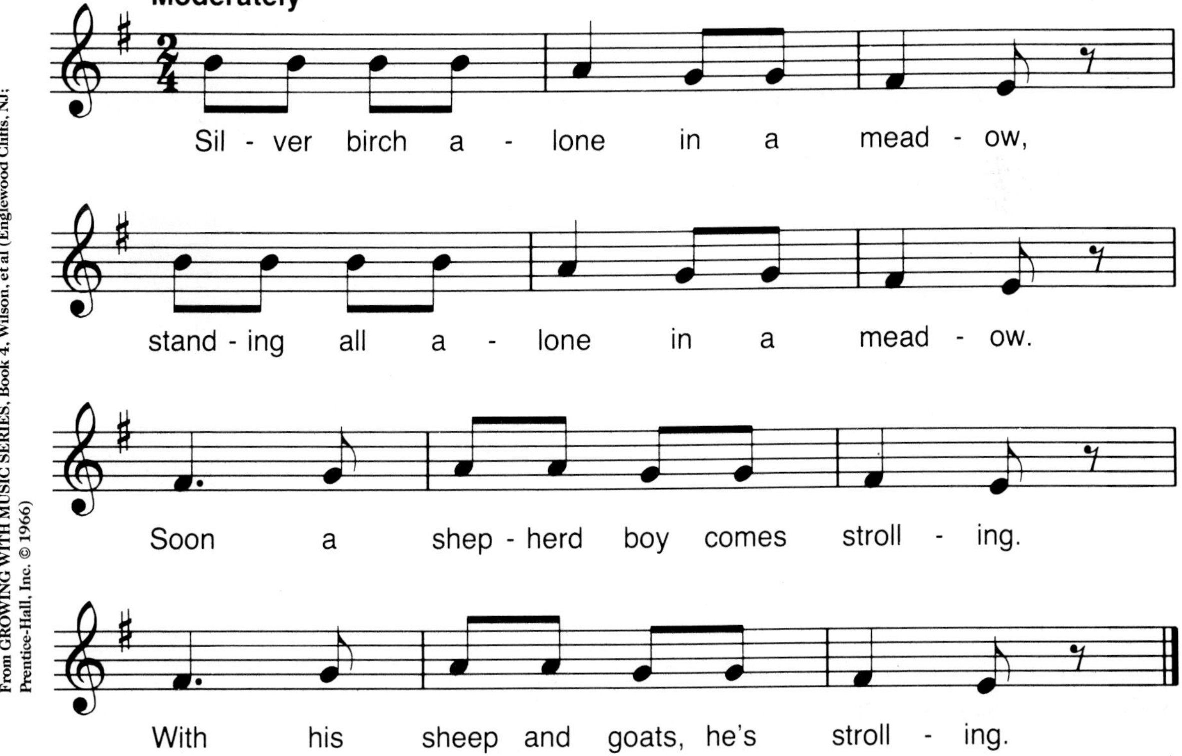

From GROWING WITH MUSIC SERIES, Book 4, Wilson, et al (Englewood Cliffs, NJ: Prentice-Hall, Inc. © 1966)

Singing Warm-Ups

Lullaby Round

Traditional Round

From GROWING WITH MUSIC SERIES, Book 4, Wilson, et al (Englewood Cliffs, NJ; Prentice-Hall, Inc. © 1966)

The Tonal Center

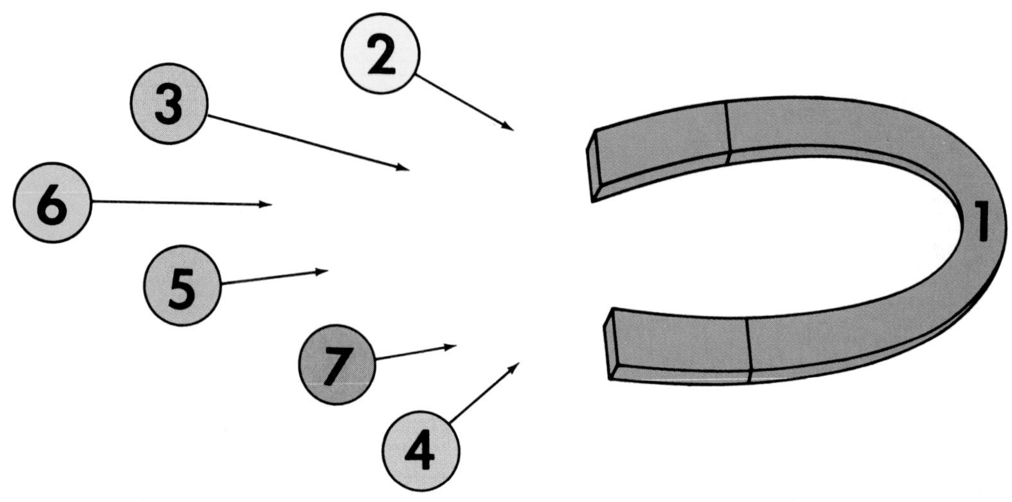

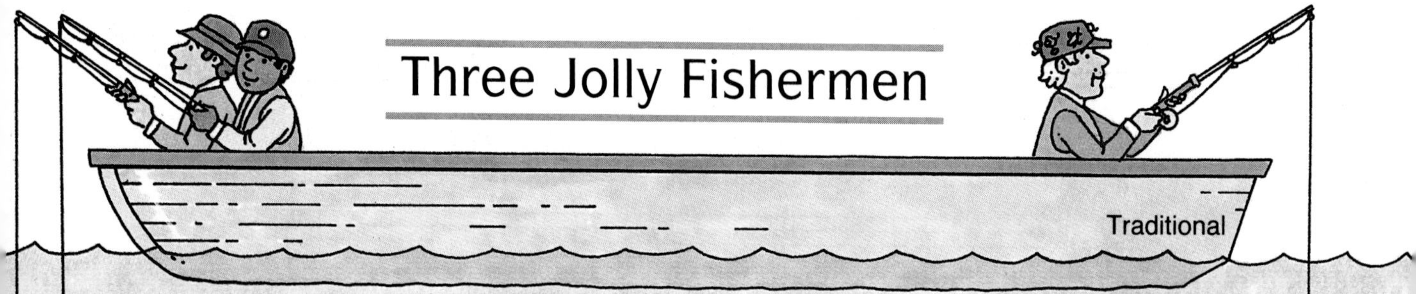

Three Jolly Fishermen

Traditional

Listen for the **tonal center**.

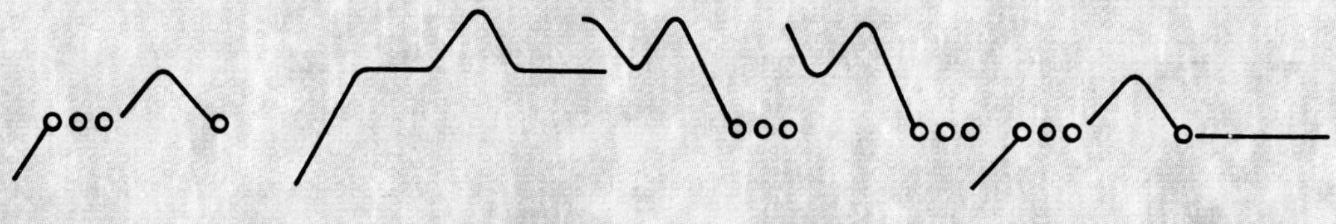

Sing the song with words.

There were three jol-ly fish-er-men.
There were three jol-ly fish-er-men.
Fish-er, fish-er, men, men, men.
Fish-er, fish-er, men, men, men.
There were three jol-ly fish-er-men.

Pop Goes the Weasel

Traditional

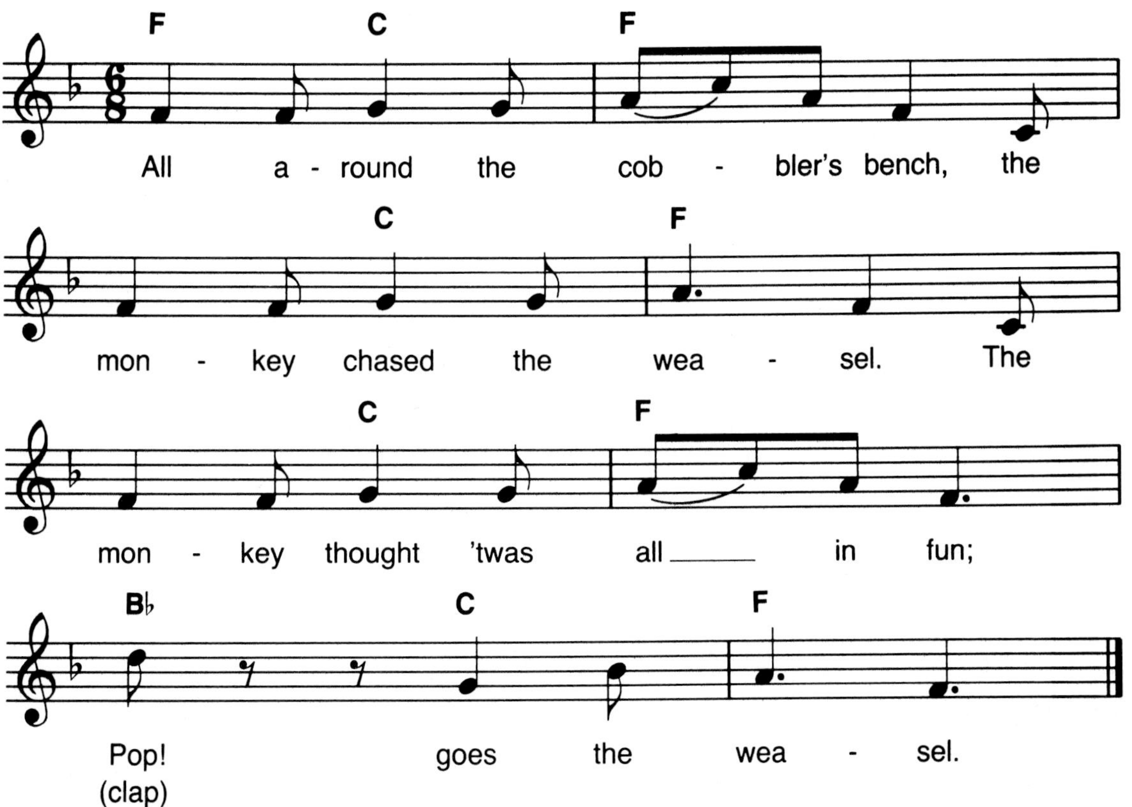

LISTENING

"Variations on Pop Goes the Weasel"

by Lucien Caillet

Bye Bye, Blackbird

Words by Mort Dixon

Music by Ray Henderson

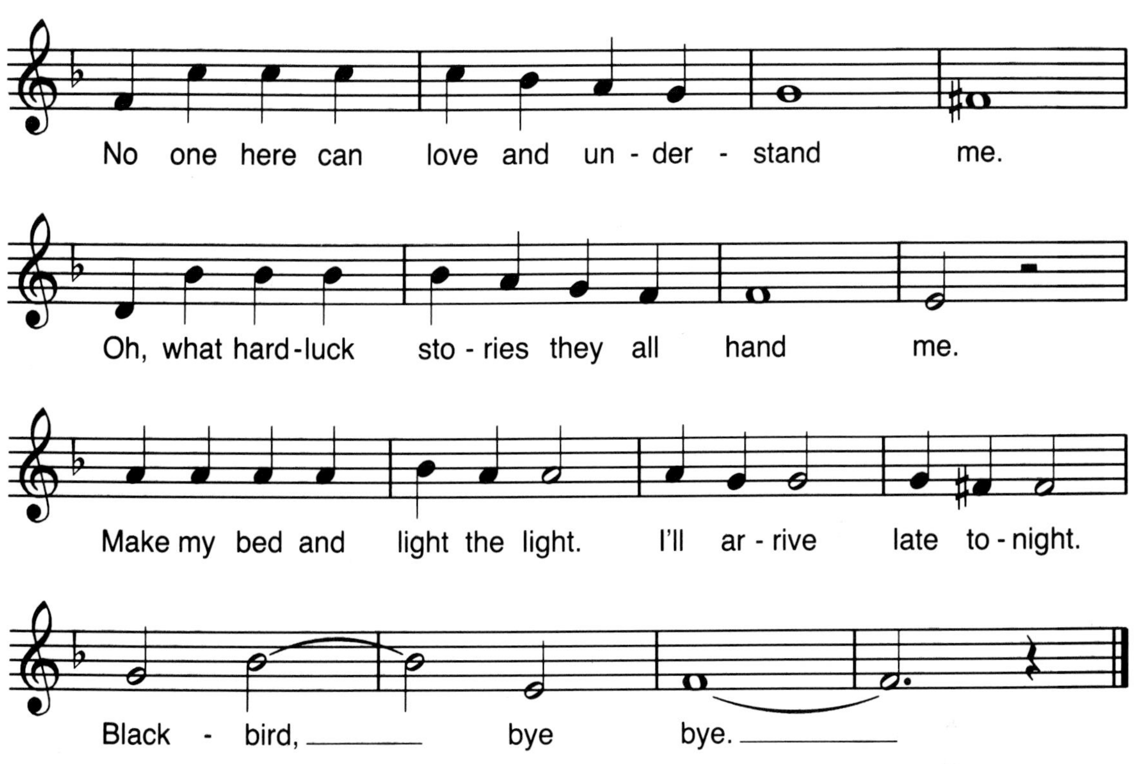
No one here can love and un - der - stand me.
Oh, what hard-luck sto - ries they all hand me.
Make my bed and light the light. I'll ar - rive late to - night.
Black - bird, bye bye.

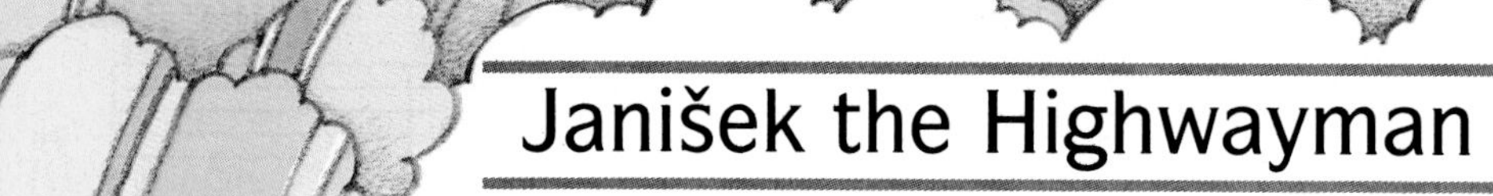

Janišek the Highwayman

Béla Bartók
Transcribed by Benjamin Suchoff

f

(clap) Who's rid-ing down the street?

No one I'd like to meet! Jan - i - šek the high-way-man will

catch you if catch he can! (clap)

mf

Who's rid - ing down the street? No one I'd like to meet!

Jan - i - šek the high-way-man will catch you if catch he can!

(clap)

p

Who's rid - ing down the street? No one I'd like to meet!

Jan - i - šek the high-way-man will catch you if catch he can!

(clap)

Play these patterns on resonator bells or piano.

Introduction and First **interlude**

f

Second **interlude**

Coda

G
C

C
F

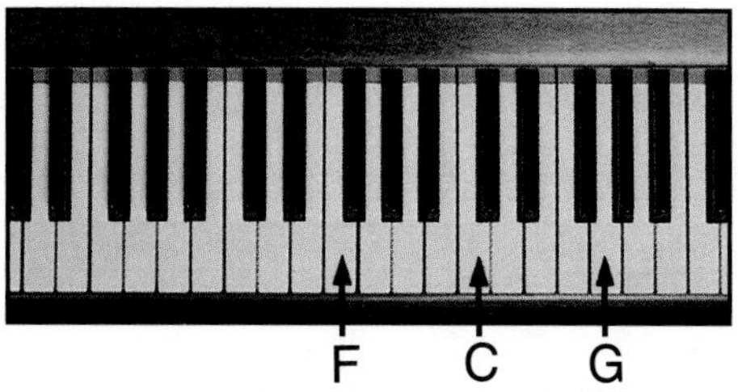

F C G

How did Bartók vary his single melody in "Janišek the Highwayman"?
How did he vary the single melody used in "Bear Dance"?

The Wells Fargo Wagon

From "The Music Man"
By Meredith Willson

I wish, I wish I knew what it could be.
I wish I knew what he was com - in' for.
I got a box of ma-ple su-gar on my birth-day.
I got some sal-mon from Se - at - tle last Sep - tem - ber.
In March I got a gray mack - i - naw.
And I ex - pect a new rock - in' chair.
And once I got some grape-fruit from Tam - pa.
I hope I get my rais - ins from Fres - no.
Mont-gom-'ry Ward sent me a bath-tub and a cross - cut saw.
The D. A. R. have sent a can-non for the court-house square.
O - ho, the Wells Far - go Wag-on is a - com - in' now.
O - ho, the Wells Far - go Wag-on is a - com - in' now.
Is it a pre - paid sur-prise or C. O. D.?
I don't know how I can ev - er wait to see.

Add this pattern as an accompaniment. Use a woodblock or coconut shells:

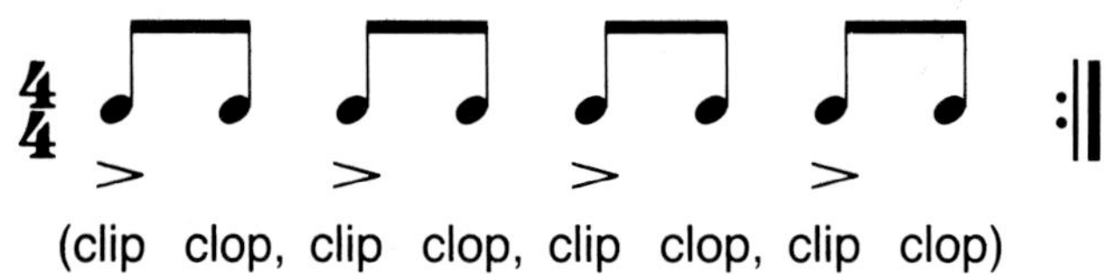

Do Your Ears Hang Low?

Add this rhythm pattern to the song.

LISTENING

Turkey in the Straw

Traditional

Listen to "Turkey in the Straw." Compare it with the melody of "Do Your Ears Hang Low?" What do you notice?

The Happy Wanderer

Words By Antonia Ridge

Music by Friedrich W. Moller

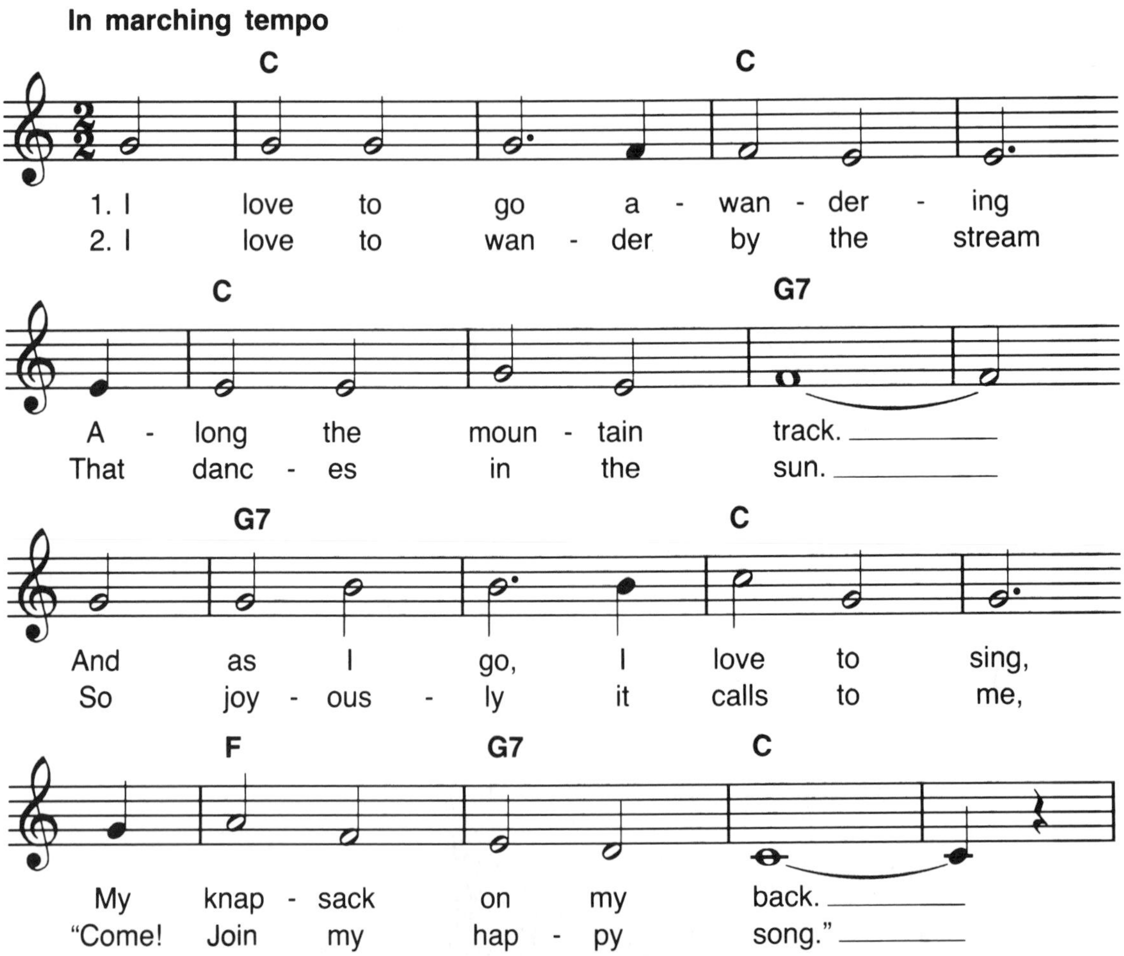

In marching tempo

C C

1. I love to go a - wan - der - ing
2. I love to wan - der by the stream

C G7

A - long the moun - tain track. ______
That danc - es in the sun. ______

G7 C

And as I go, I love to sing,
So joy - ous - ly it calls to me,

F G7 C

My knap - sack on my back. ______
"Come! Join my hap - py song." ______

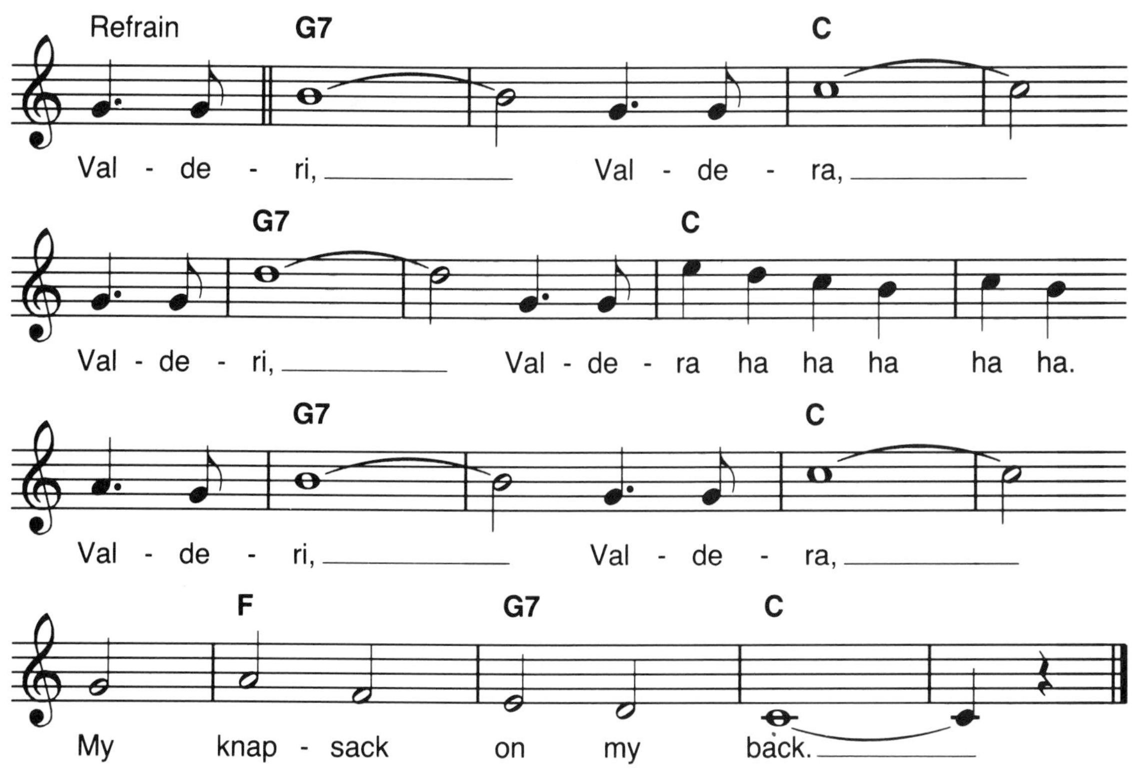

3. I wave my hat to all I meet
   And they wave back to me.
   And blackbirds call so loud and sweet
   From every greenwood tree.
   Refrain

4. High overhead, the skylark wing;
   They never rest at home.
   But just like me they love to sing,
   As o'er the world we roam.
   Refrain

Review 1

Gather 'Round

Words and Music by Margaret Dugard

f *mf*

Raise your voice with a joy-ous_ ring-ing, Gath-er 'round hear the chil-dren sing-ing,

f

Ding, dong, ding ring-a-ling, Ding, dong, ding ring-a-ling,

p

Give thanks and sing. Give thanks and sing.

mf *f*

Young folks gath-er 'round. Old folks gath-er 'round.

Gath-er 'round and join us sing-ing, Ding, dong, ding ring-a-ling

Ding, dong, ding ring-a-ling, Give thanks and sing.

Give thanks and sing.

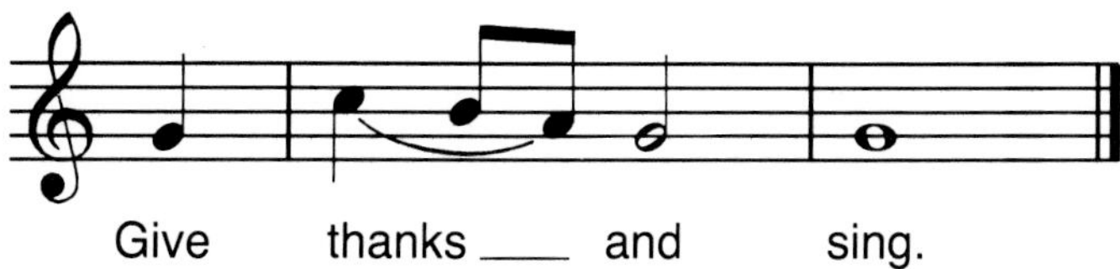

Can you learn this part to sing with "Gather 'Round"? Sing it with numbers. The first pitch is "5."

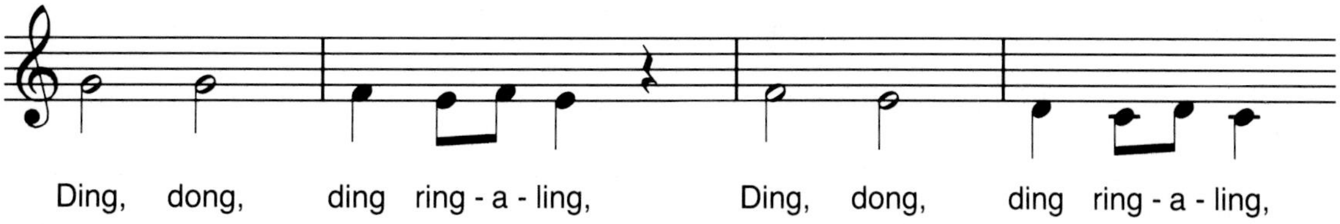
Ding, dong, ding ring - a - ling, Ding, dong, ding ring - a - ling,

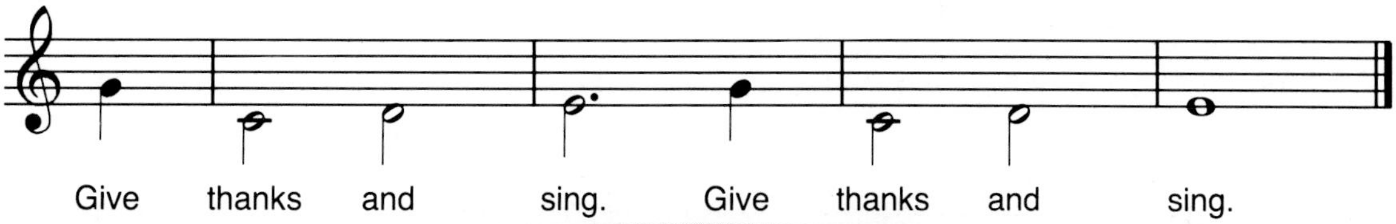
Give thanks and sing. Give thanks and sing.

LISTENING

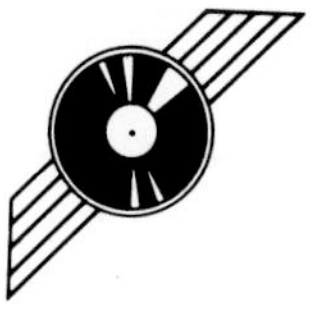

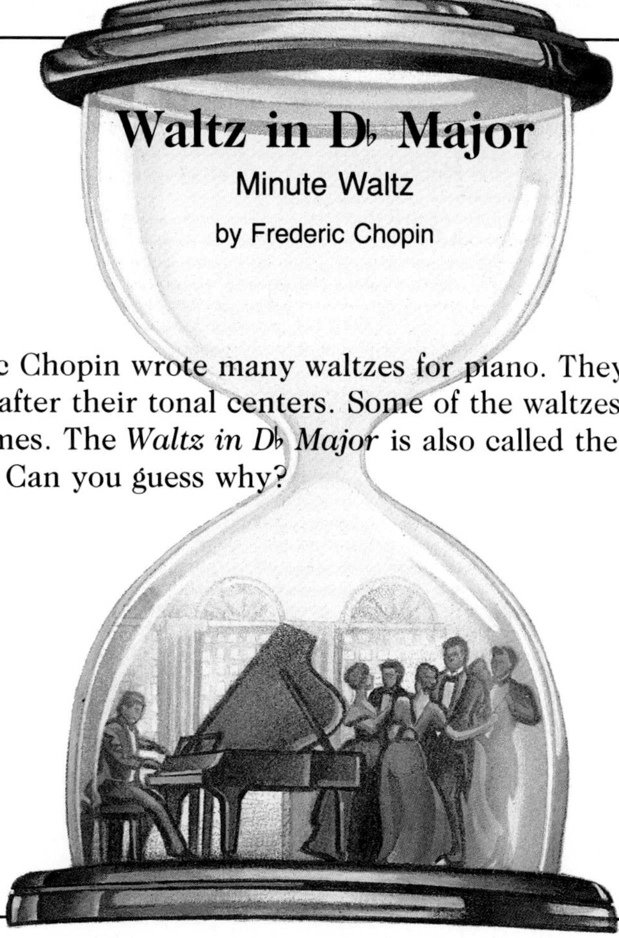

Waltz in D♭ Major

Minute Waltz

by Frederic Chopin

Frederic Chopin wrote many waltzes for piano. They are named after their tonal centers. Some of the waltzes have nicknames. The *Waltz in D♭ Major* is also called the "Minute Waltz." Can you guess why?

The Second Quarter

LISTENING

Meringue Boom

Caribbean Folk Tune

Listen to the steel drums from Trinidad.
Can you hear the same melody repeated?
Can you hear a different melody?

To follow the form of this music,
count eight beats for each letter.

A	A	B	B	B	A	A	B	B	B	B
A	A	B	B	B	B	A	A	B	B	B
improvisation									A	A
B	B	B	A	A	B	B	B	B	B	B

Jesusita en Chihuahua

Mexican Folk Tune

How many different melodies do you hear mariachis from Mexico playing?

Each section gets 32 counts.

Call	Introduction	
1	A	A staccato brass melody is joined by legato strings.
2	A	The section is repeated.
3	B	New melody: brass and strings alternate **phrases**.
4	A	The original melody returns.
5	C	Strings play a contrasting, legato melody.
6	C	The legato melody is repeated with mellow brass.
7	D	A quick, running melody: brass ask musical questions and are answered by strings.
8	C	The legato melody returns with muted brass.
9	A	The original melody returns to complete the piece.

Are You Sleeping?

Traditional Words

French Folk Tune

Sing this song in unison, then as a round.

Use the rhythm pattern of the words to create a percussion piece.

Some people may hold instruments while three players perform.

Group I wood sounds	Group II ringing sounds	Group III drumlike sounds

Perform the percussion piece as a three-part round.

Sing "Are You Sleeping?" in the following way.

How many different ways is the melody varied?

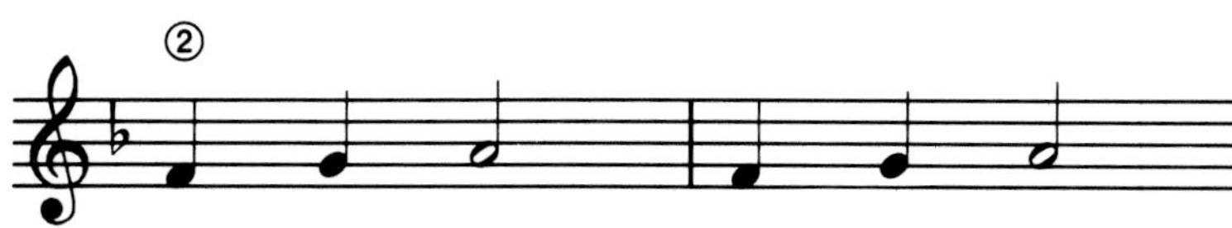

Perform the following parts as you sing.

Introduction (2 measures) and accompaniment

Piano or Timpani

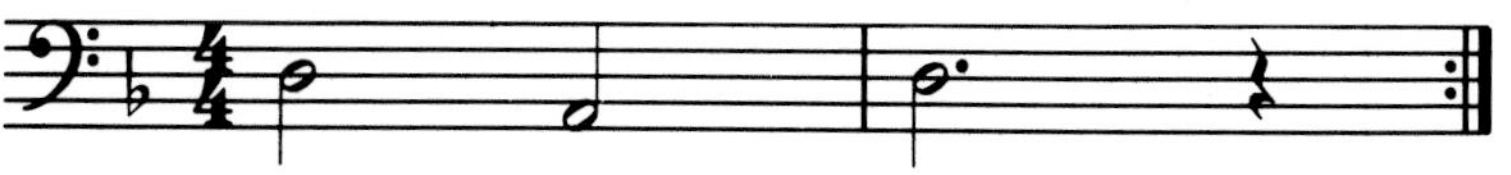

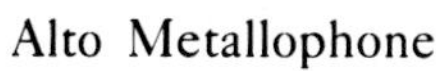

Soprano Glockenspiel

LISTENING

Symphony No. 1 in D Major [excerpt]

by Gustav Mahler

Listen to this music.
What do you hear that is the same, almost the same, or different from the way you performed "Are You Sleeping?" the first time?

Allelujah

Round by E. B.

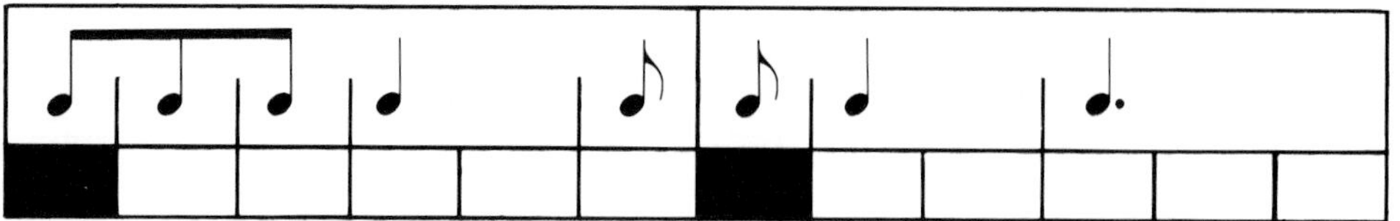

Which bell is Step 1?

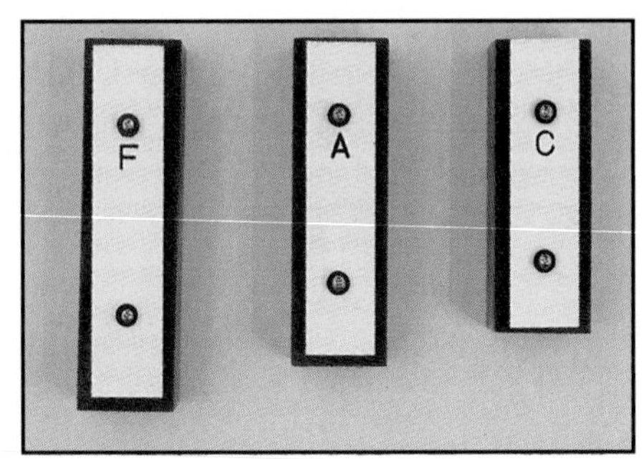

Tune up.

Melody

Chord

Sing Together

Traditional Round
Adapted by E. B.

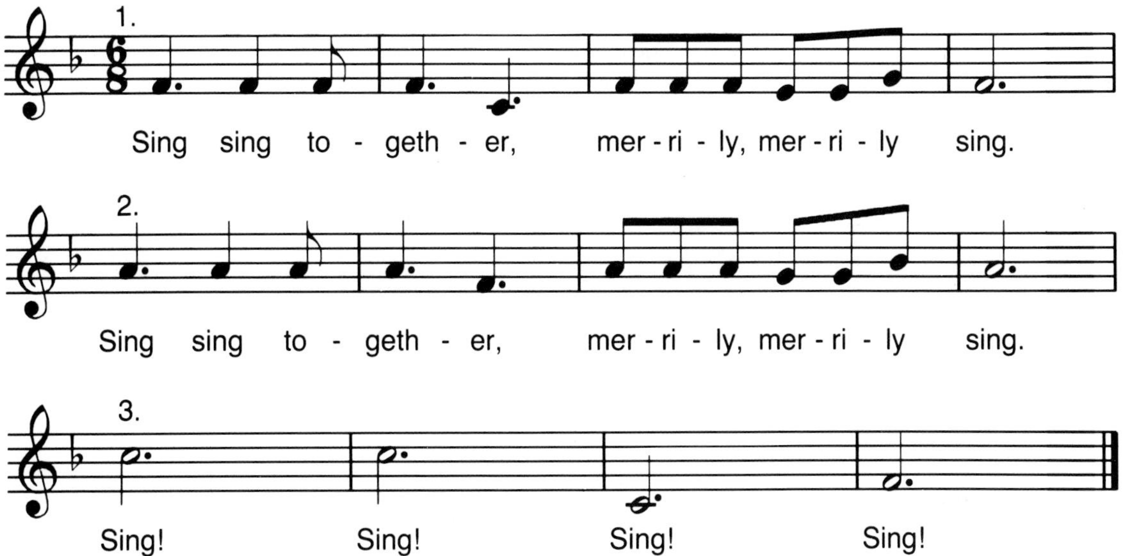

Accompany this round.

Begin with this chord.

When will you need to change this chord? How can you decide?

Which bells will you use for each chord?

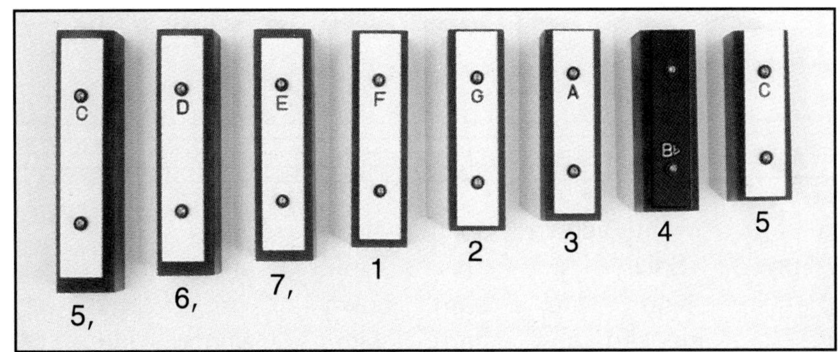

Acadian Songs and Dances (excerpt)

by Virgil Thomson

The songs on these pages may be accompanied by two chords.
When will you use each?

I V7

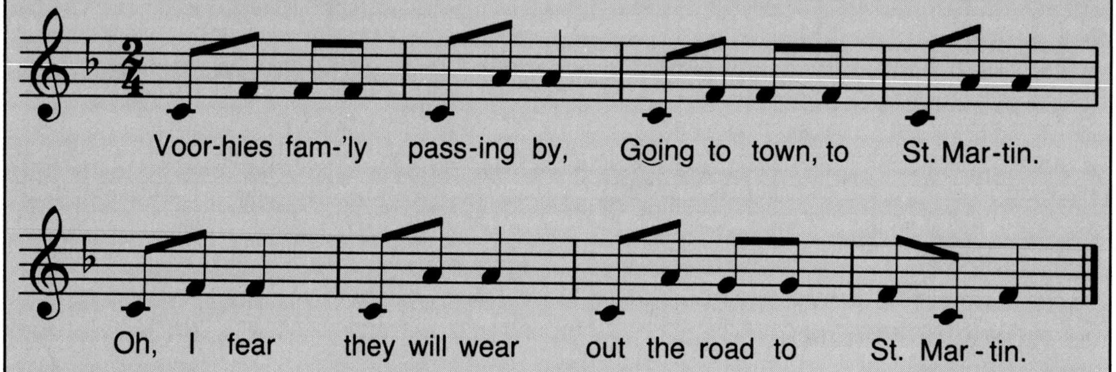

Voor-hies fam-'ly pass-ing by, Going to town, to St. Mar-tin.

Oh, I fear they will wear out the road to St. Mar-tin.

Polly Wolly Doodle

Traditional

Sing Pol - ly wol - ly doo - dle all the day.
My Sal - ly is a spunk - y gal,
With curl - y eyes and laugh - ing hair,
I thought I heard a chick - en sneeze,
He sneezed his head and tail right off,
Sing Pol - ly wol - ly doo - dle all the day.
Refrain
Fare thee well, fare thee well, Fare thee
well, my fair - y fay. For I'm
going to Loui - si - an - a, for to see my Su - sy - an - na,
Sing Pol - ly wol - ly doo - dle all the day.

One Cold and Frosty Morning

Alabama Folk Song

Use your knowledge of the major scale to learn this melody.
It uses the pitches of the C scale.

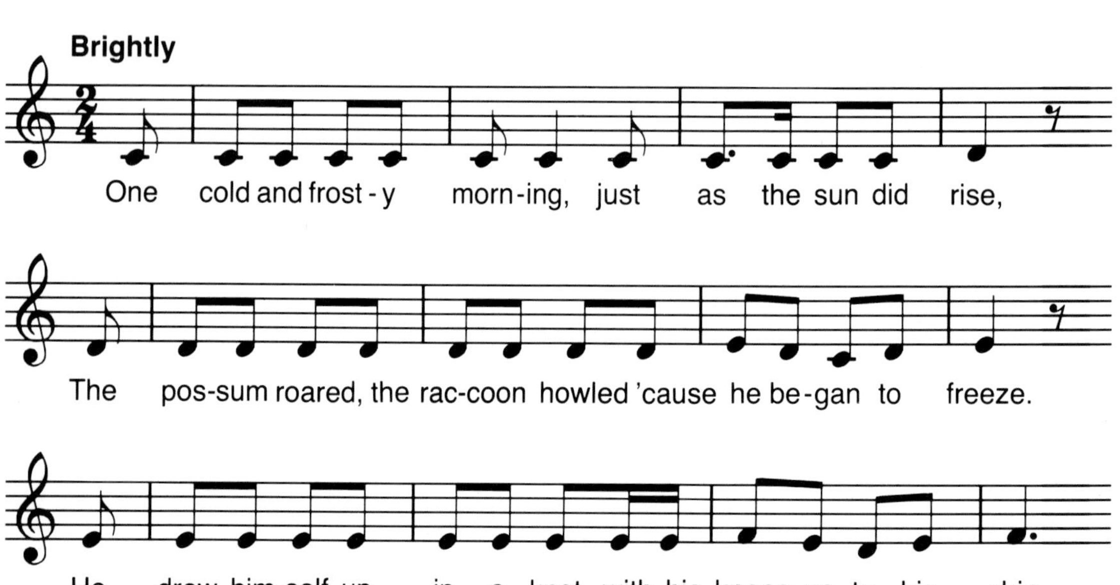

Use your knowledge of **chords** to add harmony to this song.

You will need to use three chords.

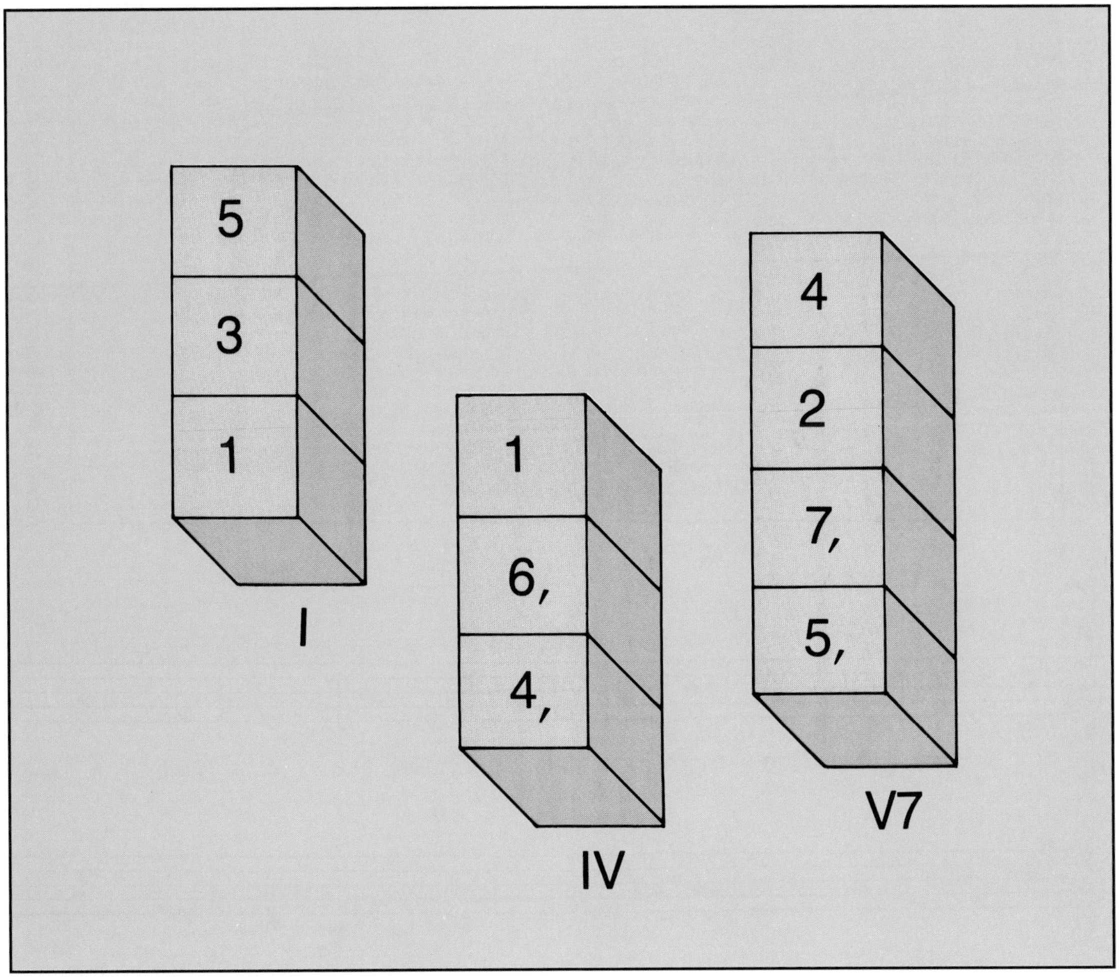

5
3
1
I

1
6,
4,
IV

4
2
7,
5,
V7

The Colorado Trail

Cowboy Song
Arranged by Kurt Miller

Cowboy Meditation, polychromed bronze, 22″ X 20″ X 9″, 1964, © Harry Jackson, artist, © Wyoming Foundry Studios, Inc., 1964.

Weep, all ye lit - tle rains, Wail, winds, _ wail,
All a - long, a - long, a - long the Col - o - ra - do Trail.

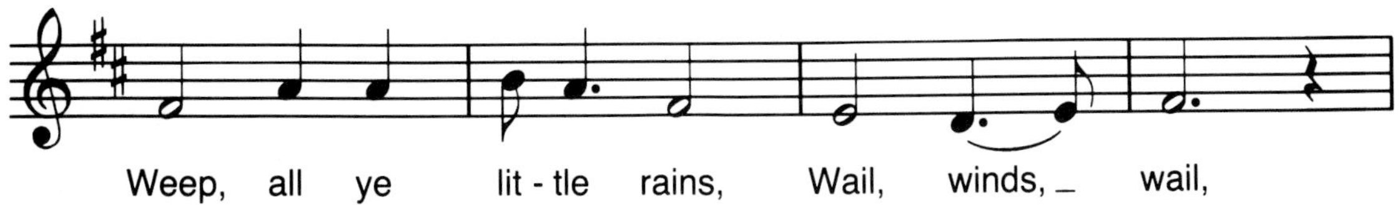

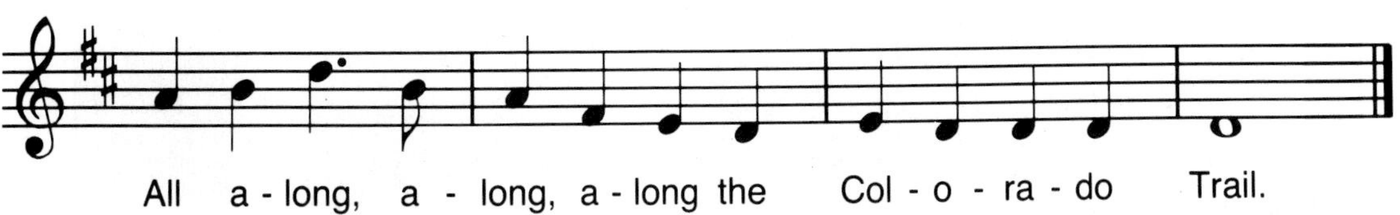

Listen for this **descant.**
Can some people sing it while others sing the melody?

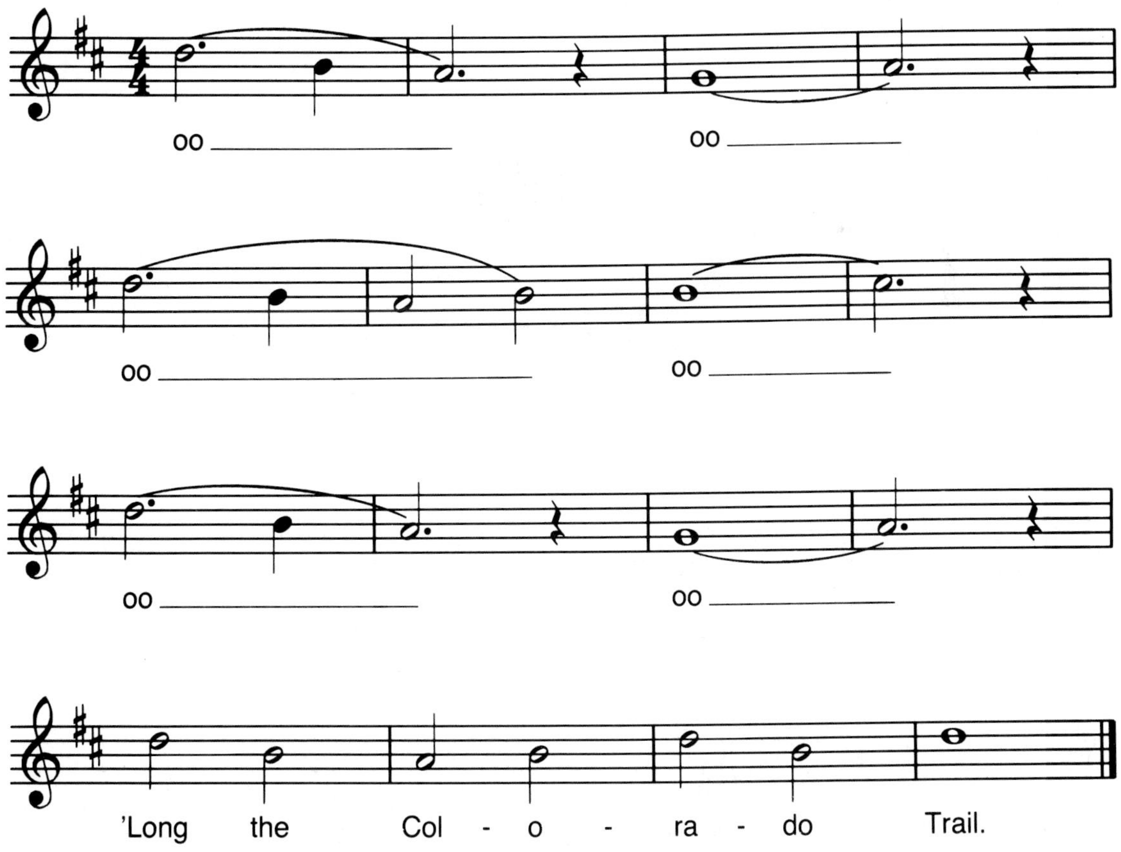
oo
oo
oo
oo
oo
oo
'Long the Col - o - ra - do Trail.

Woke Up This Morning

1960s Civil Rights Anthem

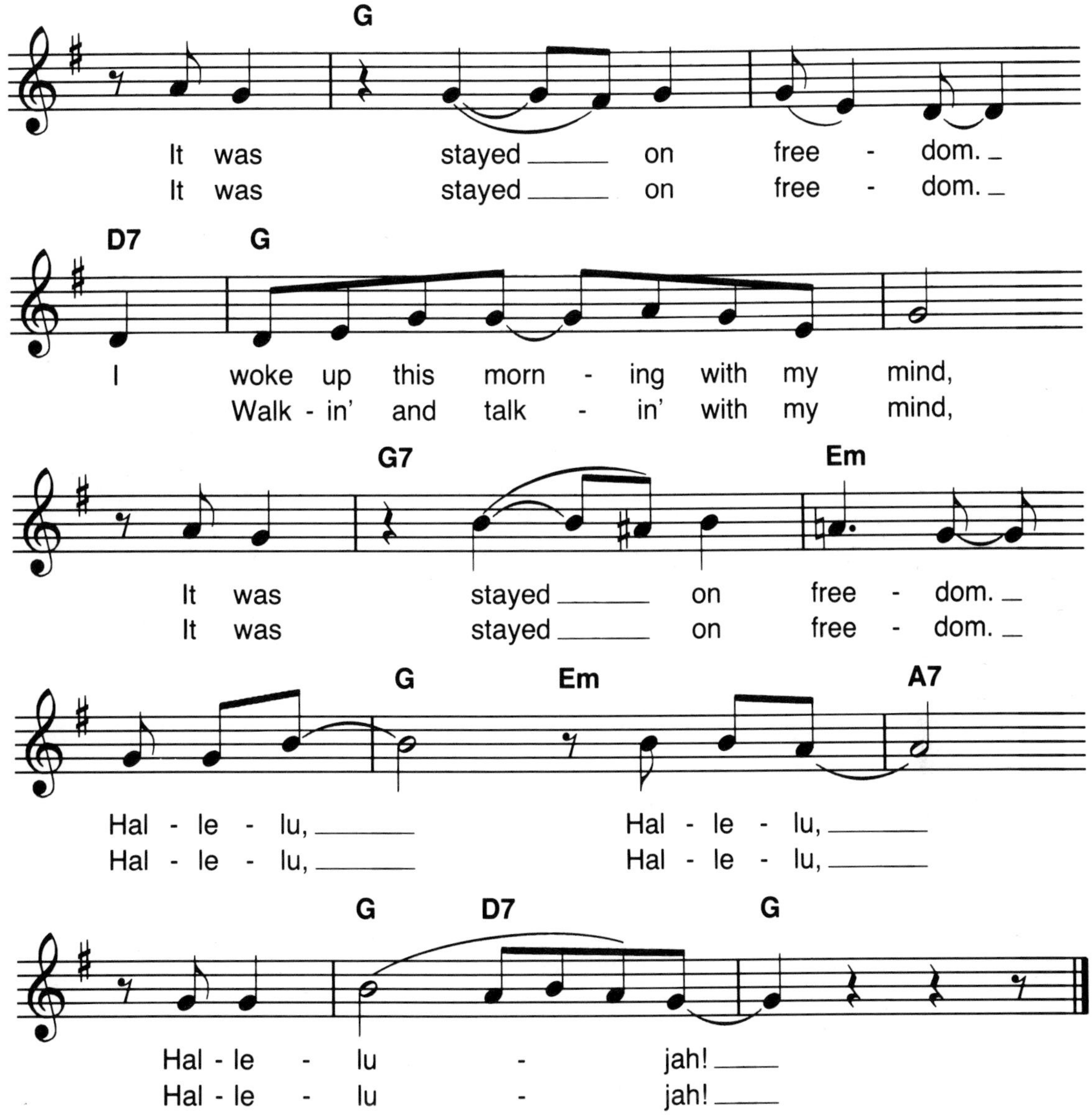

G

It was stayed ___ on free - dom. _
It was stayed ___ on free - dom. _

D7 G

I woke up this morn - ing with my mind,
Walk - in' and talk - in' with my mind,

G7 Em

It was stayed ___ on free - dom. _
It was stayed ___ on free - dom. _

G Em A7

Hal - le - lu, ___ Hal - le - lu, ___
Hal - le - lu, ___ Hal - le - lu, ___

G D7 G

Hal - le - lu - jah! ___
Hal - le - lu - jah! ___

LISTENING

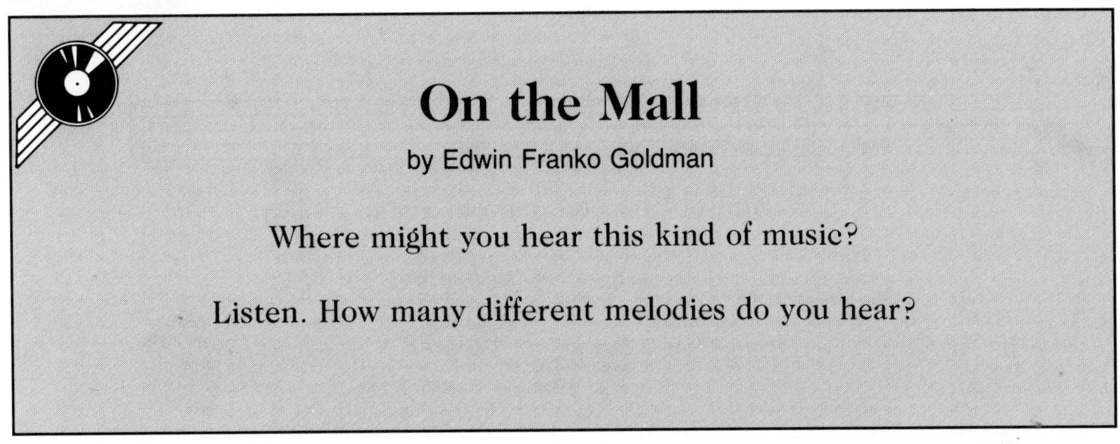

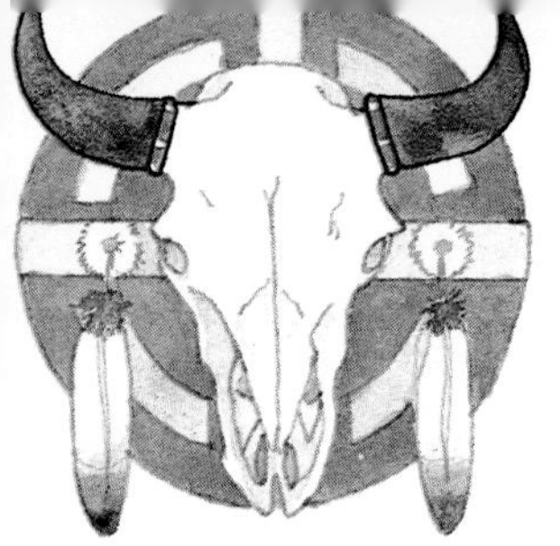

Face-Dance Song

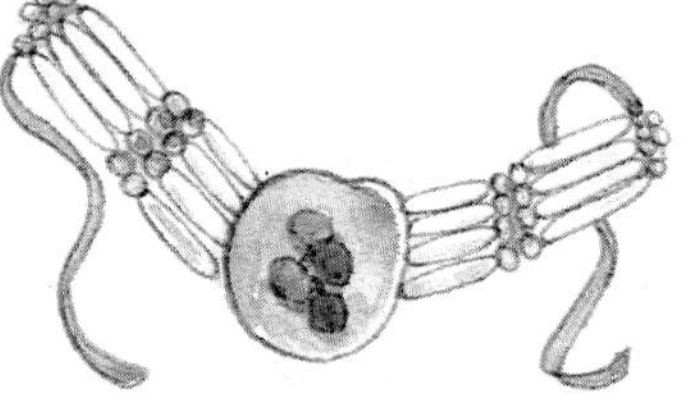

Transcribed and Arranged
by Louis W. Ballard

As you learn this song,
can you find clues that help you decide when and where it was first sung?

Look at the words. Can you **see** any clues?
Listen to the music. Can you **hear** any clues?

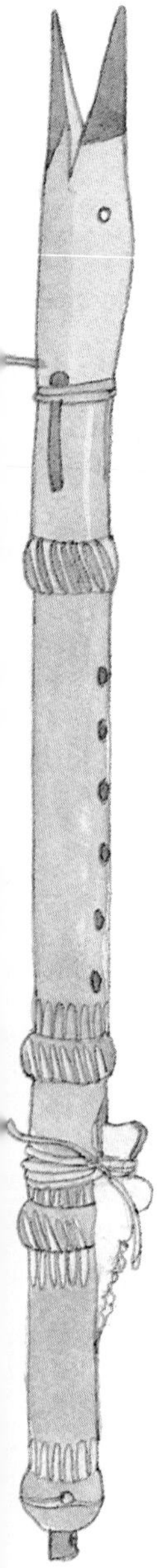

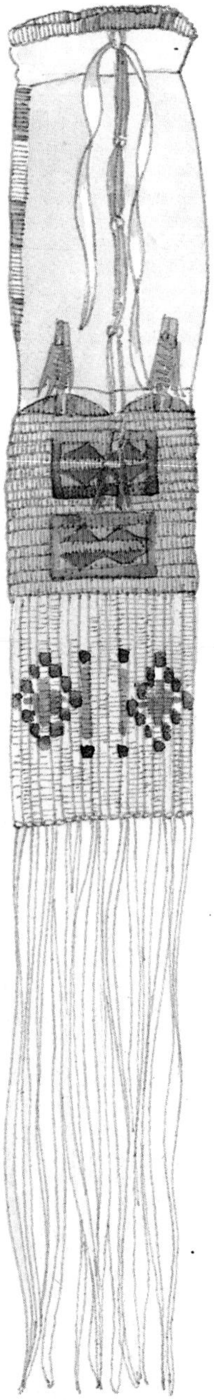

Ha - na t'si wah, Ha - na ___ t'si wah, ___
Ha - na ___ t'si wah, Ha - na t'si wah.
Yo - ho wa - ni na - ah yo - ha hey,
Yo - ho wa - ni na yo - ha hey,
Yo - ho wa - ni na - ah yo - ha hey.

Sioux Grass Dance

La Raspa

Mexican Folk Dance

How well can you follow dance instructions?
Learn the movements for this Mexican dance.

Dance with a partner.

Step I
L-hop; right heel out

Step II
R-hop; left heel out

A-section of the music

B-section of the music

Step
Clap
6
8
repeat

How many times will you dance each section?

Tinikling

Philippine Folk Dance

PLAYERS
Two players sit on the floor and hold the ends of two bamboo poles.

Introduction:
Begin when the music begins.
Slide poles together on Beat 1.
Lift the poles apart and tap the boards on Beats 2 and 3.

Sections A and B:
Continue playing the "pole rhythm."

3/4

click tap tap click tap tap

DANCERS
Two dancers on either side of the poles face each other.

Introduction:
Listen for 4 measures. Then tap right toes between the poles:

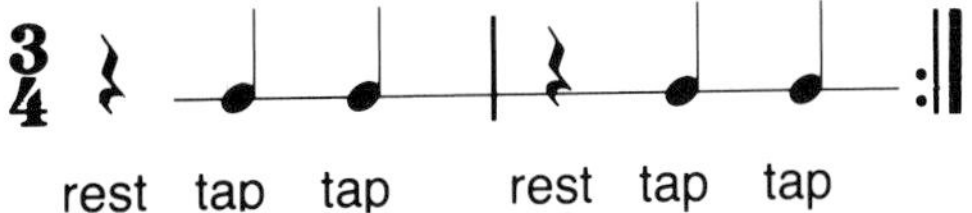

Section A:
Measure 1: Start with left foot.

1 ♩ Hop on left foot outside of poles.
2 ♩ Step between poles with right foot.
3 ♩ Step between poles with left foot.
Repeat, starting with *right* foot.

Section B:
Start with left foot.
Walk outside the poles:
left, right, left, right.
Leap inside the poles:
right foot, then left foot.
Repeat, starting with *right* foot.

Songmaker

Words and Music by
Fred Willman

B♭m Dm7
Tell it in a way that the whole wide world will
Gm C7 F
Soon sing it and say:
Gm
Song - mak - er, song - mak - er,
C C7 F
Make it hap - py or sad.
B♭m Dm7
Tell of the times that are good, my friend, but
Gm C7 F
Don't be a - fraid of the bad.

The Cat Came Back

Traditional

Verse

Dm C Dm C

1. Old Far - mer John - son had trou - bles all his own.
2. sent that old cat far a - way in a bal - loon.

Dm C Dm C

He had a lit - tle cat that would-n't leave his home.
Gave him to the man who lives _ in the moon.

Dm C Dm C

He tried and he tried to give that cat a - way!
The man left the moon. Said, "That's e - nough of that!

Dm C Dm C

He gave it to a man go - ing far, far a - way. _
I'll nev - er share my home with an old yowl - in' cat!" _

Refrain
Dm C Dm C
But the cat came back _ the ver - y next day! _
Dm C Dm C
The cat came back! _ Thought he was a gon - er.
Dm Dm C
But the cat came back! _ He just would-n't stay a - way. _
Dm
1.
2.
He _
Add these ostinatos as an accompaniment.
Bass Xylophone
Alto Xylophone
Soprano Glockenspiel

My Momma Told Me

Traditional Song Game

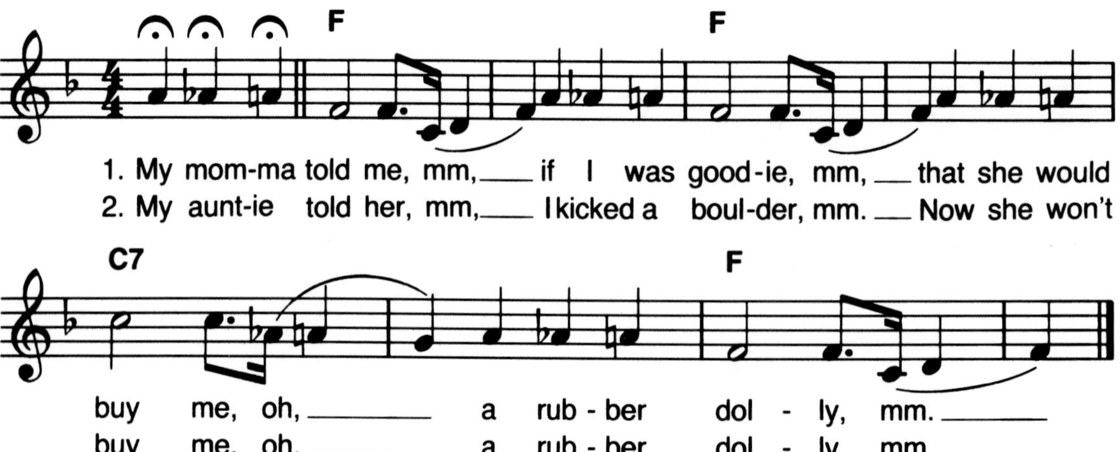

Perform a dance: Make a circle.
Walk counterclockwise.

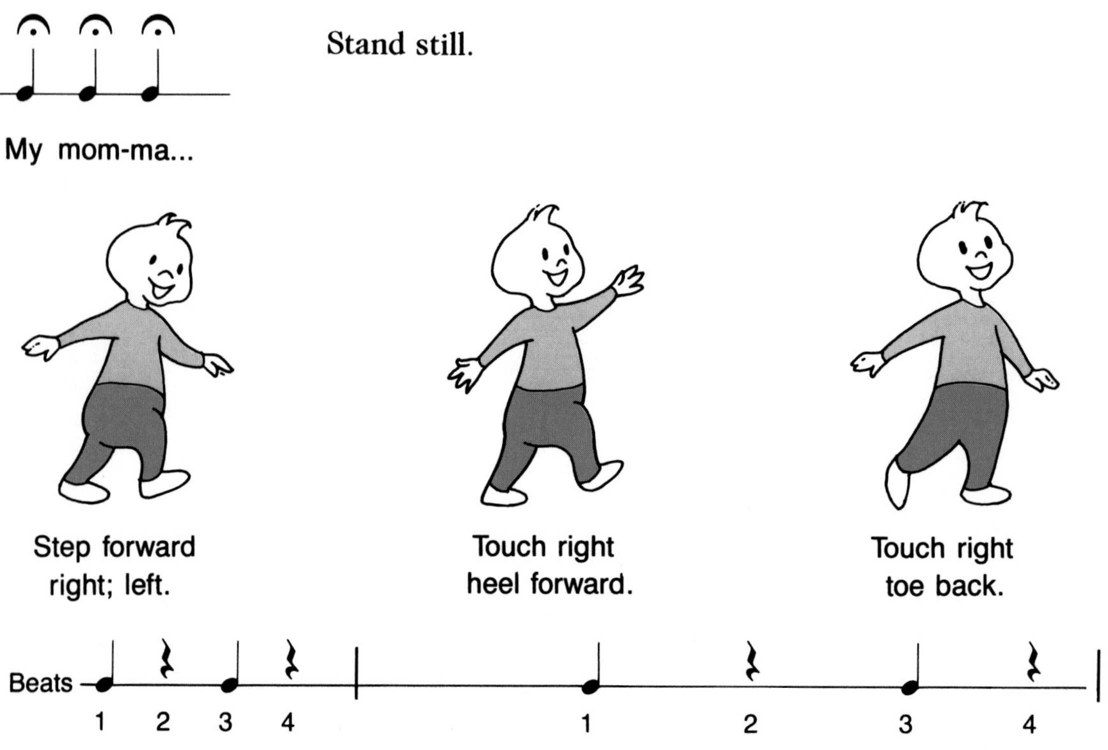

Repeat this pattern throughout Verse I.

Verse II

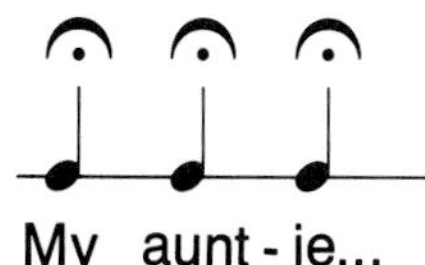

Stand still.

Turn in a circle, shaking hands on:
"...told her, mm,
I kicked a boulder, mm.
Now she won't..."

"Buy me, oh, a rub-ber dol-ly, mm"

Side step and point direction.

Point heels and fingers up.

then down to end.

Interlude

Clap beat and chant:

Choose one person to move to the center, dance, and find an instrument to play. All others keep clapping the beat.

Instruments of the Orchestra

The instruments of the orchestra are grouped into families. Each family has at least one instrument in every range:

low, middle, and high.

Listen to the sound of each family of instruments as you look at the pictures on pages 60, 61, 62, and 63.

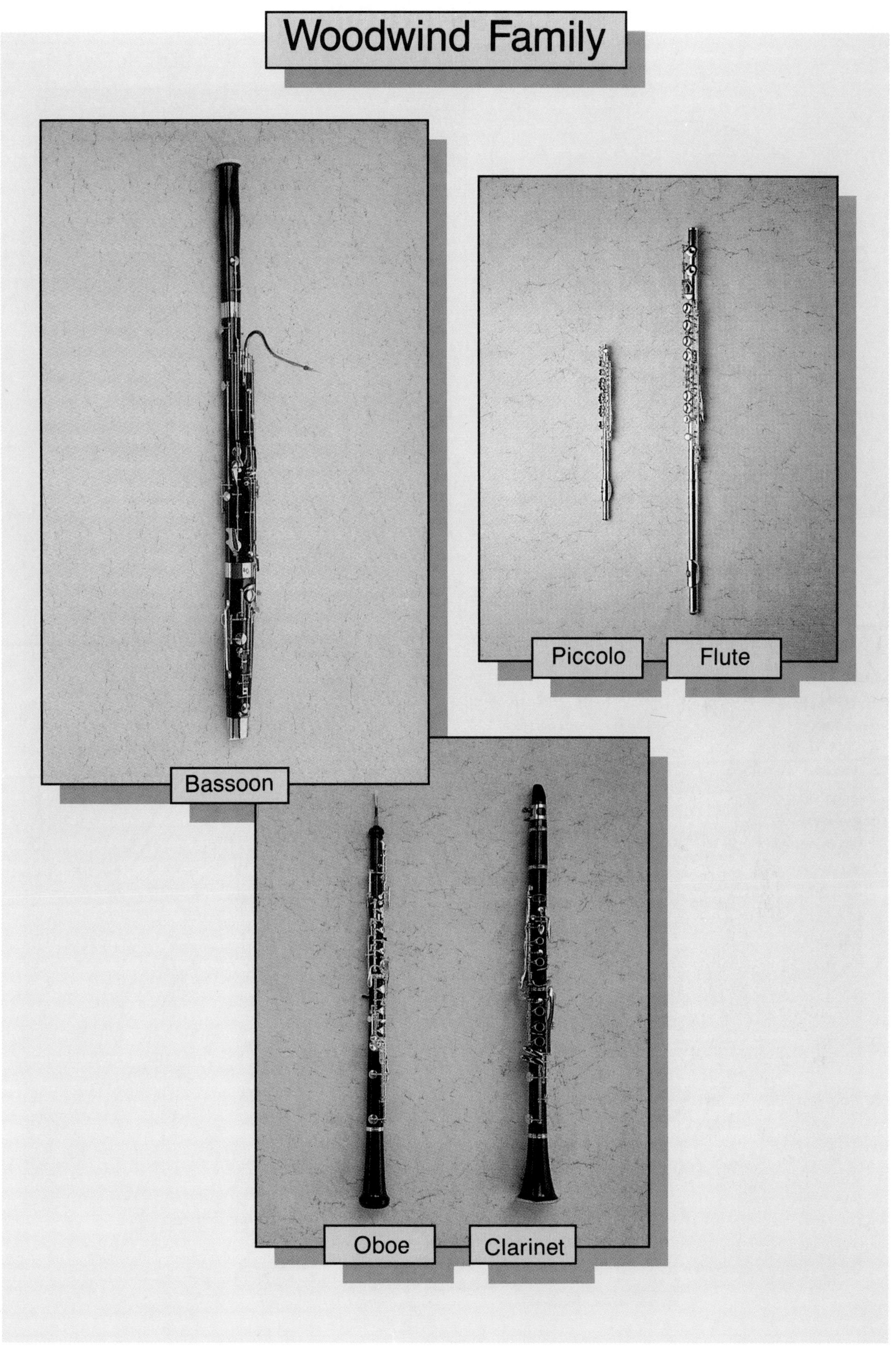
Woodwind Family
Bassoon
Piccolo
Flute
Oboe
Clarinet

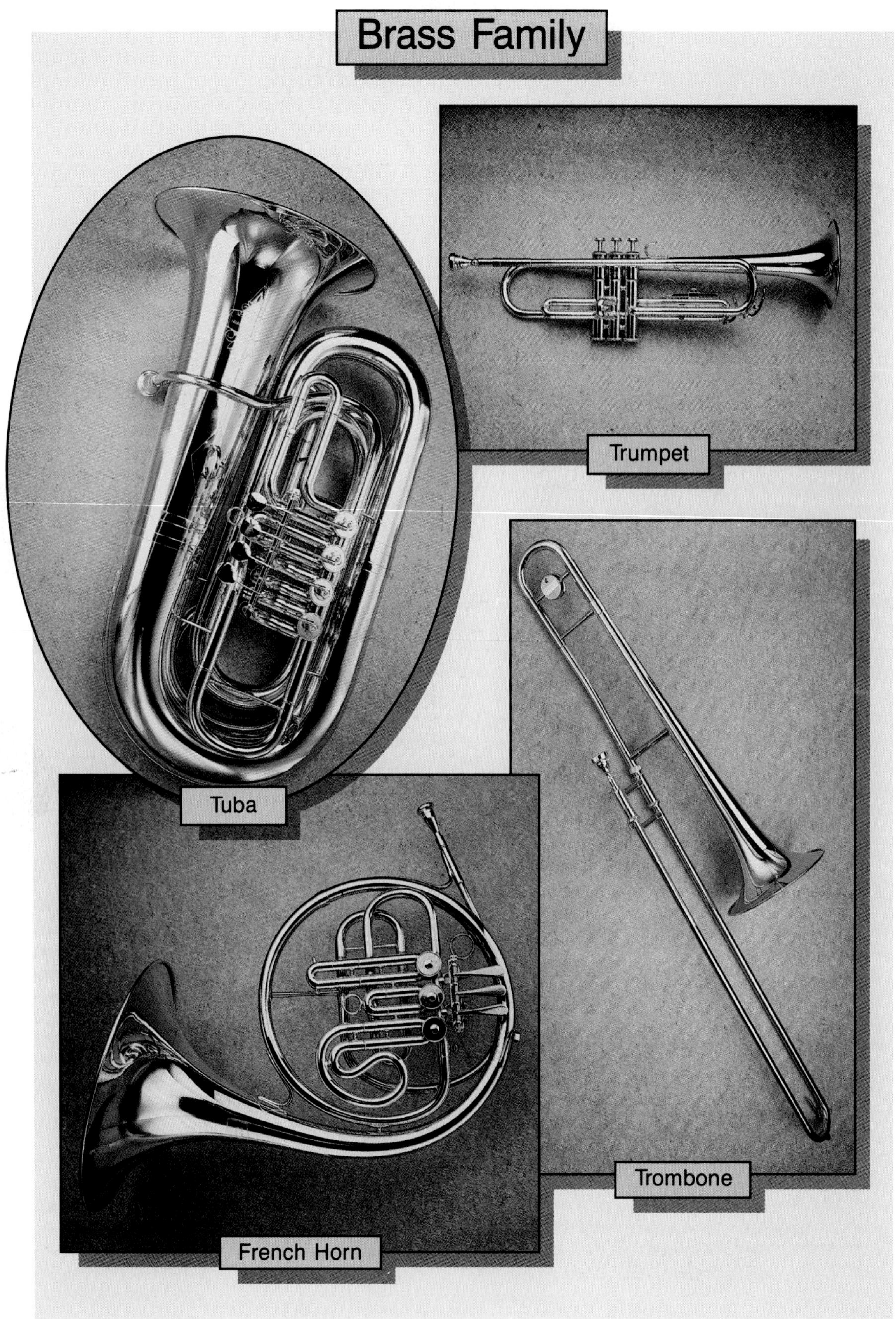
Brass Family
Trumpet
Tuba
Trombone
French Horn

Percussion Family

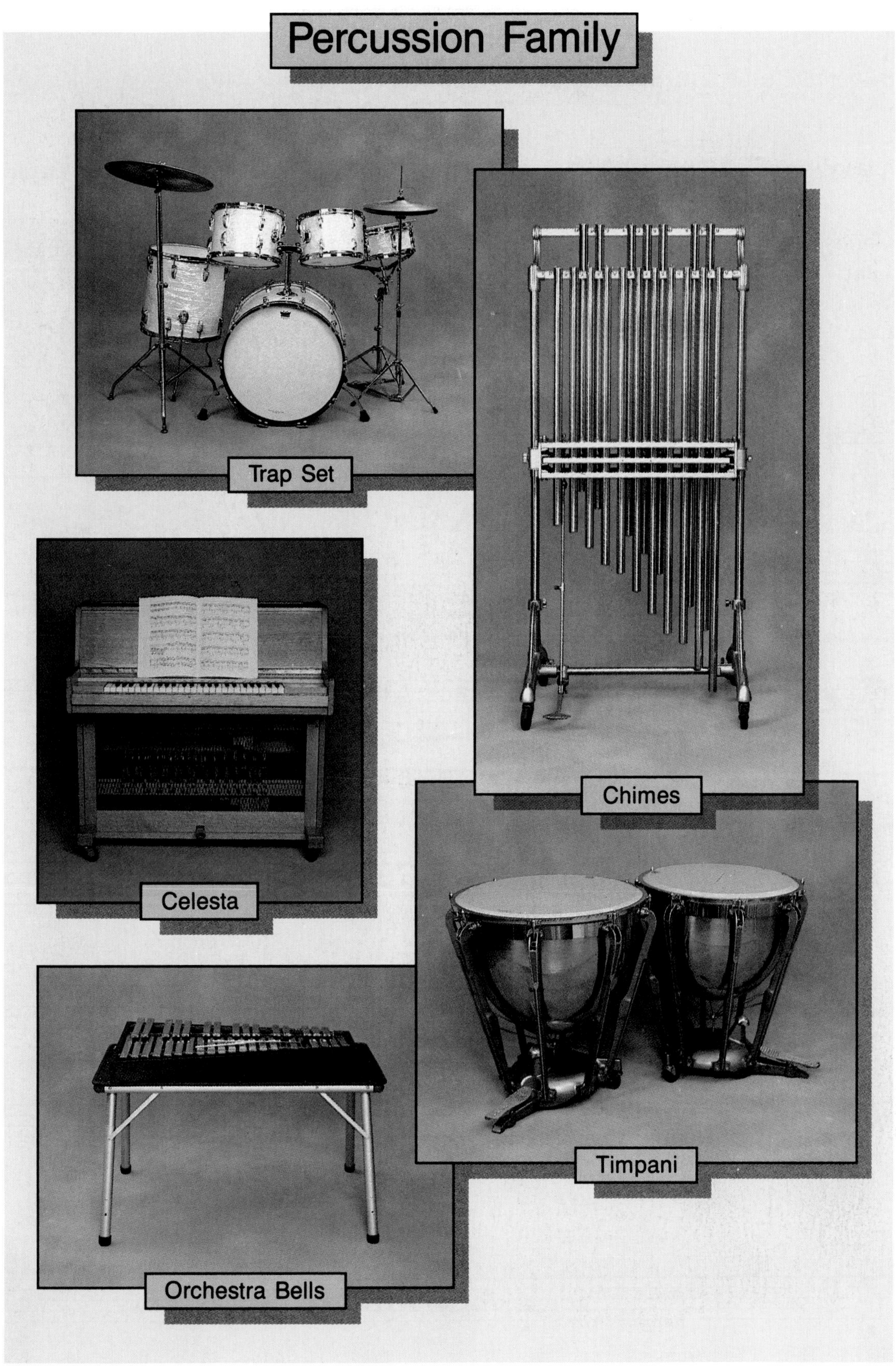

The Instruments

Arranged by Julius G. Herford

Words and Music by Willy Geisler

Choose your favorite instrument.
Learn its song.
When all know their parts, sing them together.
Can you make your voice sound like the instrument you chose?

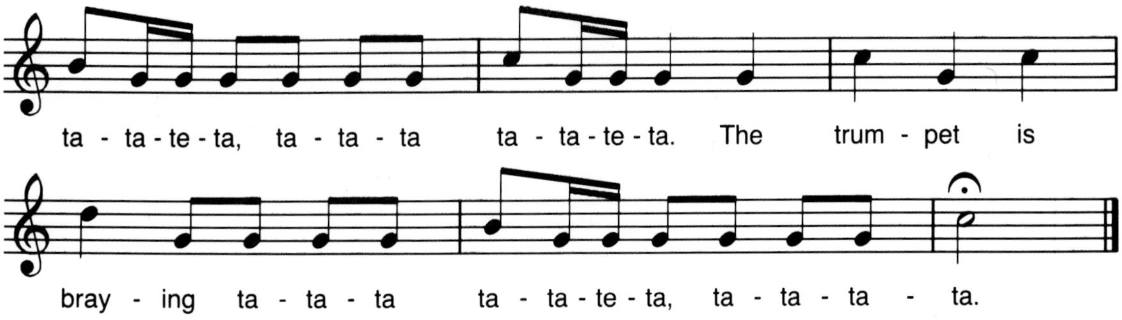
ta - ta - te - ta, ta - ta - ta ta - ta - te - ta. The trum - pet is
bray - ing ta - ta - ta ta - ta - te - ta, ta - ta - ta - ta.

4

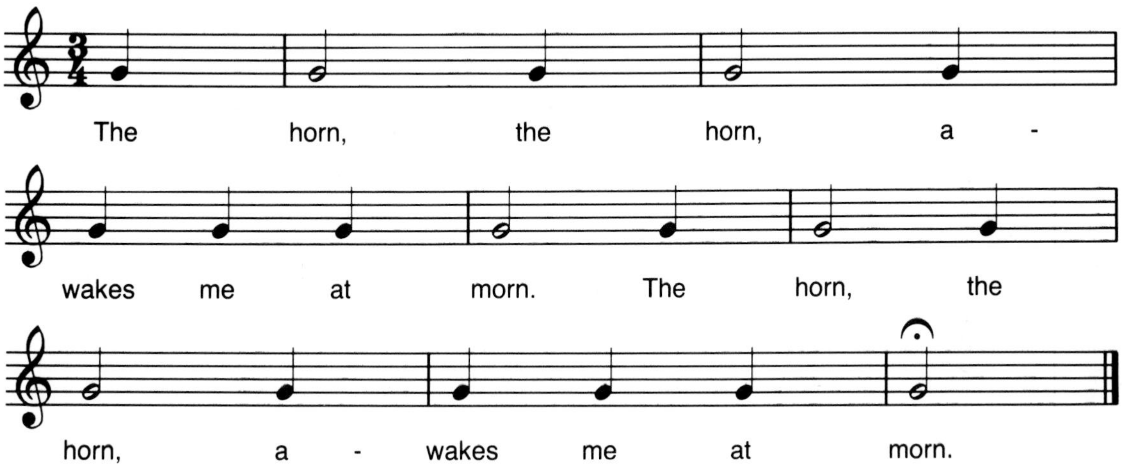
The horn, the horn, a -
wakes me at morn. The horn, the
horn, a - wakes me at morn.

5

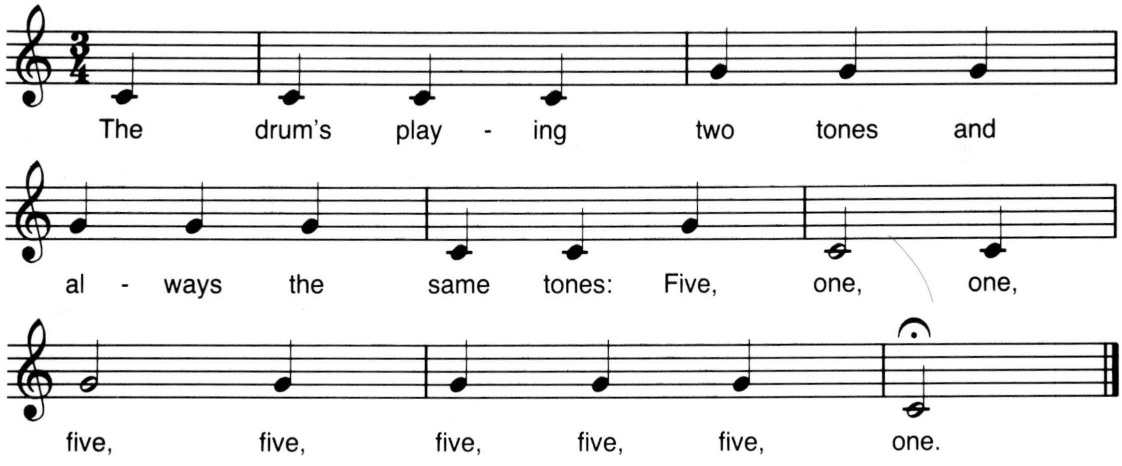
The drum's play - ing two tones and
al - ways the same tones: Five, one, one,
five, five, five, five, five, one.

If you chose the flute, sing its song while the others hold their last pitch.

The flute's play - ing sweet - ly with tone — so clear.

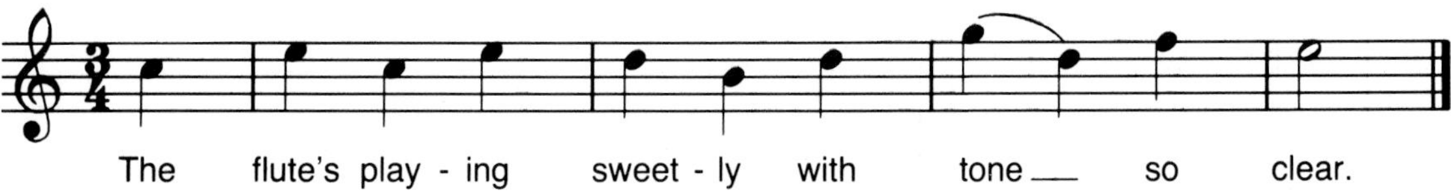

Concerto for Orchestra, Second Movement

by Béla Bartók

Béla Bartók composed music for different pairs of instruments in the orchestra. Can you name each pair?

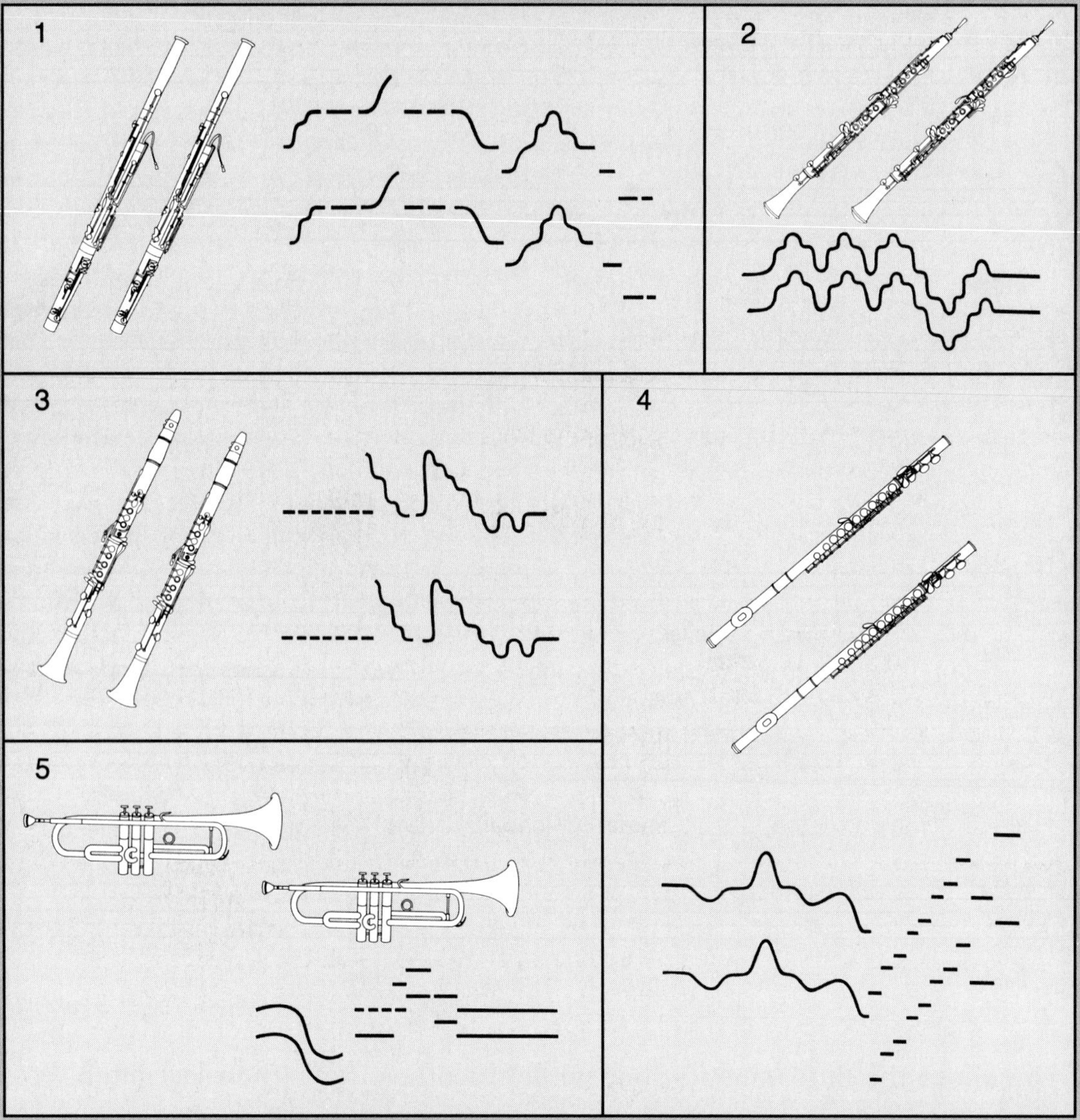

1

2

3

4

5

This music is sometimes called "A Game of Pairs." Why is this a good title?

After the game, a chorale is played by brass instruments.

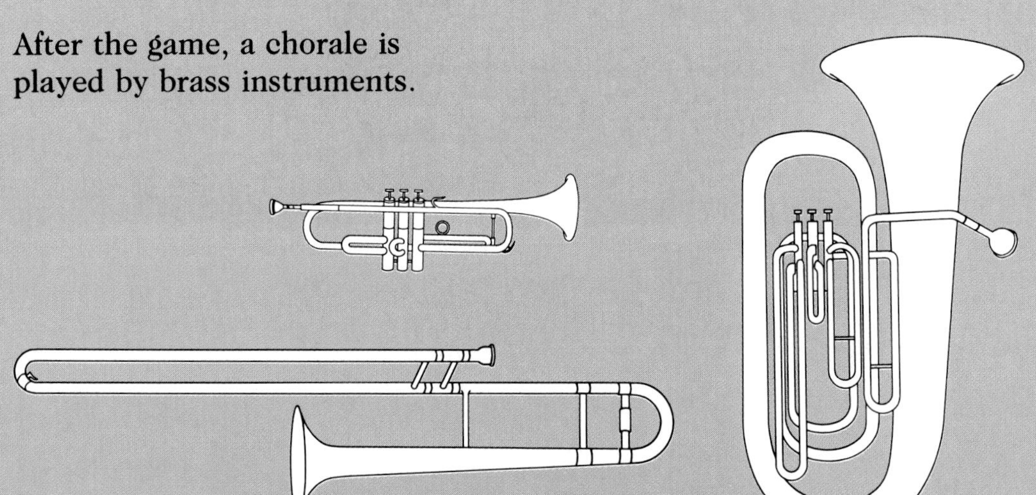

The game begins again.
Do you hear the same instruments?
Do you hear the same melodies?

Create "A Game of Pairs" of your own for resonator bells.

Decide the size of the interval you will use for your game.

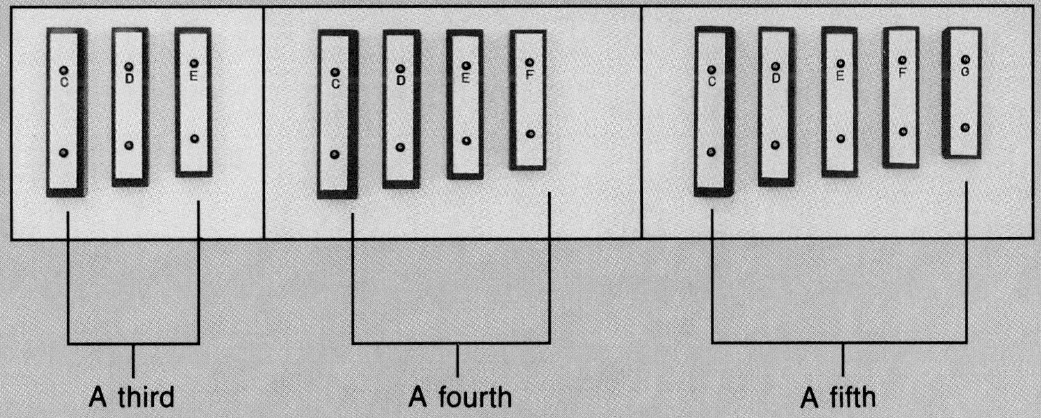

Play a melody that moves up and down.
Play it with two mallets at the same time.
Be sure to keep your mallets
the same distance apart all the time.

Review 2

Sing Along

Words and Music by Malvina Reynolds

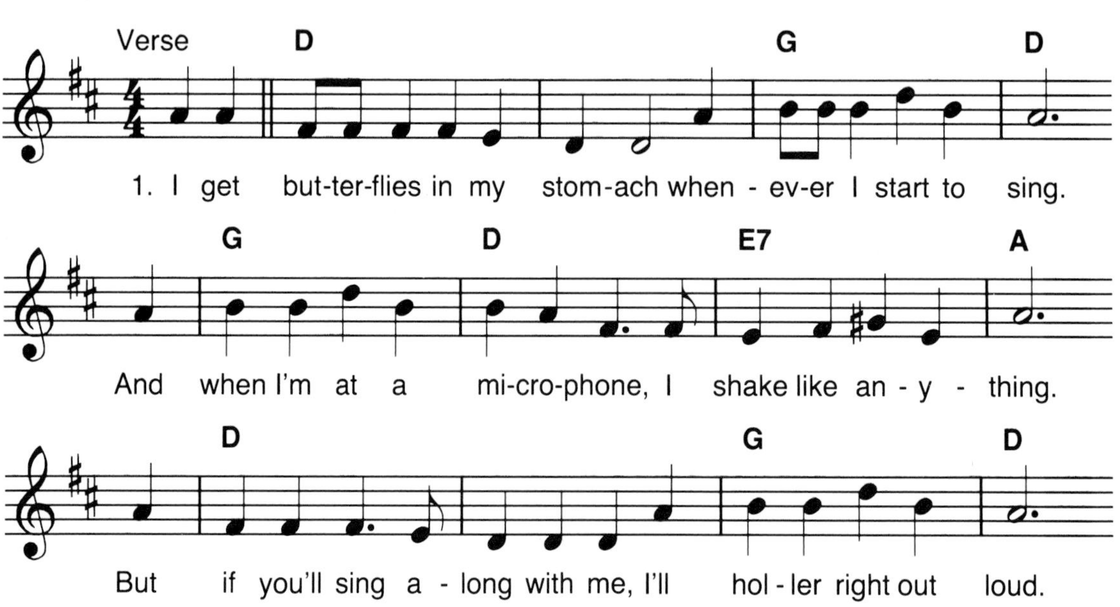

2. Oh when I need a raise in pay and have to ask my boss,
If I go to see him by myself I'm just a total loss.
But if we go together, I'll do my part right pretty.
Cause I'm awfully nervous, lonesome. But I
Make a fine committee. (Refrain)

3. My congressman's important: he hobnobs with big biz.
He soon forgets the guys and gals who
Put him where he is.
I'll just write him a letter to tell him what I need.
With a hundred thousand signatures,
Why even he can read! (Refrain)

The Third Quarter

Be a Song Leader 1

Set the starting pitch.

Have you ever gone camping or
on a field trip with your friends?
Everyone wants to sing.
Someone has to be the leader and get everyone started.
Can you be the leader while the class
sings "She'll Be Coming 'Round the Mountain"?
Hum a pitch you think is right for the starting pitch.
Lead everyone in singing the song.
Was the melody too high? too low? Try again!

She'll Be Coming 'Round the Mountain

Traditional

5, 6, 1 1 1 1 6, 5, 3, 5, 1
She'll be com-ing round the moun-tain when she comes. (toot toot)

1 2 3 3 3 3 5 3 2 1 2
She'll be com-ing round the moun-tain when she comes. (toot toot)

5 4 3 3 3 3 2 1
She'll be com-ing round the moun-tain,

1 1 6, 6, 6, 6, 2 1
She'll be com-ing round the moun-tain,

7, 6, 5, 5, 5, 5, 3 2 6, 7, 1
She'll be com-ing round the moun-tain when she comes.

You can set the pitch by "thinking" a sound.
If you have an instrument handy,
you can play the starting pitch.

Set the starting pitch for "On Top of Old Smoky" on the bells.
To do this:

1. Find the lowest scale number in the song.
   Find the highest.
   Find the tonal center.

2. Where is the tonal center? Is it low? high? in the middle?

3. Find a bell you think will be a good pitch for the tonal center.

4. Play the bell. Hum the pitch. Lead the class.

On Top of Old Smoky

Kentucky Folk Song

1 1 3 5 1′ 6 6 4 5 6 5
On top of Old Smo-ky all cov-ered with snow,

11 3 5 5 2 3 4 3 2 1
I lost my true lov-er by court-ing too slow.

Be a Song Leader 2

Set the beat.

You know how to set the starting pitch for a song.
To be a good song leader, you also need to know how to set the beat.
To set the beat, you need to know whether beats are grouped in twos, threes, or fours.
How are the beats in "On Top of Old Smoky" grouped?
"Think" the melody and tap the heavy and light beats.
Which picture below matches your tapping pattern?

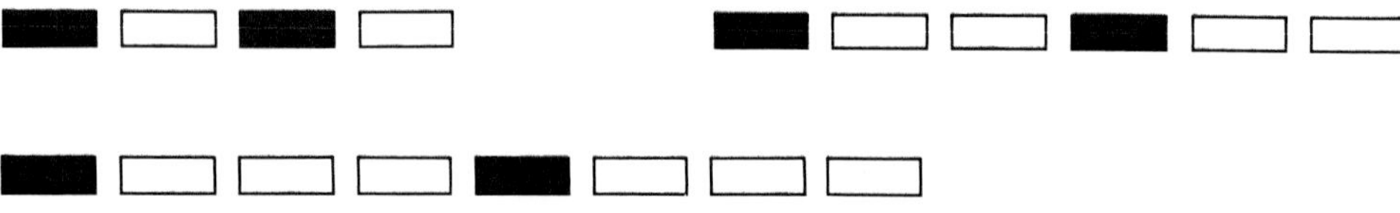

Show the singers how the beats are grouped by using one of these conducting patterns.

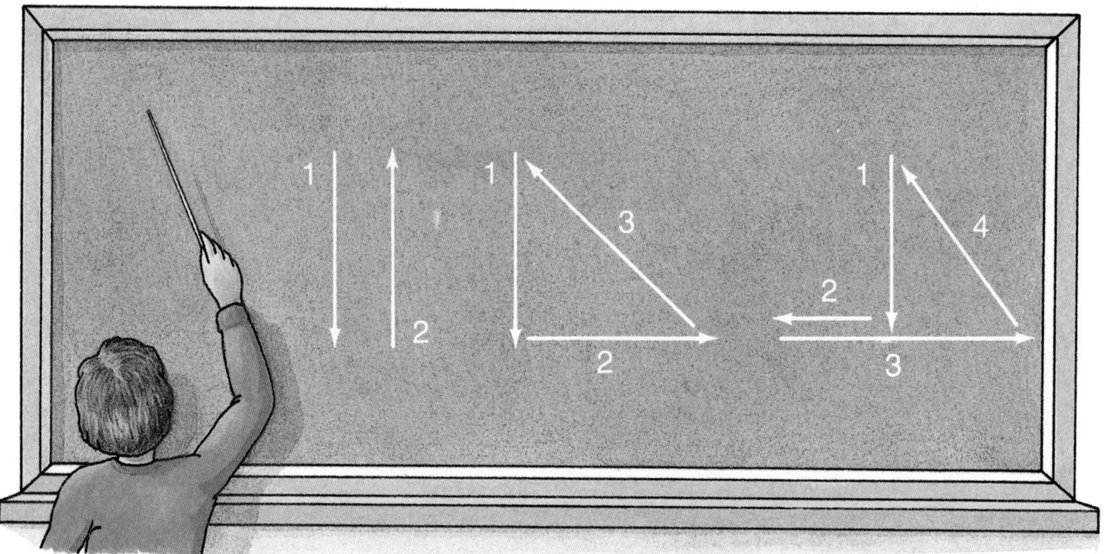

Be sure to hum the starting pitch before you signal the group to begin singing.
What about "She'll Be Coming 'Round the Mountain"?
How will you conduct that song? In twos? threes? fours?

Here is a list of "Favorite Songs to Sing."

Work in small groups.
Choose one of the songs.

How will you choose the starting pitch?
Review the suggestions on pages 70 and 71.

How will you decide whether the song moves
in twos, threes, or fours?
Practice the conducting pattern.

Take turns being the song leader.
Choose one person to lead the whole class.

Setting the Beat

Review these songs. Who will be the song leader?

She'll Be Coming 'Round the Mountain

Traditional

On Top of Old Smoky

Kentucky Folk Song

You know how the beats are grouped in these two songs.
Look at the first phrase of each song.
Can you find a musical symbol that is a clue for this information?

Is it

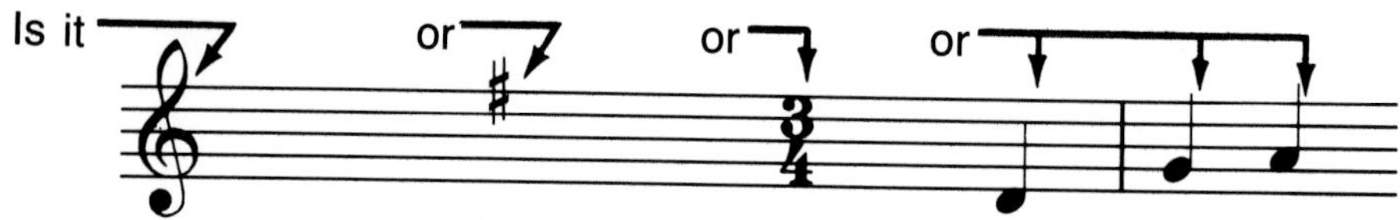

The clue is the $\frac{3}{4}$ **meter signature**.

The top number tells you to count the beats in groups.
The bottom number tells you the note that moves with the beat.

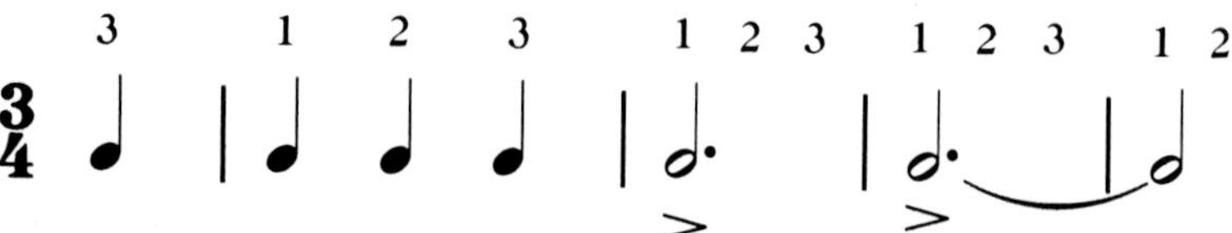

Some People

Traditional

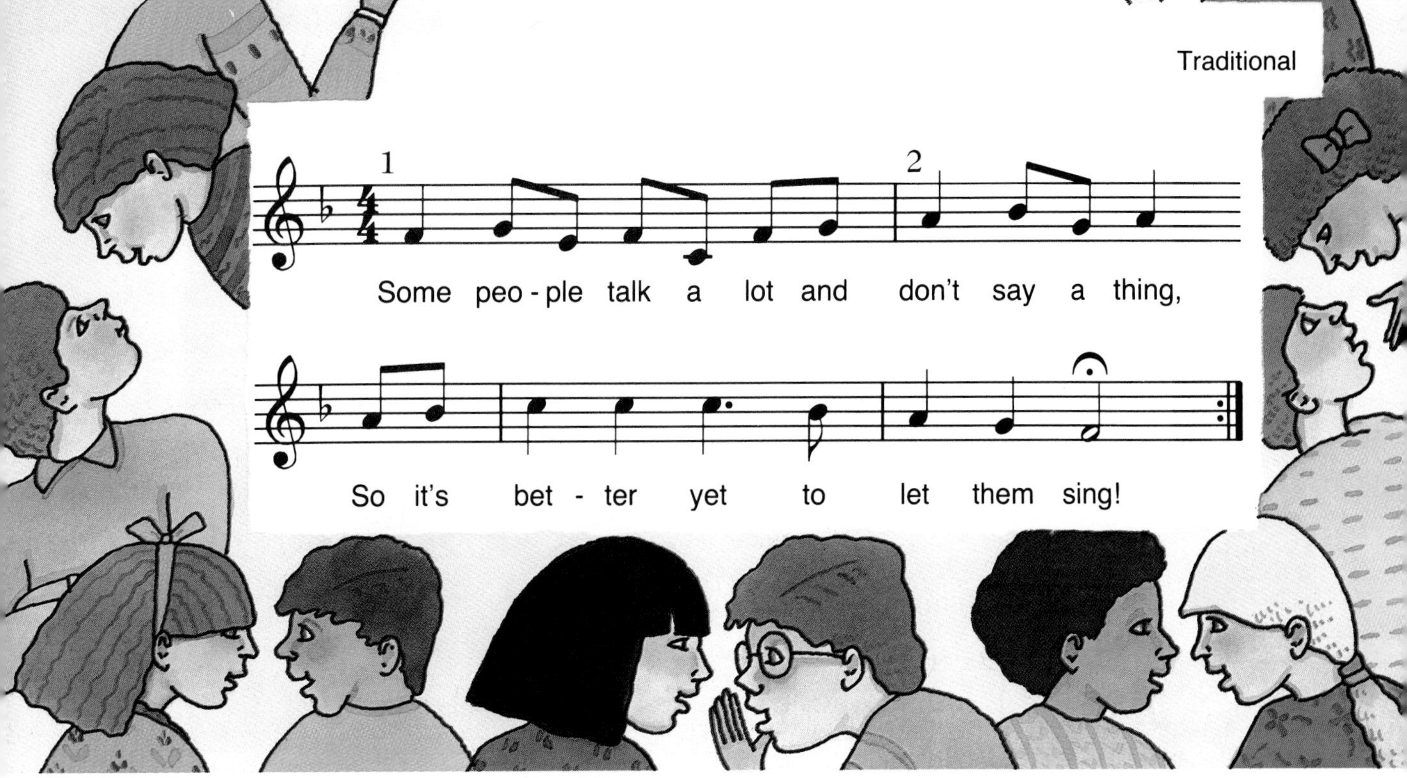
1
2
Some peo - ple talk a lot and don't say a thing,
So it's bet - ter yet to let them sing!

LISTENING

Unsquare Dance

by Dave Brubeck

Listen to an unsquare dance.
Why is this a good title?
Listen for the patterns below:

fid - dle fid - dle bass fid - dle
(hand) clap (hand) clap (hand) clap - ping

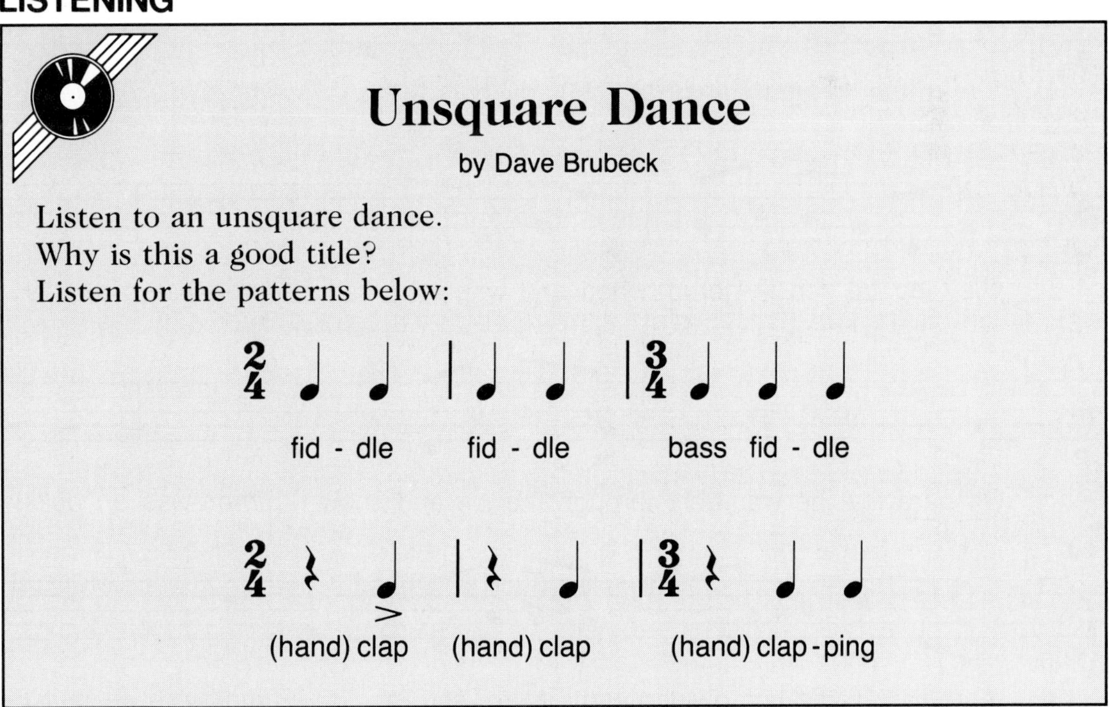

Hurdy-gurdy Man

Translation by Merritt Wheeler

Music by Franz Schubert

What is the meter signature of this song?
What does the top number tell you? the bottom number?

Play a drone autoharp accompaniment by pressing two keys at the same time.

Use this rhythm throughout the song.

There are many measures in this song
when a voice does not sing.
How many beats will you count for each of these measures?
Use these bells to create a melody.
Play it during the measures when the voice is resting.

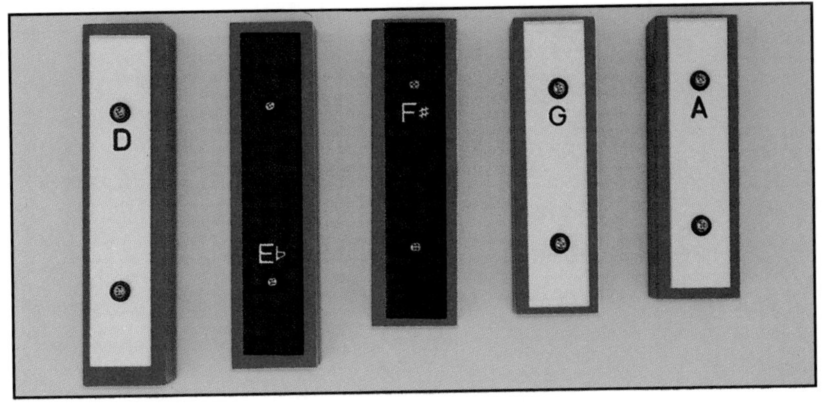

Listen to "Hurdy-gurdy Man" with Schubert's
piano accompaniment.
Compare the accompaniment he created with
those you made up.

Whether the Weather

Traditional

Learn the rhythm of this song while tapping the short sounds.

Wheth - er the weath - er be cold
Or wheth - er the weath - er be hot
Or wheth - er the weath - er be fair
Or wheth - er the weath - er be not,
We'll weath-er the weath-er what - ev - er the weath-er,
Wheth - er we like it or not!

My Name Is Yon Yonson

Traditional

Longer sounds may be shown by adding together shorter notes:

The "+" is not a music symbol.
To add notes together we use a "musical plus sign" called a **tie**.
It looks like this:

Find the musical addition symbols as you speak the rhythm of this song.

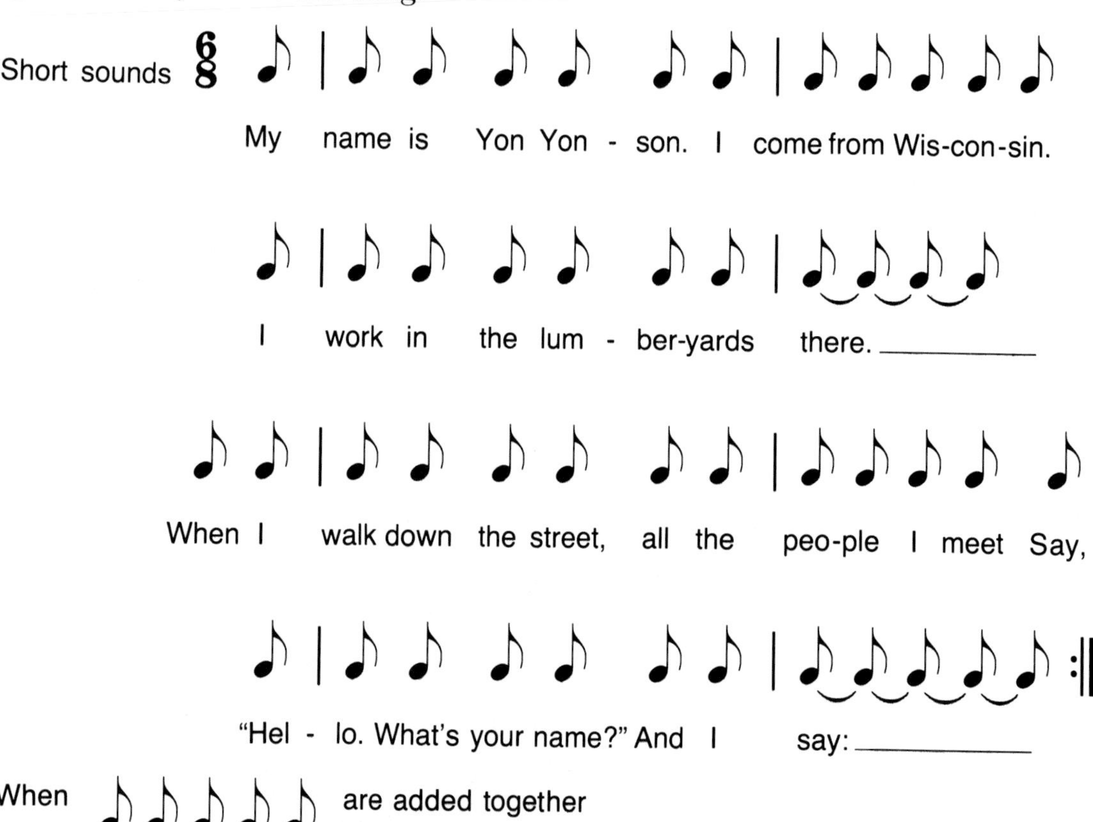

When are added together they may also look like this:

Tap the short sounds (♪) as you sing this song.

Notice how the long sounds are now written.

Follow Me

Traditional Carol

Learn to sing and play this two-part song.
Begin by learning to play Part 2 on the bells.

Which bells will you need to use?

Do you know how to choose the right bells?
Each bell has a letter name.
Each line and space on the staff has a letter name.
Can you match the bells with the staff?

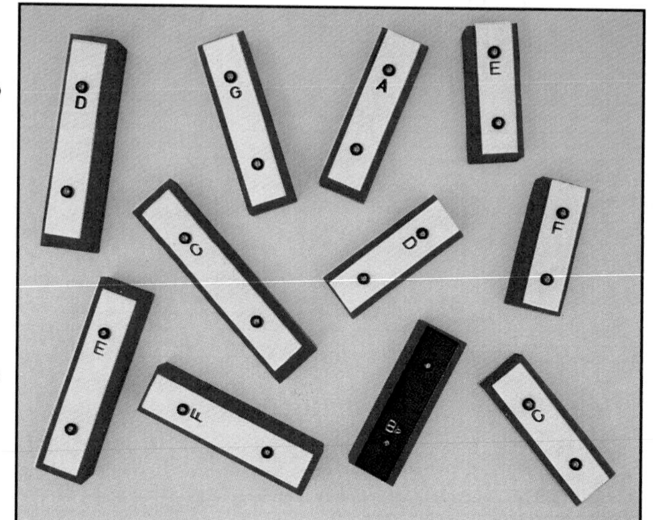

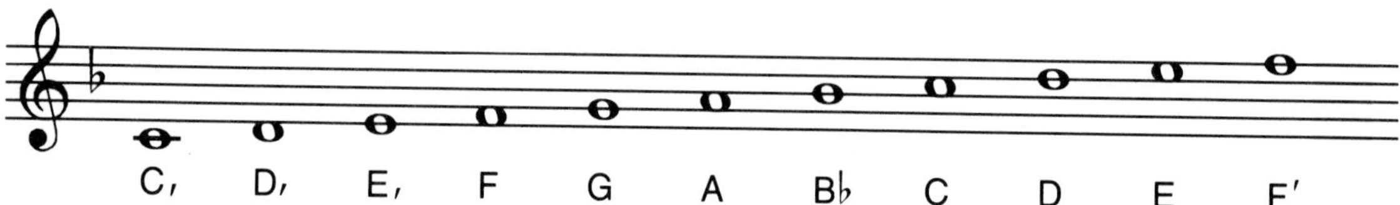

Learn Part 1 by singing the scale numbers.
Can you decide which note is the tonal center?
If you know which note on the staff is "1," can you name the scale numbers for the other notes in the song?

She'll Be Coming 'Round the Mountain

Traditional

Find a Pitch

Can you sing the songs on this page and the next by using scale numbers?

1. Locate the tonal center, scale step 1.
2. Figure out the scale step numbers for all the other notes.
3. Locate the bell you need to give the sound of the first pitch. The "Pitch Facts Guide" sheet will help you learn how to do this.

3. Gabriel, blow your trumpet loud!
4. Daniel in the lion's den.

Bye Bye Blues

Words and Music by Fred Hamm,
Dave Bennett, Bert Lown, and Chauncey Gray

Just we two, ___

Smil - ing through. ___

Don't sigh, don't cry.

Bye bye blues. ___

Musical Decisions

Tempo
After a performer has learned to sing a song, there are still many musical decisions to be made.

One of them is choosing the best speed, or *tempo,* for a song. Listen to "Chickery Chick." What tempo decision did this performer make?

Chickery Chick

Words by Sylvia Dee

Music by Sidney Lippman

Here are words and pictures that describe different tempos.
Use a metronome and define each tempo term.

The numbers indicate how many beats per minute.
Each "tick" equals one beat.

Musical Decisions

Dynamics

Chant these numbers.
What will you change each time
you chant a different number?

ppp 1111 *pp* 2222 *p* 3333 *mp* 4444 *mf* 5555

f 6666 *ff* 7777 *fff* 8888

French Cathedrals

Traditional French Round

Sing the song and follow the dynamic markings.

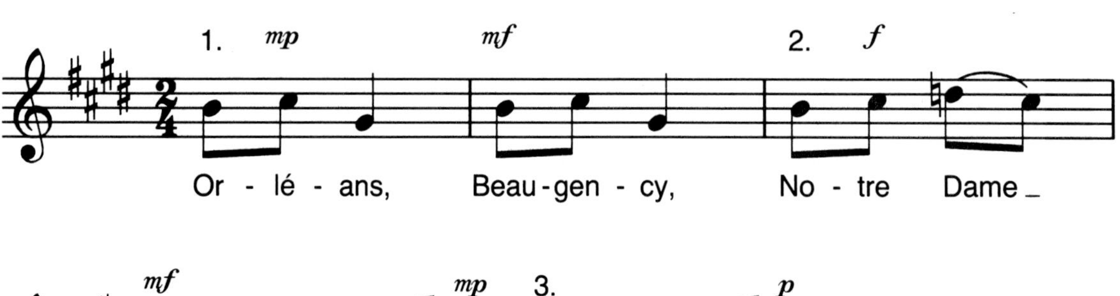

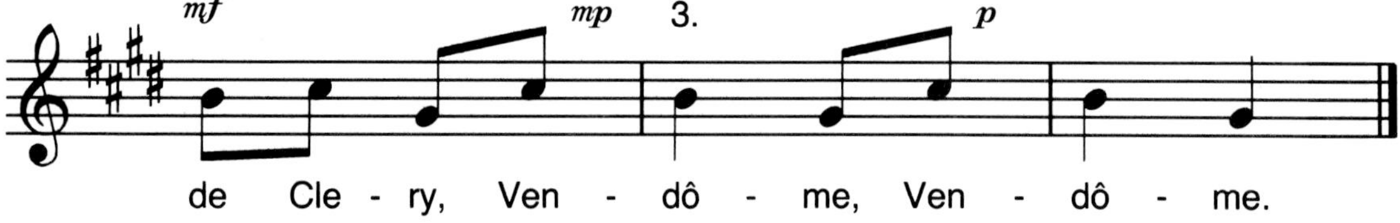

Articulation

Experiment with different ways of singing "French Cathedrals."

How will you start and stop the sounds?

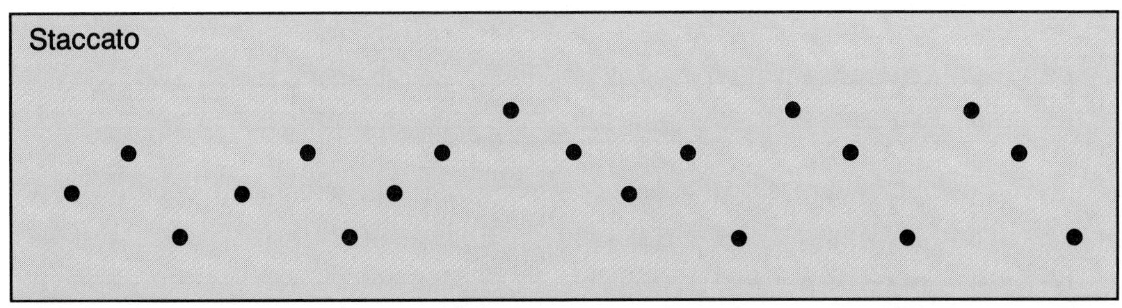

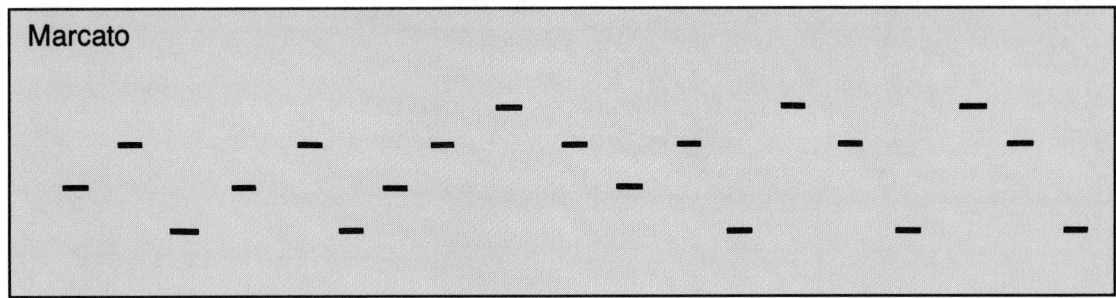

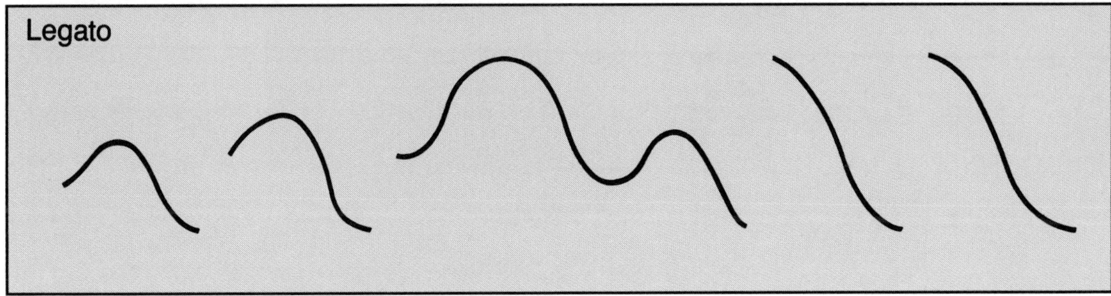

The musical term "articulation" describes how sounds start and stop.

There are different ways to articulate sounds.

Can you decide what each term means?

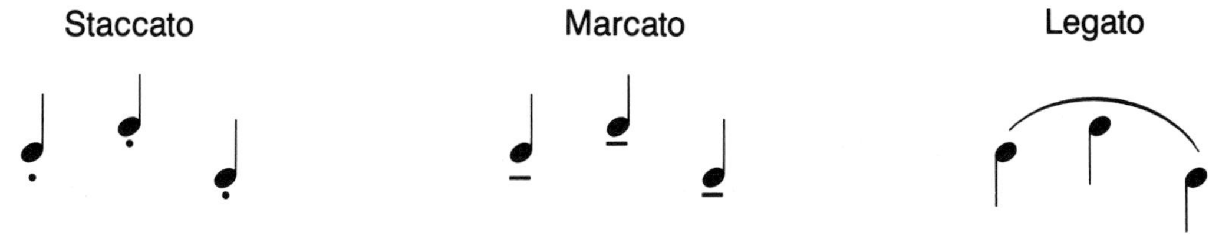

Variations on Hot Cross Buns

by F. Wayne Scott

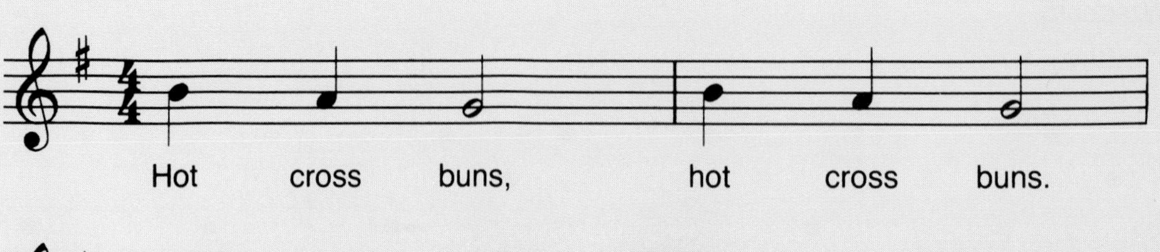

A composer makes musical decisions about:

Melody	Tempo
Rhythm	Dynamics
Harmony	Articulation
Form and Style	

What decisions did the composer make in his "Variations on Hot Cross Buns"?

Schnitzelbank

German-American Song

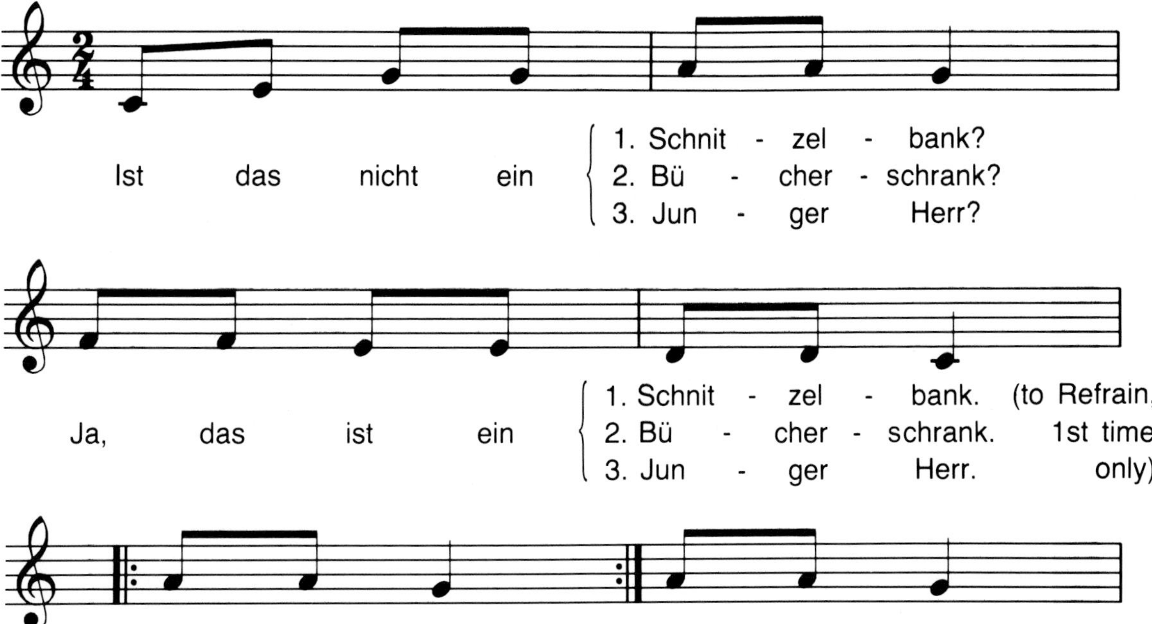

3. Junger Herr
4. Schwarzer Bär
5. Blaues Meer
6. Eisenbahn
7. Stolzer Hahn
8. Wasserfall
9. Gummiball
10. Fledermaus

Refrain

Lacadel Was a Ponderous Bear

B.A.

Perform this poem with music.
Choose two performers to play the piano ostinato throughout the piece.
Choose three performers to create a black-key improvisation after each verse.

Lacadel was a ponderous bear,
A ponderous bear who lived in a lair.
He consumed six months rations,
Slept the rest in great fashion,
And didn't pay bills for a "yair."
Nope, didn't pay bills for a "yair."

He merely rolled over
And slept like a loafer.

Improvisation 1 

Rising up ravenous one early spring day,
Lacadel hurried to the honey-pot tray.
In great disbelief and emitting a growl,
Lacadel read with a furrowed brow:
"Borrowed your honey just for the day,
Hope you don't mind, it was right on my way!"

He calmly sat down in a group of one
and had himself a bear tan-trum.

Improvisation 2 

Lacadel roared and Lacadel simpered,
His lower lip quivered, and he pitifully whimpered.
He took his loss but was really chagrined,
"I'll grind this thief in a pretzel bend!"
The thief came sneakin', honey pot in hand,
Tiptoeing back to where this began.

"Gotcha thief! Oh, pardon me.
Such a lovely, fair bear . . . . Do stay for tea!"

Improvisation 3

The Little Train of the Caipira

by Heitor Villa-Lobos

Follow the call numbers as you listen.

1

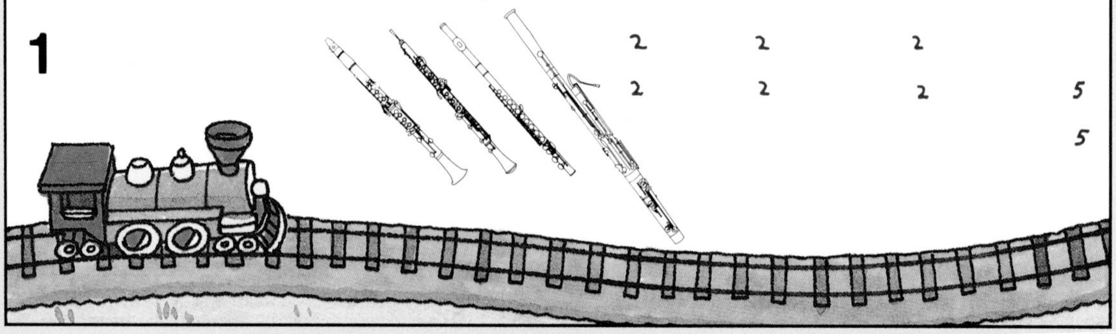

2

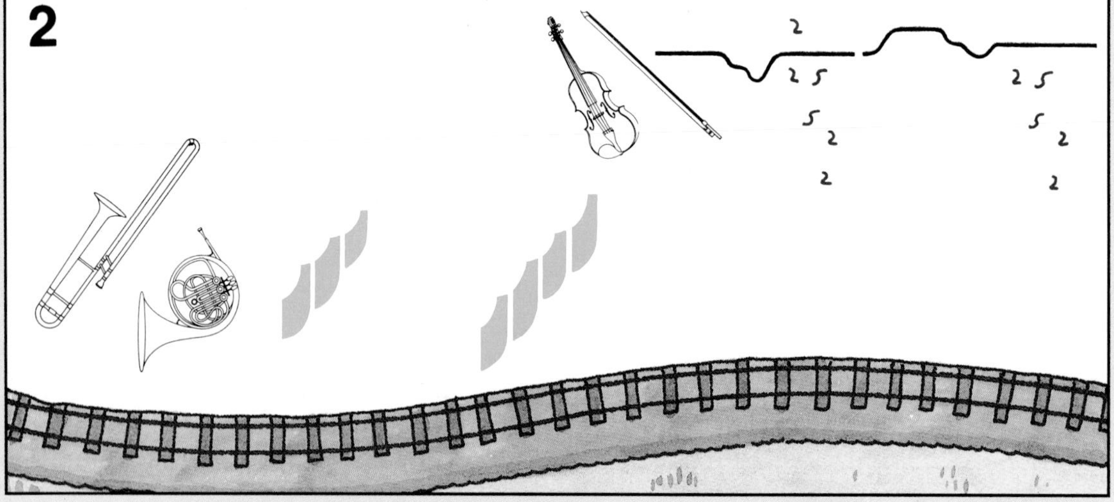

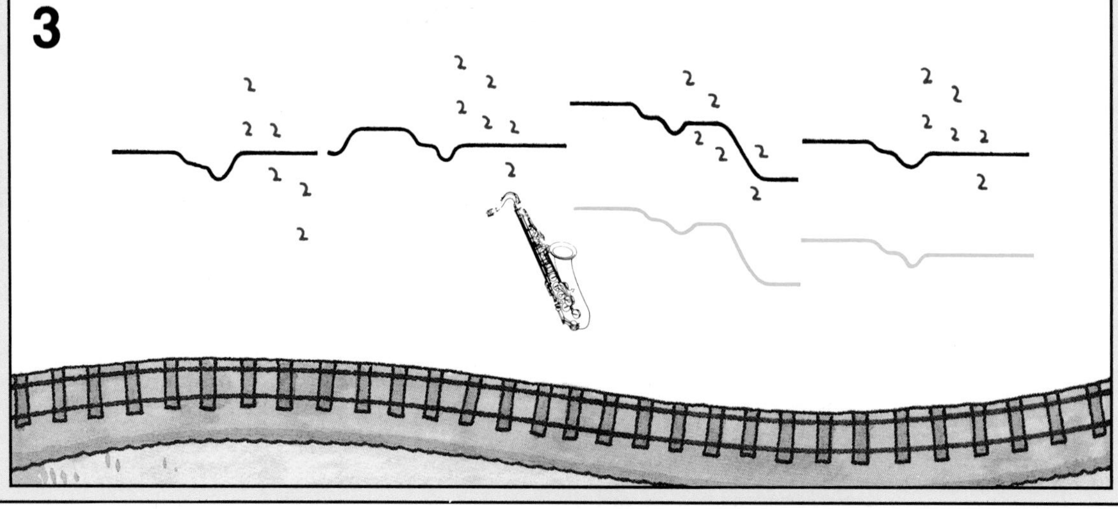

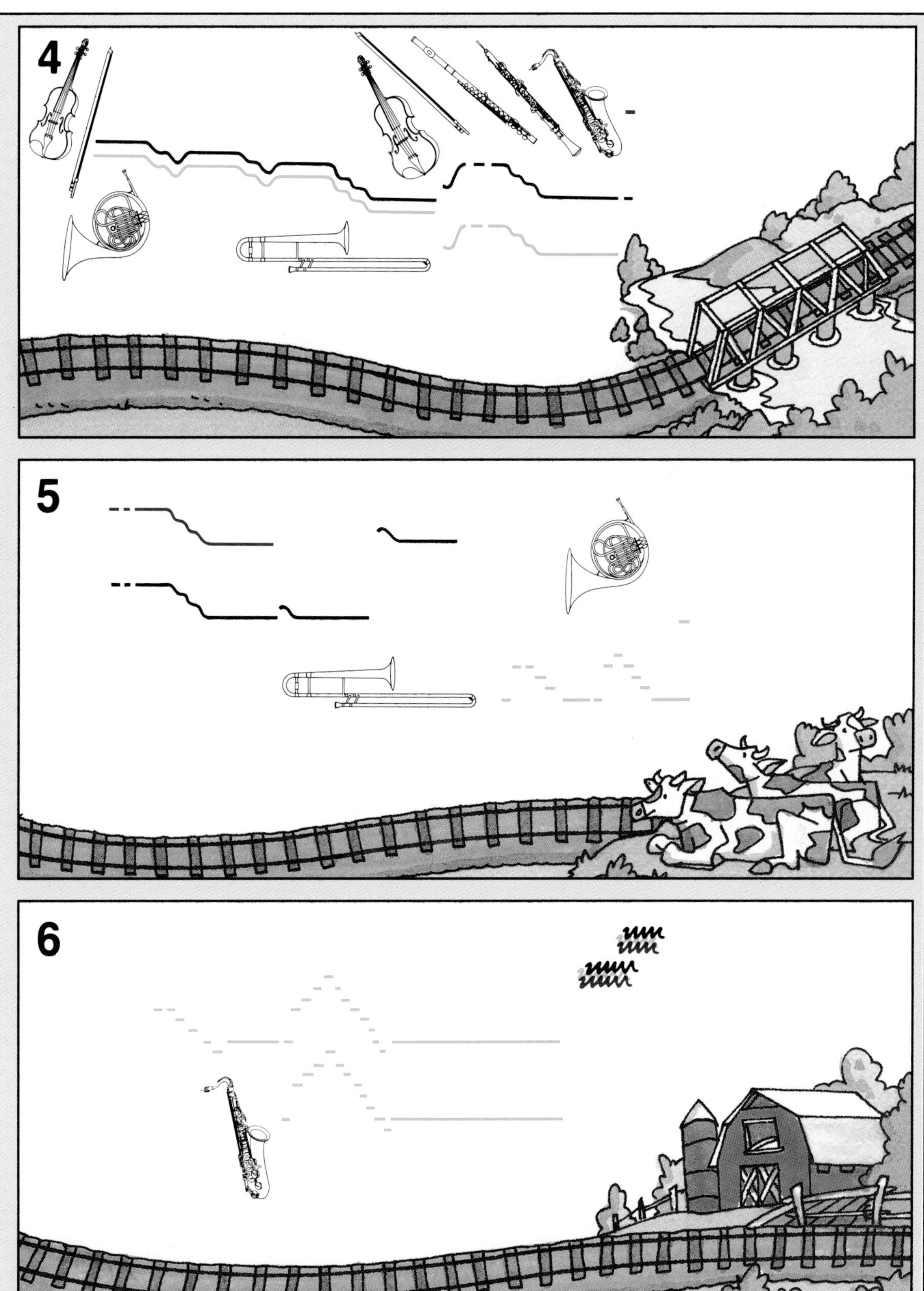

4
5
6

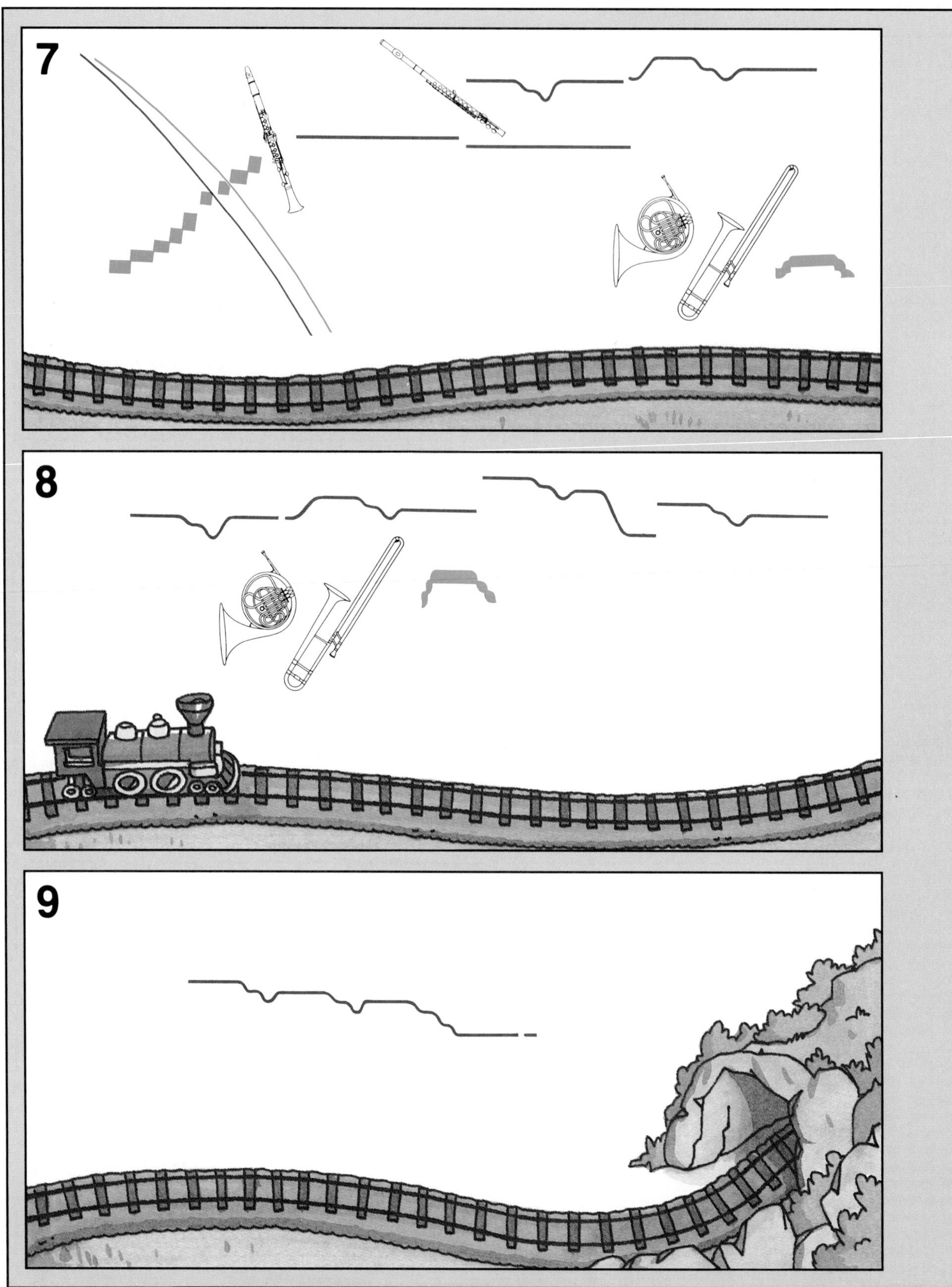
7
8
9

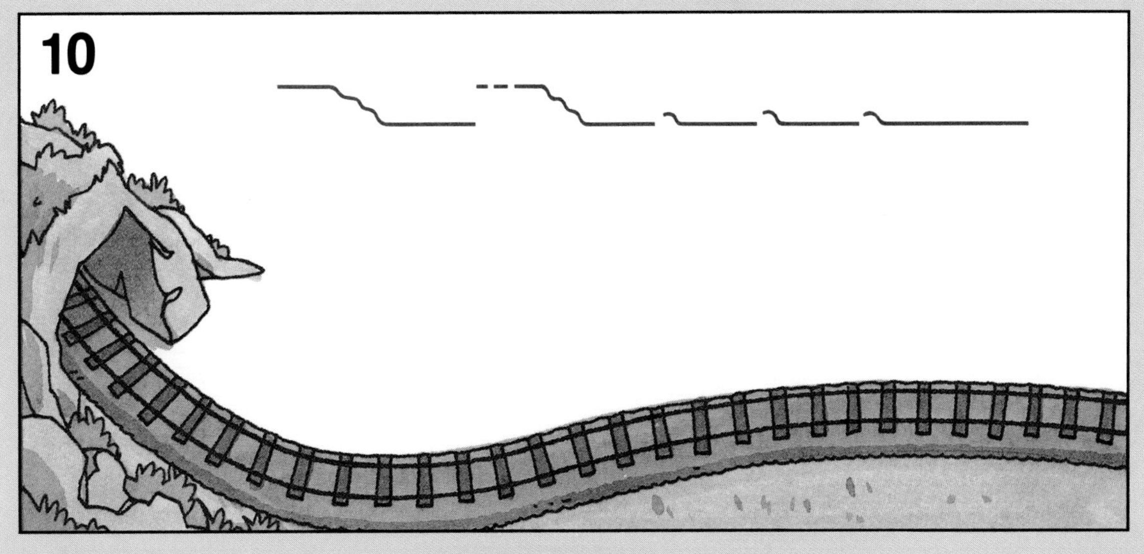

Listen to another performance.
What differences do you notice?

Review 3

You Can't Make a Turtle Come Out

Words and Music by Malvina Reynolds

Andante

1. You can't make a tur - tle come out. ______
You can't make a tur - tle come out. ______
You can call him or coax him or shake him or shout.
But you can't make a tur - tle come out, come out.
You can't make a tur - tle come out. ______

2. If he wants to stay in his shell,
If he wants to stay in his shell,
You can knock on the door but you can't ring the bell.
And you can't make a turtle come out, come out.
You can't make a turtle come out.

3. Be kind to your four-footed friends.
Be kind to your four-footed friends.
A poke makes a turtle retreat at both ends.
And you can't make a turtle come out, come out.
You can't make a turtle come out.

4. So you'll have to patiently wait.
So you'll have to patiently wait.
And when he gets ready, he'll open the gate.
But you can't make a turtle come out, come out.
You can't make a turtle come out.

5. And when you forget that he's there,
And when you forget that he's there,
He'll be walking around with his head in the air.
But you can't make a turtle come out, come out.
You can't make a turtle come out.

The Fourth Quarter

A Memory Game

How well do you remember what you hear?
Play a game to find out!

Listen to two phrases.
Are they . . .

the same, similar, or different?

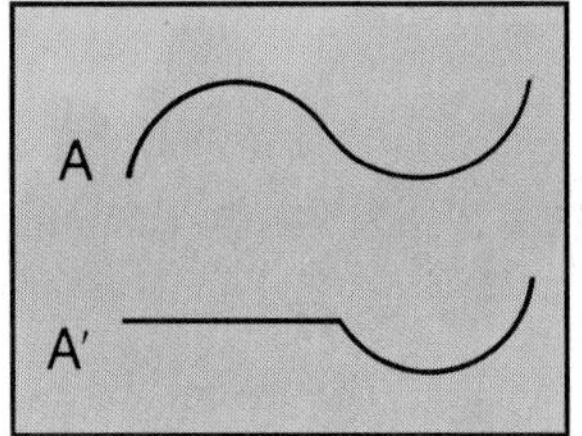

Give a Little Whistle

by Ned Washington and Leigh Harline

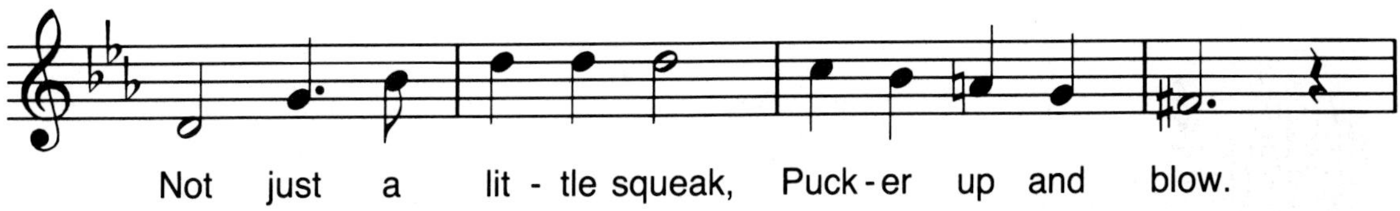

You can remember sections of a song.
Can you now remember a longer form?

Can you stretch your musical memory?
Can you remember the **A** section
when you hear a longer composition?

LISTENING

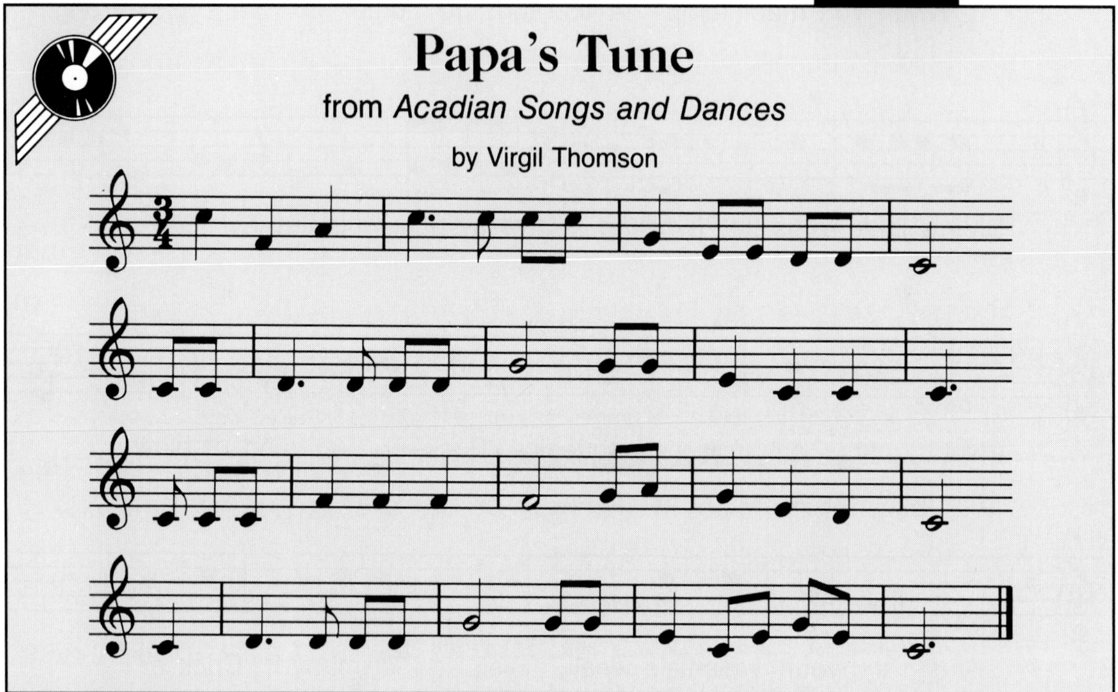

LISTENING

Creating Form

1. Create a 4-section composition.

Use this melody to play the **A** section.
Play it on these resonator bells: C, D, E, F, G, and A.
Play this autoharp chord: F

Use a chord built on the first step of the song's scale, the I chord.

Jump Down, Turn Around Southern Folk Song

2. Now plan an **A′** section. You might want to
- Change the end of the melody.
- Change the rhythm of the melody.
- Play in a new **key.**

Use these resonator bells: G, A, B♭, C, D, and E.
Use this autoharp chord:

3. Plan a **B** section.
Use the C chord for the accompaniment.
Create a new melody using these resonator bells: C, D, E, F, G, and A.
The melody must be the same length as the **A** melody.

4. Repeat the **A** section to complete your composition.

Sally Don't You Grieve
Spiritual
1. Oh, I want to go to hea-ven,
Echo
And I want to go right,
Echo
I want to go to hea-ven,
Echo
All dressed in white.
Echo

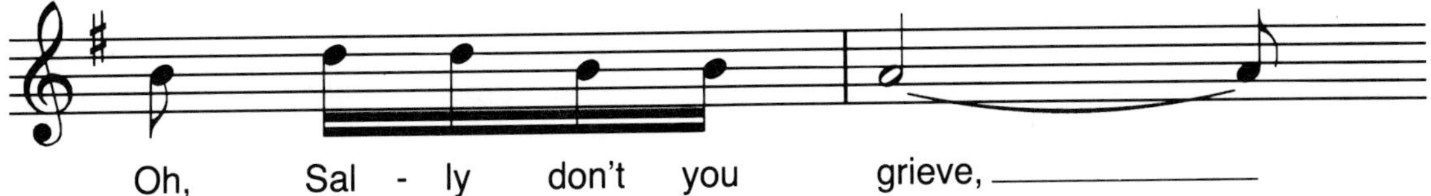

2. Oh, you can't go to heaven in a rockin' chair,
Get down on your knees and say a prayer.
Oh, you can't go to heaven in a rockin' chair,
Get down on your knees and say a prayer.
Oh, Sally don't you grieve,
Don't you grieve no more.

3. Oh, you can't go to heaven on roller skates,
You'll roll right by those pearly gates.
Oh, you can't go to heaven on roller skates,
You'll roll right by those pearly gates.
Oh, Sally don't you grieve,
Don't you grieve no more.

4. "That's all there is, there isn't any more,"
Saint Peter said, as he closed the door.
"That's all there is, there isn't any more,"
Saint Peter said, as he closed the door.
Oh, Sally don't you grieve,
Don't you grieve no more.

Allelujah, Amen

Traditional

Learn to sing and play "Allelujah, Amen."

What scale steps are used?
What pitches are used?
Which bells will you use to play the melody?

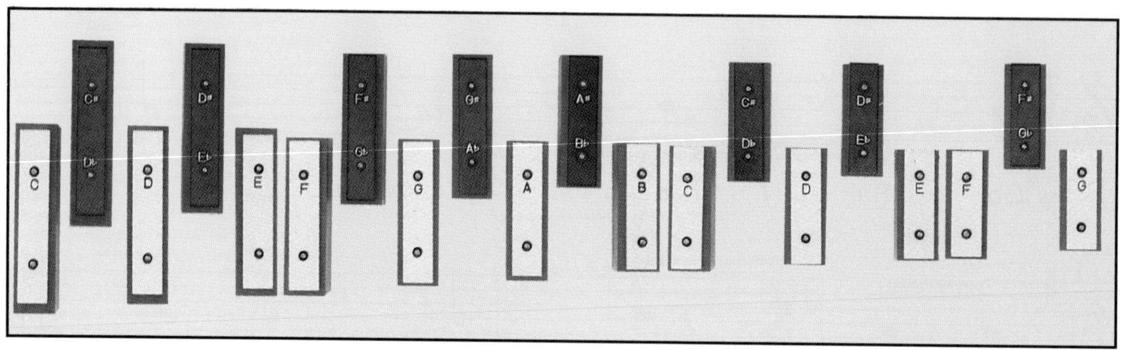

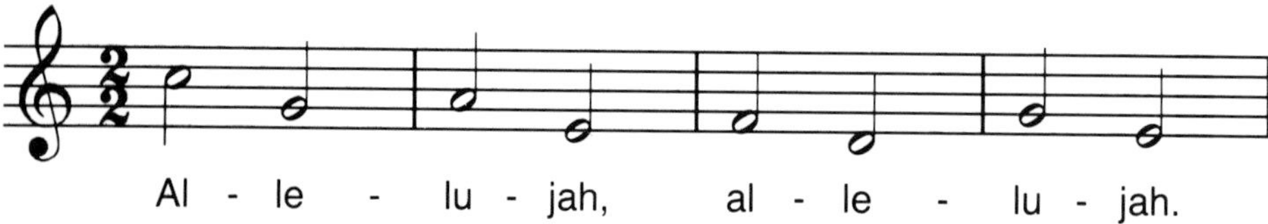

"Allelujah, Amen" is written in three different ways on page 109.

Compare the three ways.

How are they the same?
How are they different?

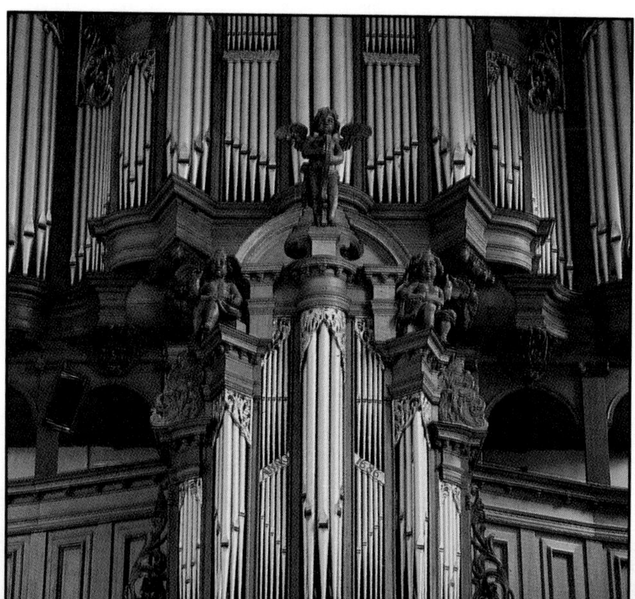

1\. Al - le - lu - jah, al - le - lu - jah.

A - men, a - men.

2\. Al - le - lu - jah, al - le - lu - jah.

A - men, a - men.

3\. Al - le - lu - jah, al - le - lu - jah.

A - men, a - men.

Buffalo Gals

American Folk Song

Learn to sing and play "Buffalo Gals."

What scale steps are used?
What pitches are used?
Which resonator bells will you use to play the melody?

Look at these three melodies.

How are they the same?
How are they different?

1.

2.

3.

Brethren in Peace Together

Jewish Folk Song

Look at the **key signature**.
On what scale is this song based?

Name the pitches used in the song.
Play them on the resonator bells, from low to high.

Does the pattern sound like the scale you named?

Someone may play this on the bells.
Others may sing it while the class sings the melody.

It is good to dwell in peace.

Lady From Baltimore

Southern Folk Song

2. Oh, she can't do the Samba;
I know she can't,
Know she can't,
Know she can't.
Oh, she can't do the Samba;
I know she can't.
Let's see what she can do.

3. Oh, she can't do the Lindy; etc.

4. Oh, she can't do the Rhumba; etc.

5. Oh, she can't Ickaboga; etc.

March of the Kings

Translated by Satis Coleman

French Folk Melody

Three great kings_ I met at ear - ly morn,_ With all their
Ce ma - tin, ___ J'ai ren-con-tré le train _ De trois grands

ret - i - nue were slow - ly march - ing. Three great
Rois qui al - laient en voy - a - ge, Ce ma -

kings ___ I met at ear - ly morn, ___ Were on their
tin, ____ J'ai ren - con-tré le train ____ De trois grands

way to meet the new - ly born. With gifts of
Rois des - sus le grand che - min. Tout char - gés

gold brought from far a - way___ And val - iant
d'or les sui-vaient d'a - bord___ De grands guer -

war - riors to guard the king - ly treas - ure, With gifts of
riers et les gar - des du tré - sor,___ Tout char - gés

gold brought from far a - way___ And shields all
d'or les sui-vaient d'a - bord___ De grands guer -

shin-ing in their bright ar - ray.
riers a - vec leurs bou- cli - ers.

LISTENING

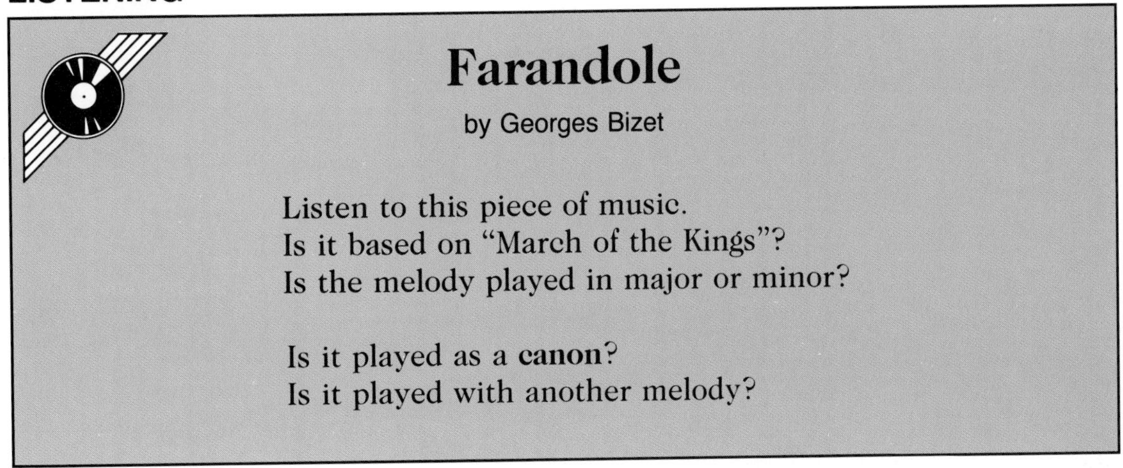

Farandole

by Georges Bizet

Listen to this piece of music.
Is it based on "March of the Kings"?
Is the melody played in major or minor?

Is it played as a **canon**?
Is it played with another melody?

Zum Gali Gali

Israeli Work Song

Melody

1. He - cha - lutz l' - maan a - vo - dah; ___
2. A - vo - dah l' - maan he - cha - lutz; ___
3. He - cha - lutz l' - maan ha - b'tu - lah; ___
4. Ha - sha - lom l' - maan ha - 'a - mim; ___

Chant

Zum ga - li ga - li ga - li, Zum ga - li ga - li,

— A - vo - dah l' - maan he - cha - lutz.
— He - cha - lutz l' - maan a - vo - dah.
— Ha - b'tu - lah l' - maan he - cha - lutz.
— Ha - 'a - mim l' - maan ha - sha - lom.

Zum ga - li ga - li ga - li, Zum ga - li ga - li.

Sing “Zum Gali Gali” in a new key.
Change the home tone from F to G.
Add an accompaniment.

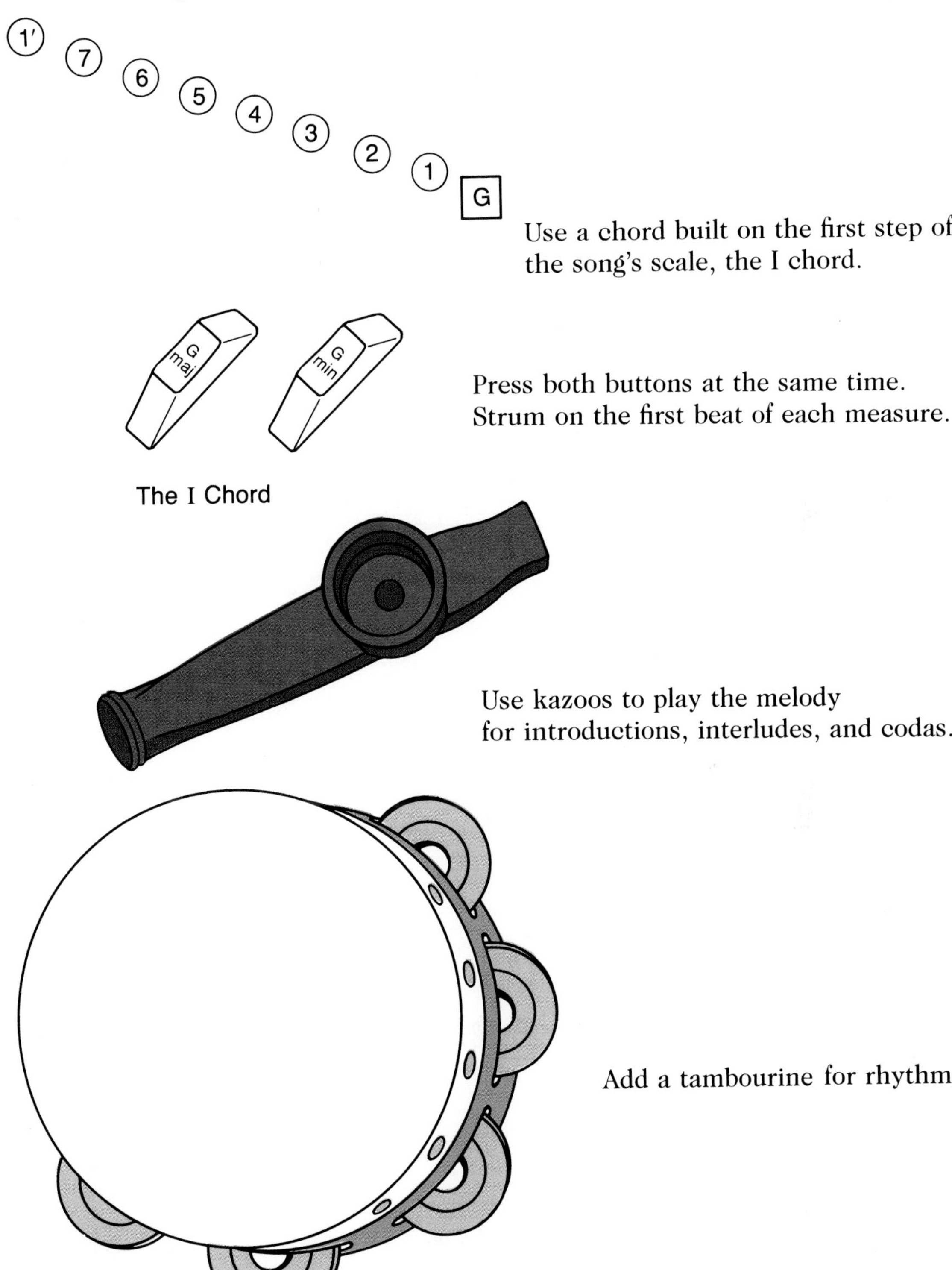

Use a chord built on the first step of the song’s scale, the I chord.

Press both buttons at the same time.
Strum on the first beat of each measure.

Use kazoos to play the melody
for introductions, interludes, and codas.

Add a tambourine for rhythm.

Down by the Riverside
Spiritual
F
1. Gon - na lay down my sword and shield, _
2. Gon - na put on my long, white robe, _
F
(Clap, clap) Down by the riv - er - side, _
C7
(Clap, clap) Down by the riv - er - side, _
F
(Clap, clap) Down by the riv - er - side, _
F
Gon - na lay down my sword and shield, _
Gon - na put on my long, white robe, _
F
(Clap, clap) Down by the riv - er - side, _
C7
F
Oh, down by the riv - er - side.

Melody: Gonna lay down my sword and shield

Melody: (Clap, clap) Down by the riverside,

Harmony: (1′ 7 6 5) Way down

Melody: (Clap, clap) Down by the riverside,

Harmony: (1′ 7 6 5) Down

Melody: (Clap, clap) Down by the riverside,

Harmony: (1′ 7 6 5) Way down

Melody: Gonna lay down my sword and shield

Melody: (Clap, clap) Down by the riverside,

Harmony: (1′ 7 6 5) Way down

Melody: Oh, down by the river-side.

Harmony: (1′ 7 6 5) Down by the river- side.

Accompany this song using two autoharp chords.

1′	F
7	E
6	D
5	C7
4	B♭
3	A
2	G
1	F

Use a chord built on the fifth step of the song's scale: the V7 chord.

V7 chord

Use a chord built on the first step of the song's scale: the I chord.

I chord

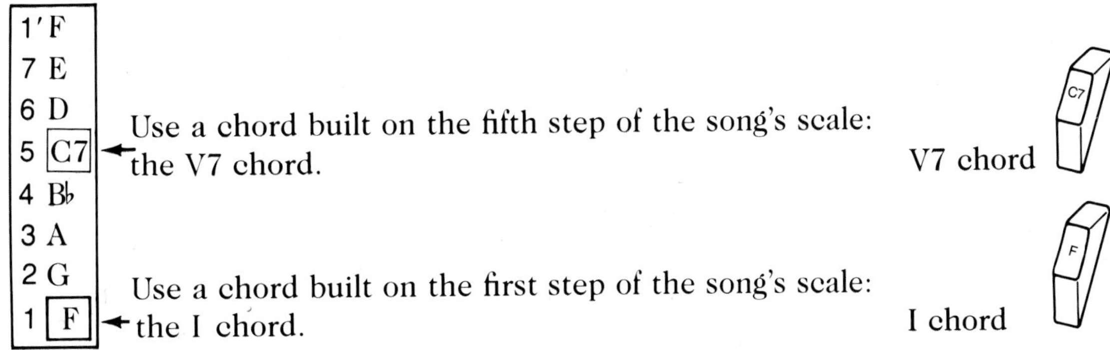

Chords not shown on pupil page

The Caravan

Syrian Folk Song

Group 1 sings the **melody** while **Group 2** sings an **ostinato.**

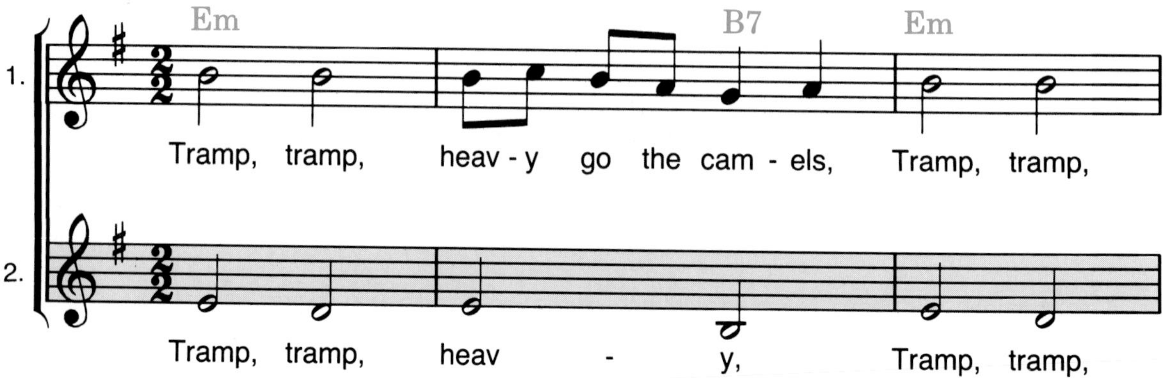

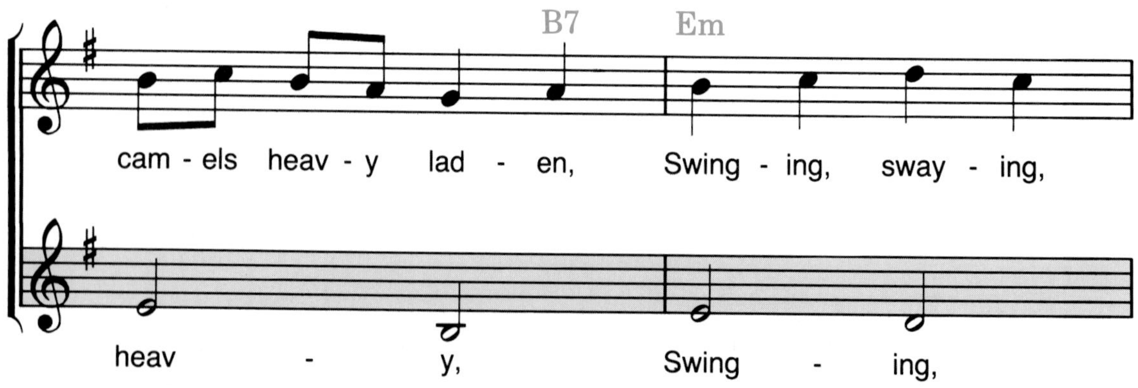

B7 Em B7 Em

1.

on the road to Bagh-dad, Heav-y goes the car - a - van.

sway - ing, Heav - y bur - den.

Em B7 Em

2.

Heav - y goes the car - a - van.

Car - a - van.

Add an accompaniment.

High-pitched drum: (Play 4 times)

Finger cymbals: (Play 4 times)

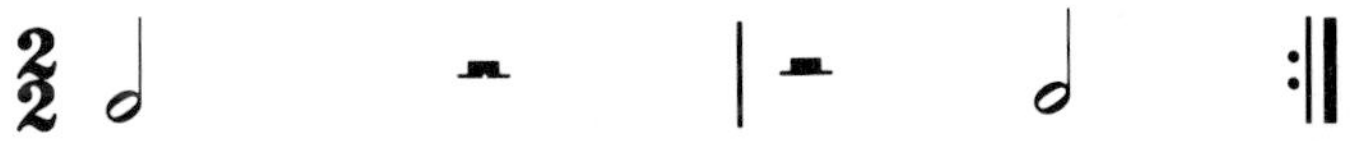

Bass Metallophone:

B
E

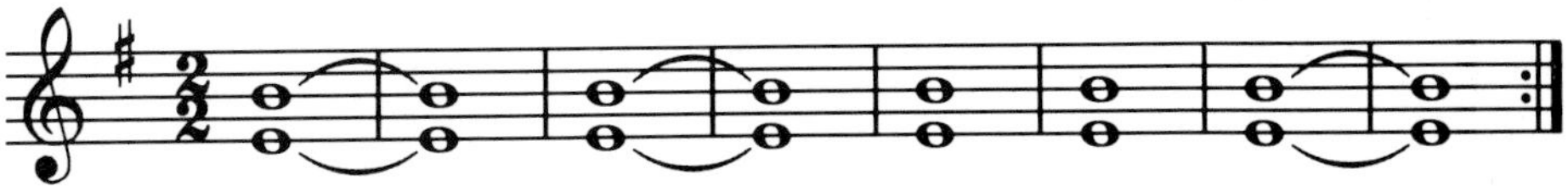

Get Along, Little Dogies

Cowboy Song

Use the information you have learned this year.
Learn the three western songs on pages 124 through 127.

1. Describe the form.
2. Study the rhythm.
3. Learn the melody.

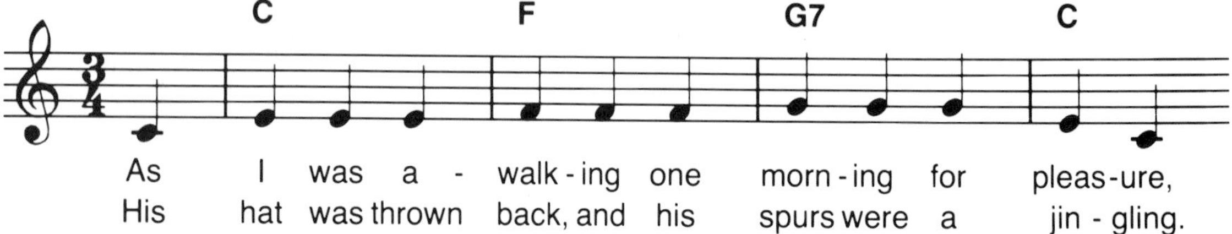

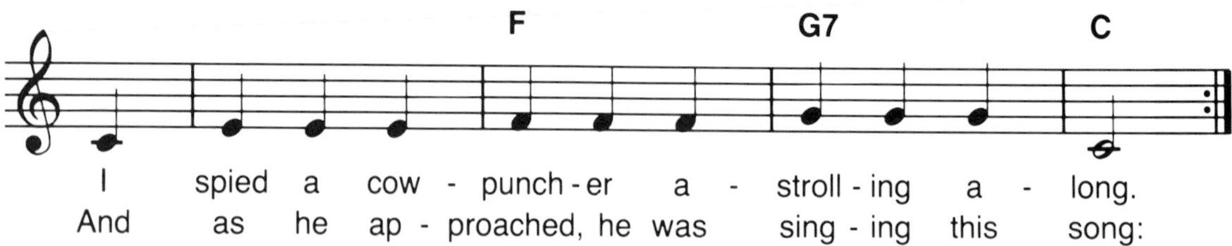

Refrain
C7
F
Whoop-ee ti - yi - yo, get a - long, lit - tle do - gies.

C7
F
It's your mis - for - tune and none of my own.

C
G7
C
Whoop-ee ti - yi - yo, get a - long, lit - tle do - gies.

F
G7
C
You know that Wy - o - ming will be your new home.

I Ride an Old Paint
American Folk Song
I ride an old Paint._ I lead an old Dan._
I'm going to Mon - tan - a to throw the Hou - li - han.
They feed in the cou - lees, they wa - ter in the draw.
Their tails are all mat - ted, their backs are all raw.
Refrain
Ride a - round, lit - tle do - gies, ride a - round_ them_ slow.
For the fier - y and snuf - fy are rar - in' to go.

My Home's in Montana

Cowboy Song

D G

When rid - ing the rang - es, my luck nev-er chang-es.
When I have par - tak - en of beans and of ba - con,

LISTENING

Cattle

by Virgil Thomson

The composer used these three songs of the West as the themes for a composition. Listen to "Cattle."

Can you find each song?
Are the melodies exactly the same as you sang them?

So Long, Farewell

from *The Sound of Music*

Words by Oscar Hammerstein, II

Music by Richard Rodgers

1.
We flit, we float, we fleet - ly flee, we fly. 4. The
So long, fare - well, Auf Wie - der - sehn, a -
2.
dieu. Good - bye, good - bye,

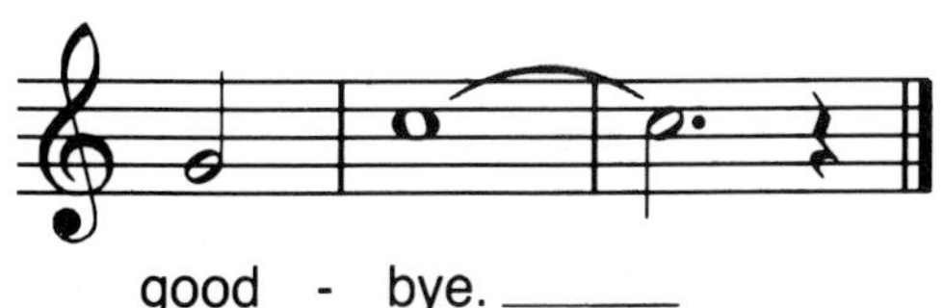
good - bye.

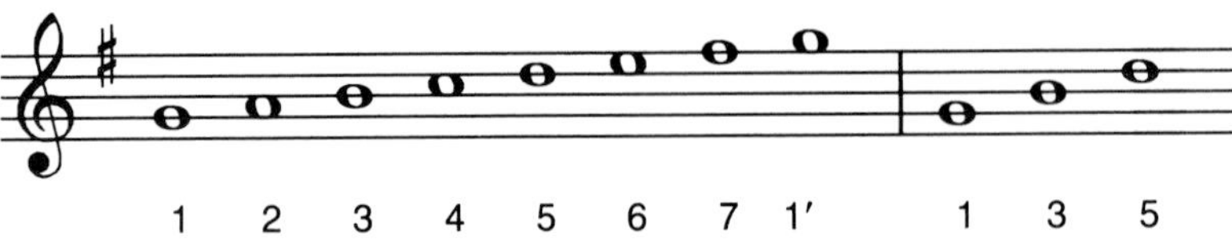

To sing "Row Your Boat," which key is more comfortable?

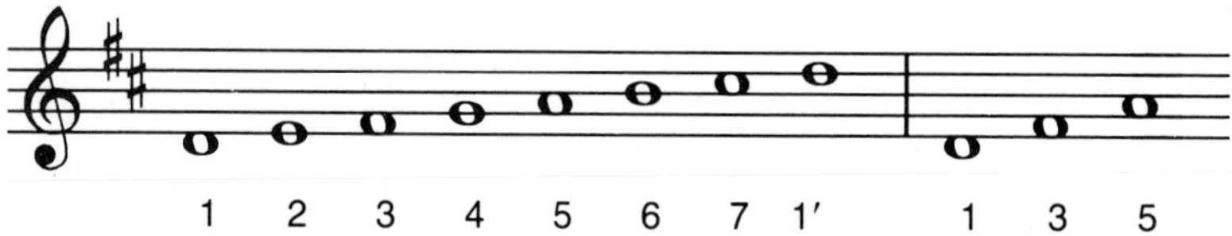

There Was an Old Woman

American Folk Song

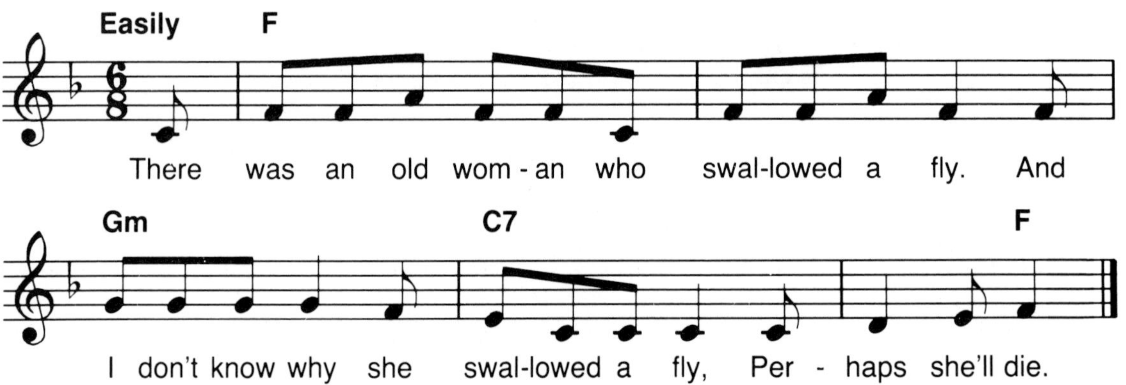

p 2. There was an old woman who swallowed a spider that wiggled and jiggled and tickled inside her! She swallowed the spider to swallow the fly, and I don't know why she swallowed the fly. Perhaps she'll die!

f 3. There was an old woman who swallowed a bird! How absurd to swallow a bird! She swallowed the bird to swallow the spider to swallow the fly, and I don't know why she swallowed the fly. Perhaps she'll die!

p 4. There was an old woman who swallowed a cat! Imagine that to swallow a cat! She swallowed the cat to swallow the bird to swallow the spider to swallow the fly, and I don't know why she swallowed the fly. Perhaps she'll die!

mf 5. There was an old woman who swallowed a dog! What a hog to swallow a dog! She swallowed the dog to swallow the cat to swallow the bird to swallow the spider to swallow the fly, and I don't know why she swallowed the fly. Perhaps she'll die!

f 6. There was an old woman who swallowed a goat! Just opened her throat and swallowed a goat! She swallowed the goat to swallow the dog to swallow the cat to swallow the bird to swallow the spider to swallow the fly, and I don't know why she swallowed the fly. Perhaps she'll die!

p 7. There was an old woman who swallowed a cow! I don't know how she swallowed a cow! She swallowed the cow to swallow the goat to swallow the dog to swallow the cat to swallow the bird to swallow the spider to swallow the fly, and I don't know why she swallowed the fly. Perhaps she'll die!

ff 8. There was an old woman who swallowed a horse! SHE'S DEAD, OF COURSE!

LISTENING

Concerto in D

Johann Altenburg

The trumpet concerto has three short movements identified by tempo markings. Listen to the composition. Which movement is *Andante*? *Allegro*? *Vivace*? Can you hear dynamic changes?

Review 4

Lament for a Donkey

Spanish Folk Tune

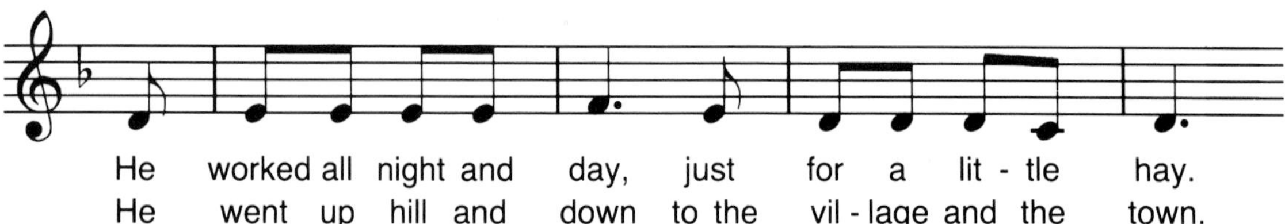

3. One hot summer day, though
Poor Tururu passed away, oh.
He breathed weary sighs
And forever closed his eyes.
He breathed such weary sighs
And forever closed his eyes.
He breathed such weary sighs
And forever closed his eyes.

4. All the village people
came together round the steeple.
Said, "We'll ring the bell
For the donkey worked so well."
They said "We'll ring the bell
For the donkey worked so well."
They said "We'll ring the bell
For the donkey worked so well."

Gypsy Rover

English Ballad

Unit 2

More Music To Explore

Perform Music

Learn to Play the Autoharp

It's as easy as "one, two, three!"
Easy as "one . . . "

- Play an expressive accompaniment as you speak these words.
- Use only: Am Min

I am the wind
I blow and I roar
I stir the low waters
And hurl them ashore.

I whirl o'er the dunes
Then settle on flowers
I lift each soft petal
Then rise to chase showers.

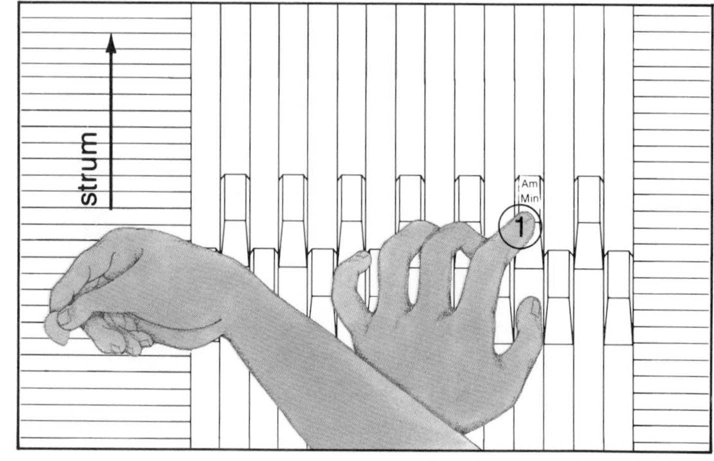

Three Blind Mice

Traditional Round

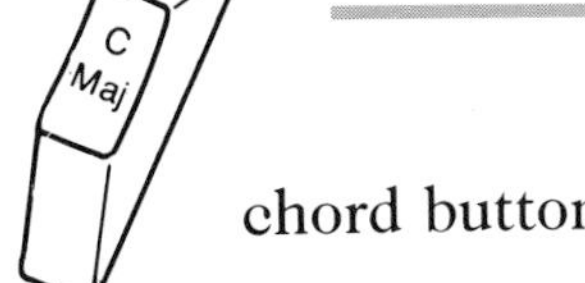

- Find the chord button.

  Press it down firmly with your left index finger.
- Use your right hand to strum the chord while you sing.

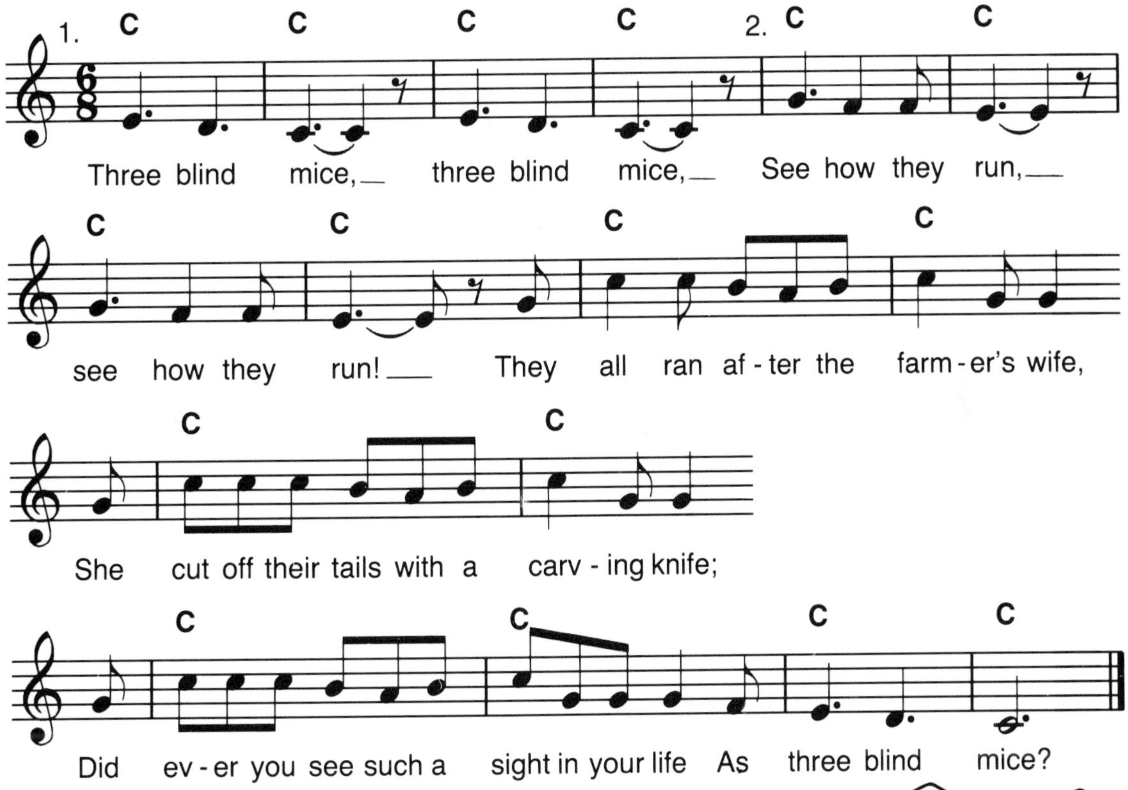

1\. C C C C 2. C C

Three blind mice,— three blind mice,— See how they run,—

C C C C

see how they run!— They all ran af - ter the farm - er's wife,

C C

She cut off their tails with a carv - ing knife;

C C C C

Did ev - er you see such a sight in your life As three blind mice?

Sing "Three Blind Mice" several times. Each time, choose a different **major** chord and change the beginning pitch of the melody.

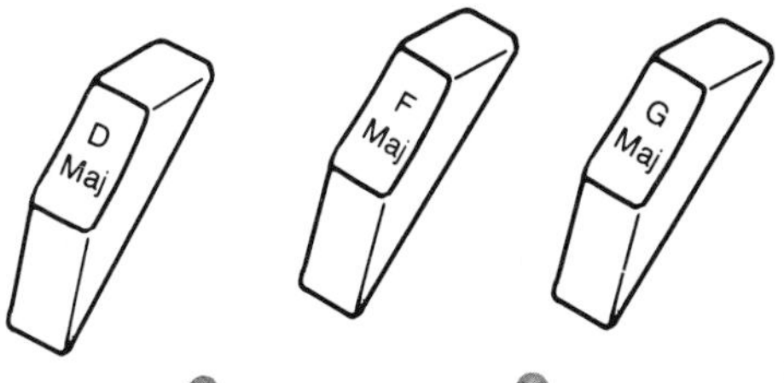

D Maj F Maj G Maj

Play these chords:
Begin singing on these pitches:

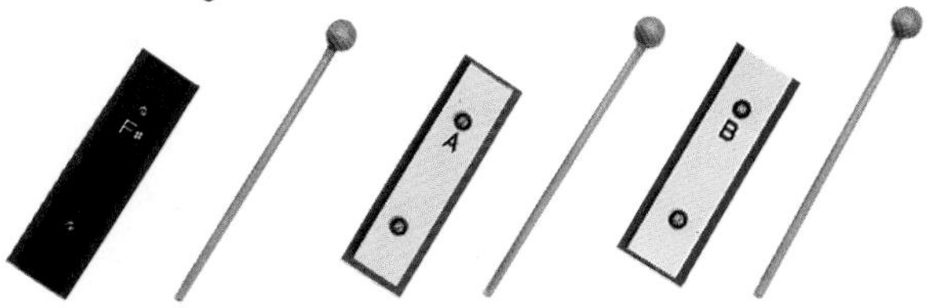

F♯ A B

What was different about your singing when you repeated the round in each of the **major** keys?

Which was your best **key** for singing?

Hey, Ho! Anybody Home?

English Round

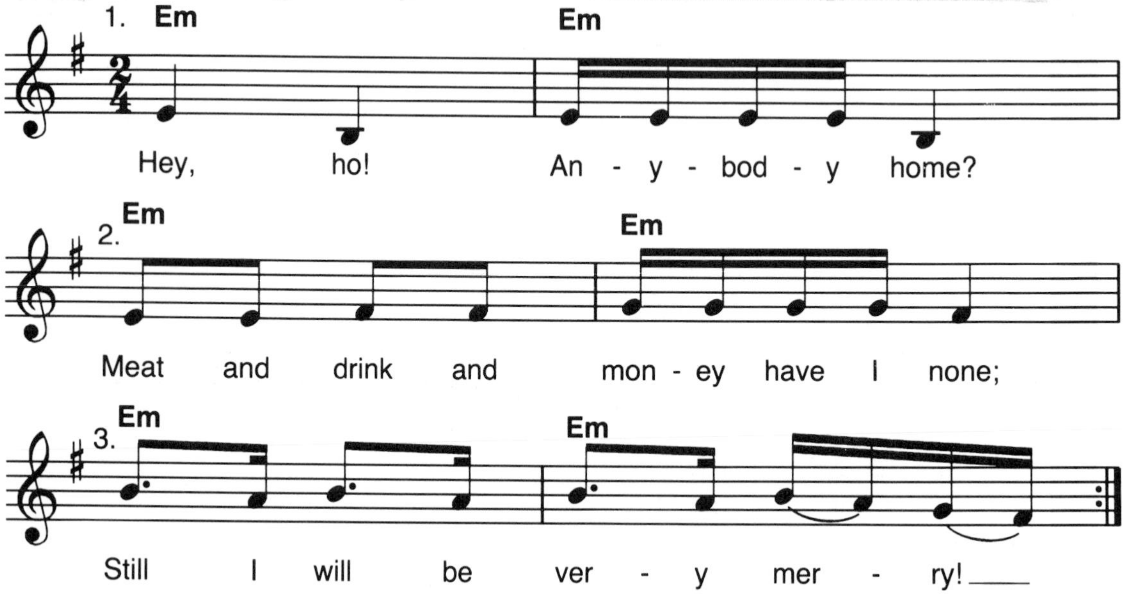

Sing and accompany "Hey, Ho! Anybody Home?"

Use one **minor** chord:

Repeat the song in different **minor keys,** changing the first pitch.

Play these chords:

Begin singing on these pitches:

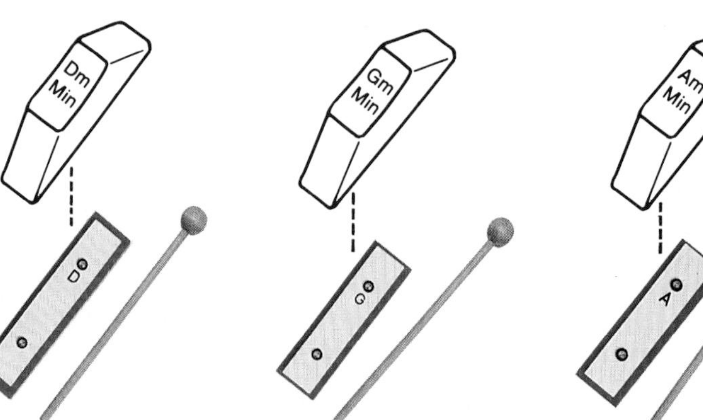

Which was your best **key** for singing?

Groundhog

Traditional

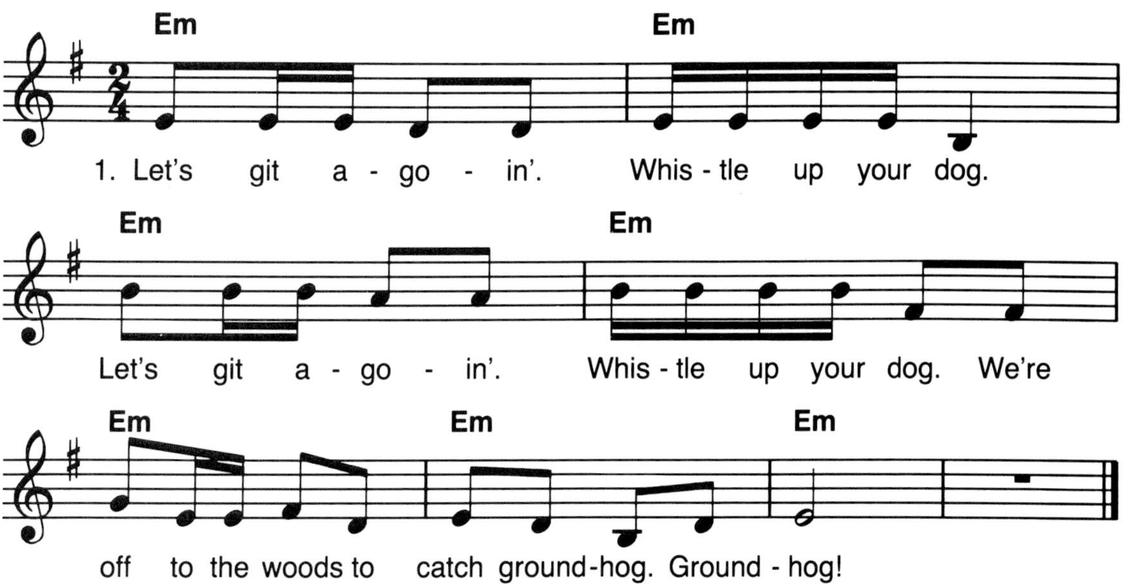

2. Everybody ready and everybody set.
Everybody ready and everybody set.
We'll catch a groundhog, you can bet. Groundhog!

3. Too many rocks and too many logs.
Too many rocks and too many logs.
Too much trouble to catch groundhogs. Groundhog!

Found a Peanut

Nonsense Song

4. Got sick . . .
5. Called the doctor . . .
6. Had an operation . . .
7. I died anyway . . .
8. Went to heaven . . .
9. Woke up . . .

What other verses can you make up to finish this song?

A Sailor Went to Sea

Traditional

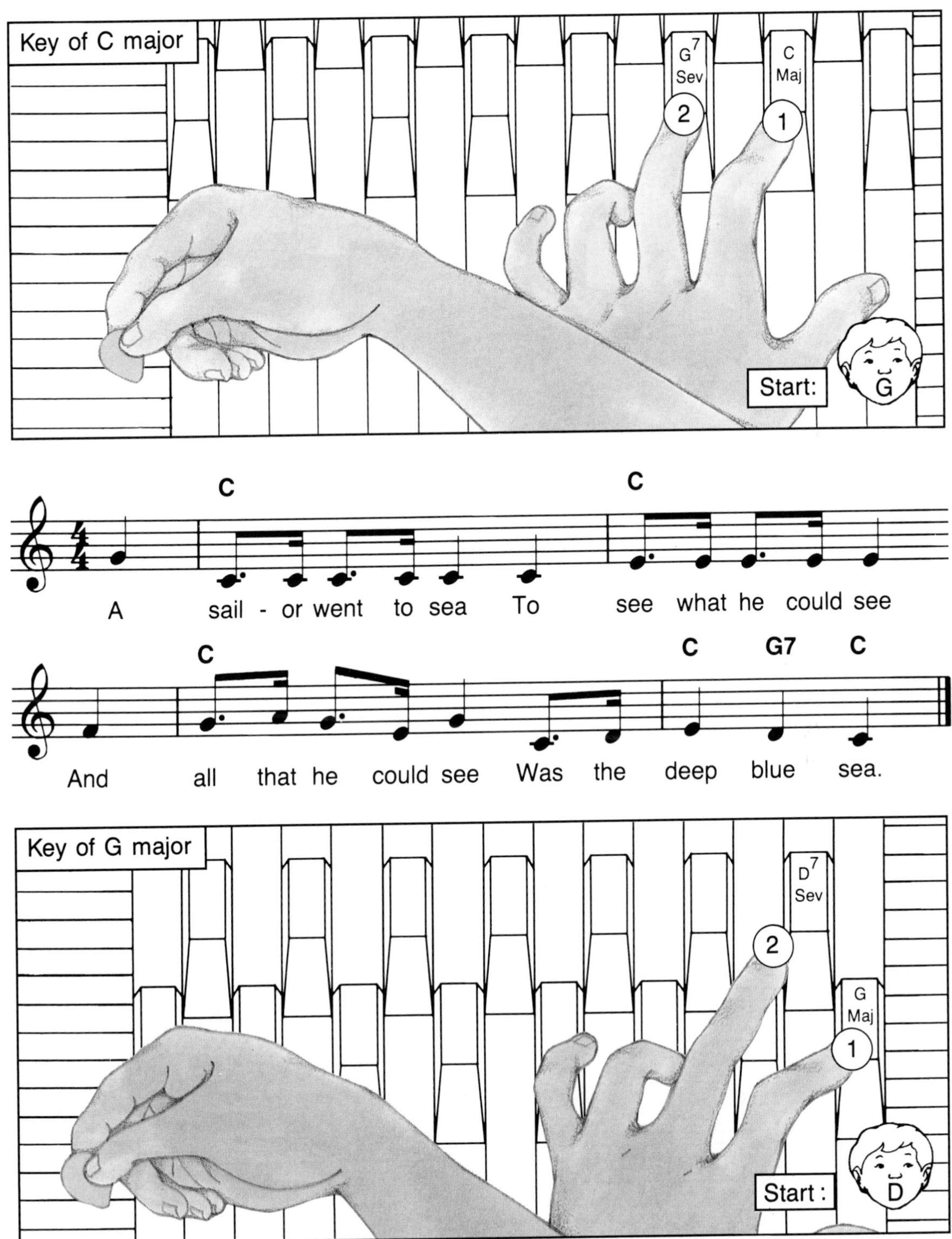

So Long It's Been Good to Know You

Words and Music by Woody Guthrie

Easy as "one, two, three!"

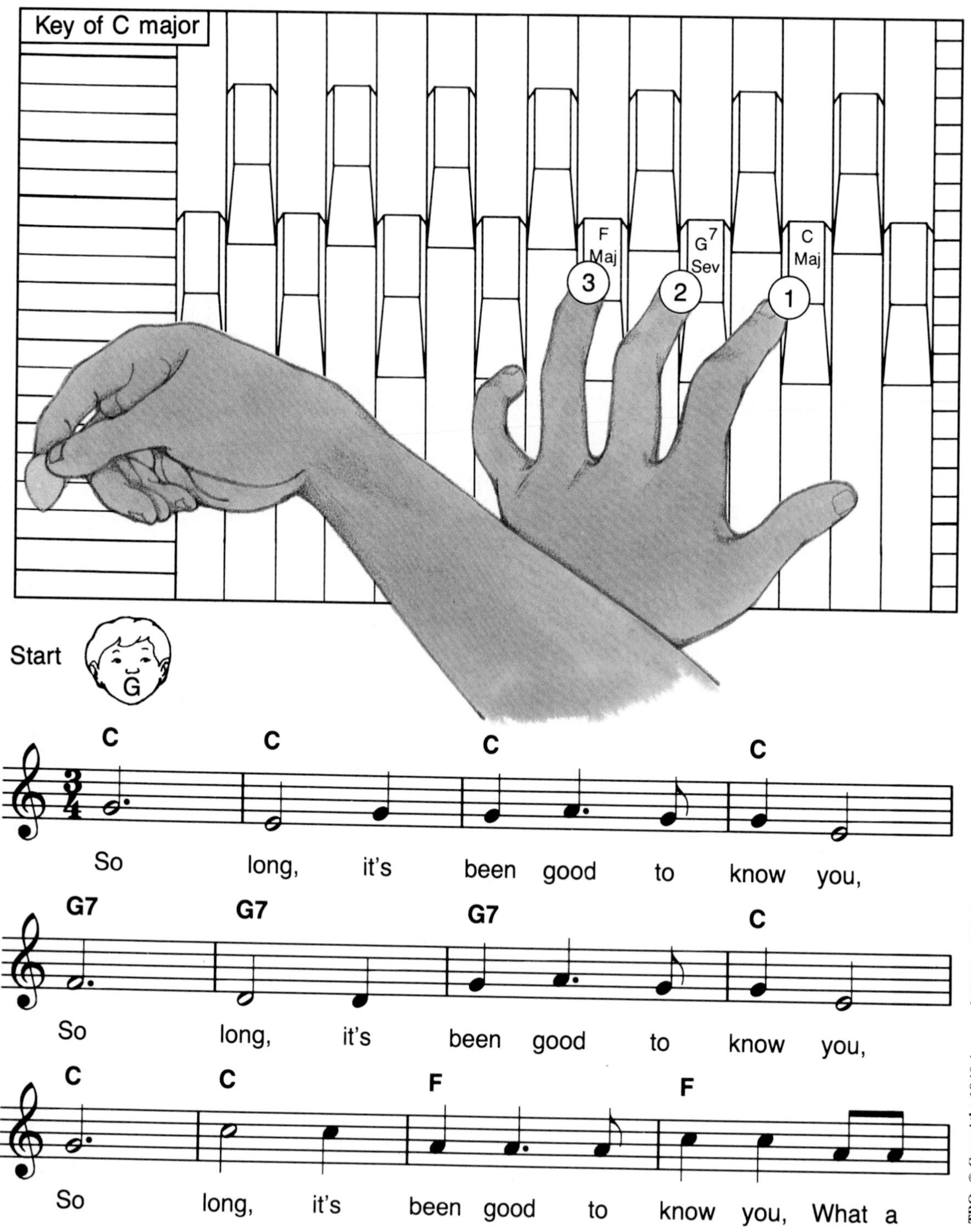

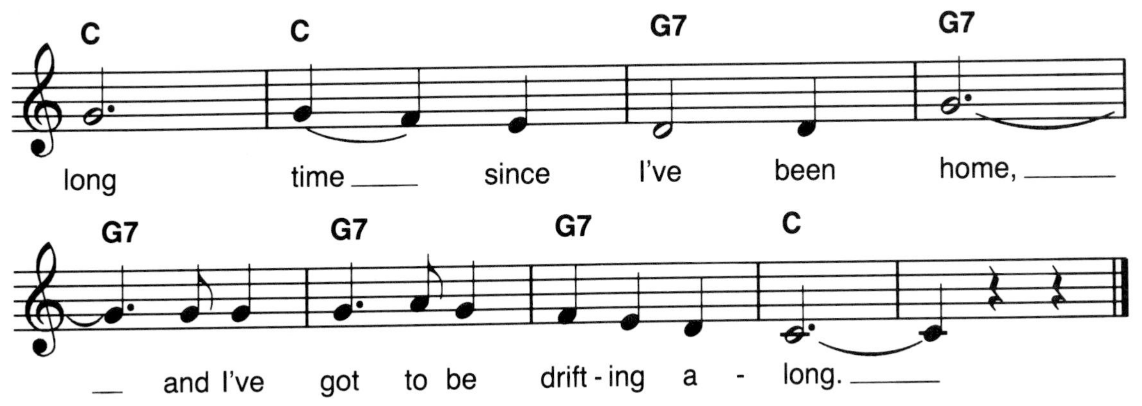
C C G7 G7
long time since I've been home,
G7 G7 G7 C
and I've got to be drift - ing a - long.

Down by the Bay
Traditional
Group 1
G
Group 2
G
Down by the bay, (Down by the bay)
D7
D7
Where the wa - ter-mel - ons grow, (Where the wa - ter-mel - ons grow)
D7
D7
Back to my home, (Back to my home)
G
G
I dare not go. (I dare not go)
C
C
For if I do, (For if I do)
G
G
My moth - er will say: (My moth - er will say)
All
D7
D7
"Did you ev - er see a bee with a sun-burned knee
D7
D7
Down by the bay?"

Old Texas

Cowboy Song

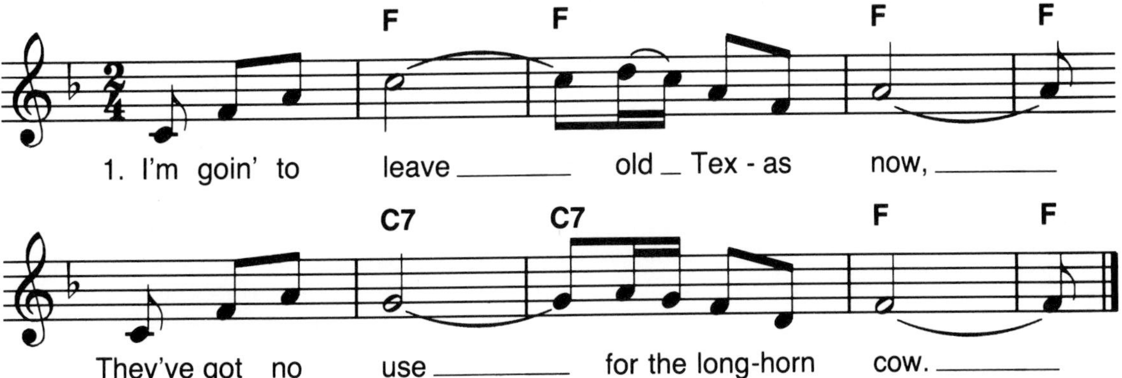

2. They've plowed and fenced my cattle range,
   And the people there are all so strange.

3. I'll take my horse, I'll take my rope,
   And hit the trail upon a lope.

4. Say *adios* to the Alamo,
   And turn my head toward Mexico.

5. I'll make my home on the wide wide range,
   For the people there are not so strange.

6. The hard hard ground shall be my bed,
   And my saddle seat shall hold my head.

Divide into two groups.
Perform this song singing
two special parts.
When do you hear
only a melody?
When do you hear harmony?

I'm on My Way

Traditional

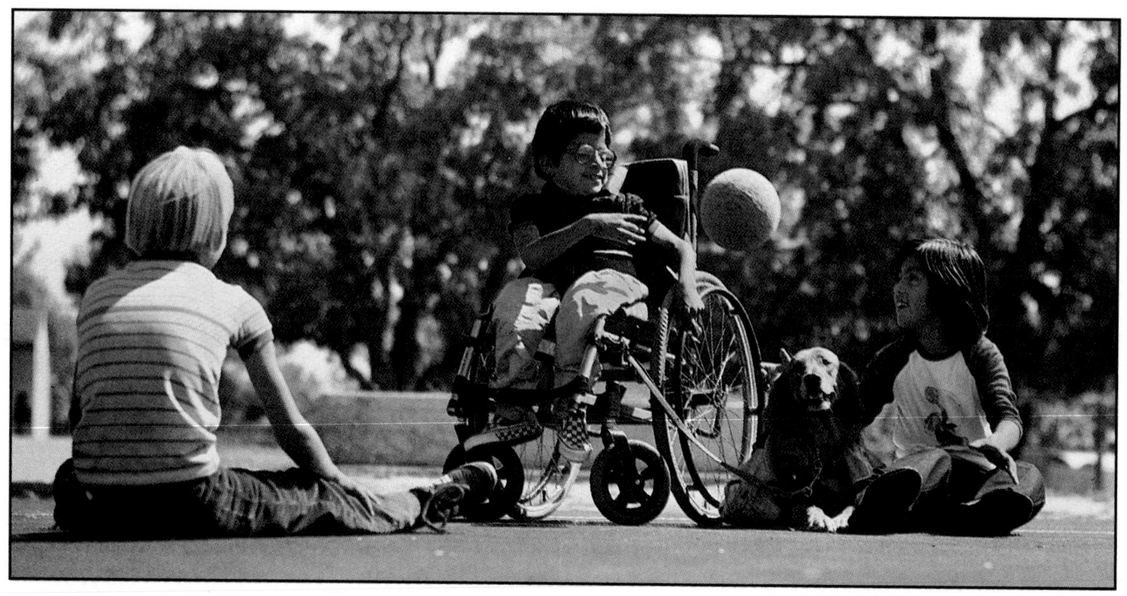

Look at this song.
How many ways can you find to add special parts?

Apusski Dusky

Traditional Nonsense Song

Make up a second part for this song.
Create special melodic echoes as Part II.
Begin the echo when you see this sign: *

Part I—The Melody

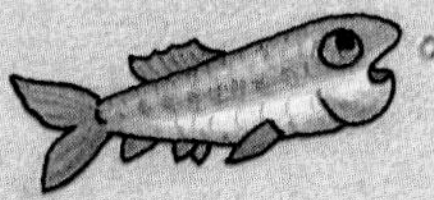

2. One wise old sardine
flicks out a warning.
Apusski dusky, apusskidu.
Swift through the water,
They dart away.
Apusski dusky, apusskidu.

3. With tails a-flashing,
Sardines are swimming.
Apusski dusky, apusskidu.
So full of joy that
They're swimming free,
Apusski dusky, apusskidu.

Grizzly Bear

Southern Work Song

Take turns being the leader.
Improvise your own "grizzly bear" story using this melody.
Be sure to keep the phrase lengths the same so that the chorus knows when to respond.

Happiness Runs

Words and Music by Donovan Leitch

Portland Town

Words Adapted by B. A.

Music by Derroll Adams

Can you sing these two pitches?

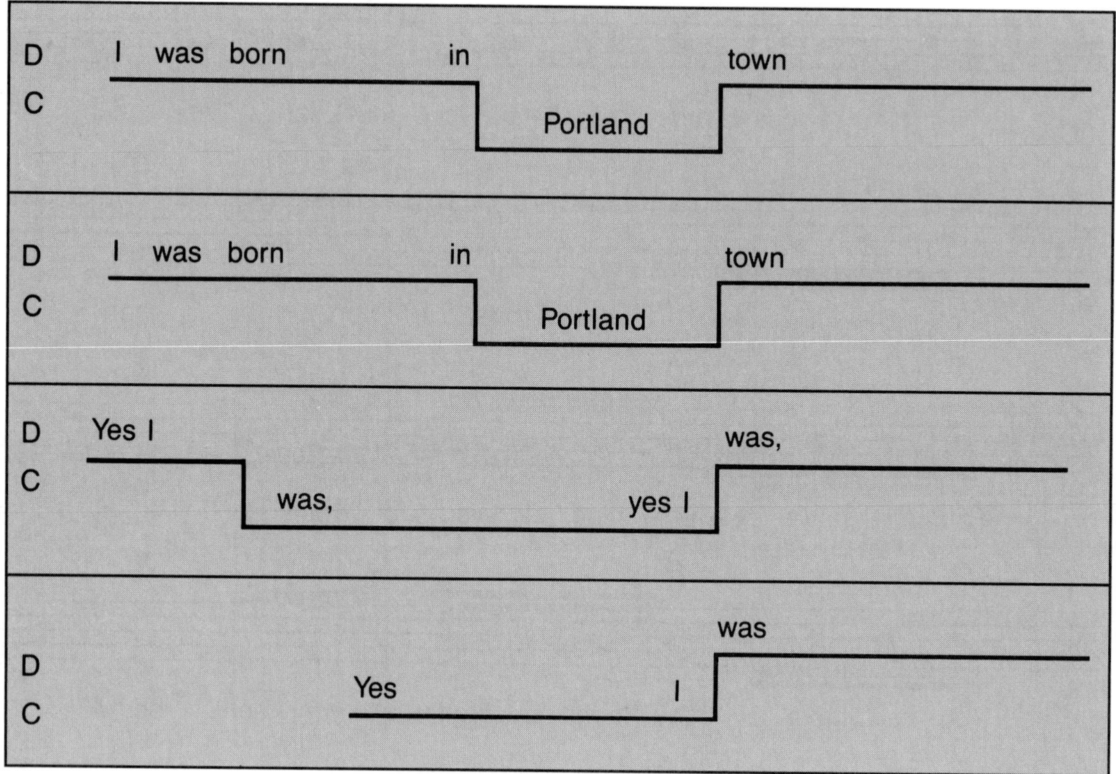

Look at Part 2.
On what pitch does it begin?
How is it the same or different from the part you have just sung?

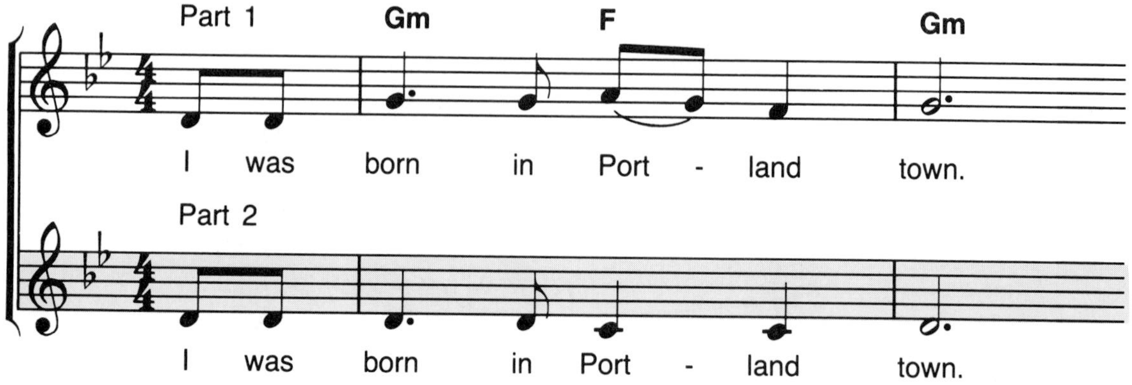

2. I got married in Portland town,
Me and my gal (guy),
We settled down.
Yes we did, yes we did,
Yes we did.

3. Had children, one, two, three,
They grew up and soon left me.
Yes they did, yes they did,
Yes they did.

4. I grew old in Portland town,
Had a good life
In Portland town.
Yes I did, yes I did,
Yes I did.

5. I was born in Portland town,
I was born in Portland town.
Yes I was, yes I was,
Yes I was.

Sing a Little

1′
7
6
5
4
3
2
1

Sing up and down the scale.

Learn this two-part scale song.
First begin low; then begin high.

Traditional

Sing a lit - tle, sing a lit - tle, la, la, la.

Sing a lit - tle, sing a lit - tle, la, la, la.

Sing a lit - tle, sing a lit - tle, la, la, la.

Sing a lit - tle, sing a lit - tle, la, la, la.

La, la, la, la, la, la, la, la, la, la.

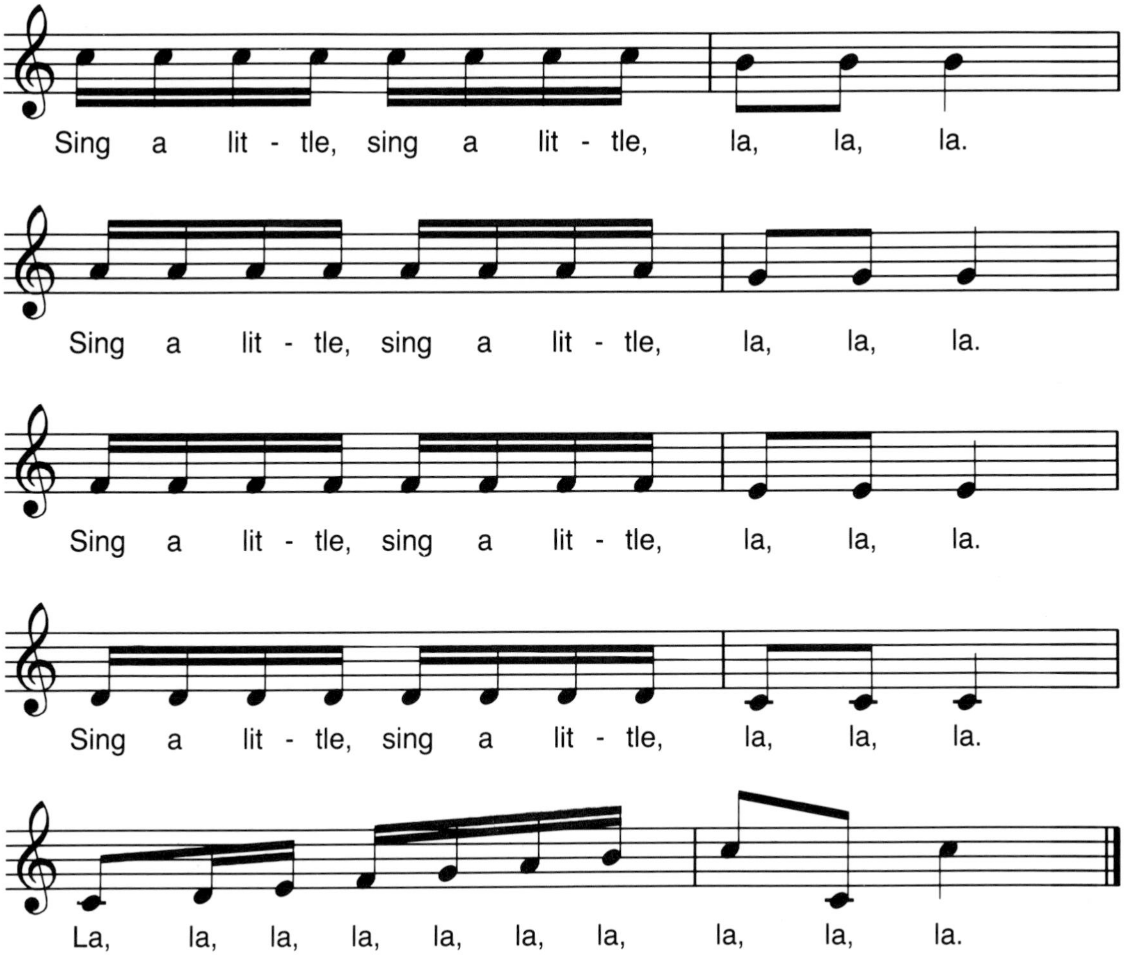

Sing a lit - tle, sing a lit - tle, la, la, la.
Sing a lit - tle, sing a lit - tle, la, la, la.
Sing a lit - tle, sing a lit - tle, la, la, la.
Sing a lit - tle, sing a lit - tle, la, la, la.
La, la, la, la, la, la, la, la, la, la.

What is the mystery tune played on the scale?

One
1 2 3 4 5 6 7 1′
Two
1 2 3 4 5 6 7 1′
Three
1 2 3 4 5 6 7 1′

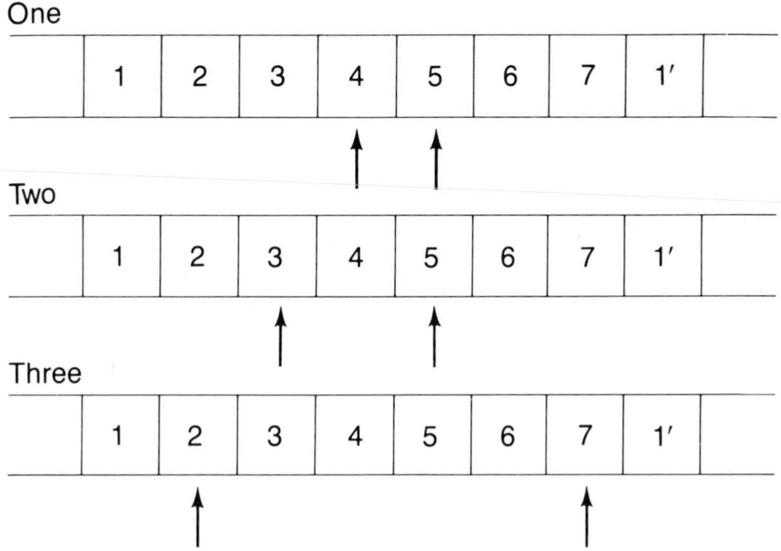

The Wizard of Oz

Once upon a time, a little girl named Dorothy and her dog, Toto, had an exciting adventure. A great wind came and blew them out of their farmhouse in Kansas. They needed help in finding their way home again. Who could help?

We're Off to See the Wizard

Words by E. Y. Harburg

Music by Harold Arlen

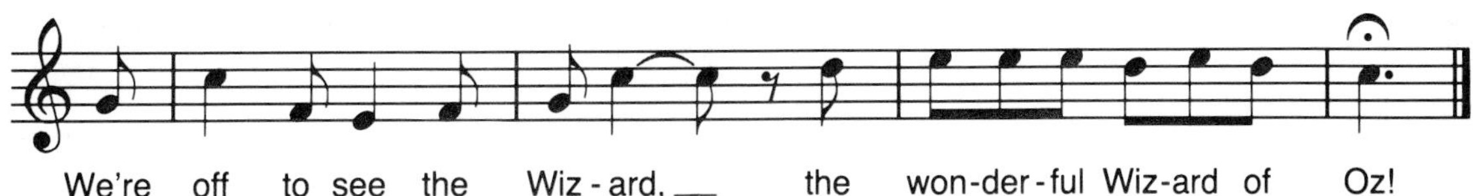

Along the way Dorothy met friends who had their own special reasons for wanting to see the Wizard of Oz.

If I Only Had a Brain

Words by E. Y. Harburg

The Straw Man

I could while away the hours
Conferrin' with the flow'rs
Consultin' with the rain

And my head, I'd be scratchin'
While my thoughts were busy hatchin'
If I only had a brain.

The Tin Man

When a man's an empty kettle
He should be on his mettle
And yet I'm torn apart

Just because I'm presumin'
That I could be kind-a human
If I only had a heart.

The Cowardly Lion

Life is sad believe my missy
When you're born to be a sissy,
Without the vim and verve

But I could change my habits,
Never more be scared of rabbits
If I only had the nerve.

The Merry Old Land of Oz

Words by E. Y. Harburg

Music by Harold Arlen

Ding-Dong, the Witch Is Dead

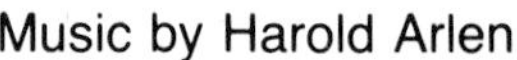

Words by E. Y. Harburg   Music by Harold Arlen

There were good witches and bad witches in the land of Oz.

Ding - Dong, the Witch is Dead! Which old witch? the wick - ed witch.
Ding - Dong, the wick - ed witch is dead. ______
Wake up, you sleep - y head, rub your eyes, get out of bed.
Wake up, the wick - ed witch is dead! ______
She's gone where the gob - lins go be - low, be - low, be - low,
yo - ho let's o - pen up and sing, and ring the bells out.
Ding - Dong! the mer - ry - o, sing it high, sing it low,
Let them know the wick - ed witch is dead. ______

Somewhere Over the Rainbow

Words by E. Y. Harburg
Music by Harold Arlen

With the help of all her good friends, Dorothy and Toto find their way back to Auntie Em and Uncle Henry and live happily ever after on their Kansas farm.

Meeting the Musicker

Adapted from *The Road to Oz* by L. Frank Baum

Create a musical theater piece from further adventures with Dorothy.

Storyteller: Dorothy and some new friends again traveled down the road to Oz. Presently, they saw a little man dressed in red, sitting on a bench before a door. The musical sounds they heard seemed to come from inside the man himself, for he was playing no instrument nor was any to be seen near him. Dorothy and her friends came up and stood in a row listening while the queer sounds came from the little man.

Instrumentalist: Breathe out on the heavy beat.

All (Class): Chant this poem in a rhythmic singsong:

3
4
Tiddle-iddle-widdle, **oom** pom-pom,
Oom pom-pom, **oom** pom-pom,
Tiddle-iddle-widdle, **oom** pom-pom,
Oom pom-pom-**pah**!

Storyteller: One of Dorothy's friends said, "Why I do believe this little man is a musicker!"

Dorothy: "How funny, when he speaks his breath makes the music."

Storyteller: "That's nonsense," said her friend, but the music began again and they all listened.

Instrumentalist: 

All: (Singsong the Musicker's song.)

2/4
My **lungs** are **full** of **reeds** like **those**
In **organs**, **therefore I** suppose
If **I** breathe **in** or **out** my **nose**
The **reeds** are **bound** to **play.**

So, **as** I **breathe** to **live,** you **know,**
I **squeeze** out **music as** I **go:**
I'm **very sorry this** is **so.**
Forgive my **constant piping, pray.**

Dorothy: "Who are you, sir?"

Storyteller: His reply came in the shape of this sound.

Instrumentalist:  3/4

All (singsong):

3/4
I'm **Allegro** da **Capo**, a **very** famous **man:**
Just **find** another, **high** or low
To **match** me if you **can.**

Dorothy: "Why I believe he's proud of it!"

Storyteller: Dorothy and her friends decided it was time to go. Even when they climbed to the top of a hill, they could still hear the Musicker's piping.

Instrumentalist:  3/4

All (singsong):

3/4
Tiddle-iddle-widdle, **oom** pom-pom,
Oom pom-pom-**pah!**
(repeat fading away . . .)

Describe Music

LISTENING

Nuages

from *Nocturnes*

by Claude Debussy

Have you ever watched the clouds float overhead and imagined that you saw people or animals or strange shapes? Listen to "Nuages." This is the French word for "clouds." Does the music suggest cloud shapes?

Listen for the melodies played by the English horn, the flute, and the viola as the rest of the instruments create "floating" music.

Clouds

Words by Christina Rossetti

White sheep, white sheep
On a blue hill,
When the wind stops
You all stand still.
When the wind blows
You walk away slow,
White sheep, white sheep
Where do you go?

Clouds

Words by Christina Rossetti

Music by Ruth Bampton

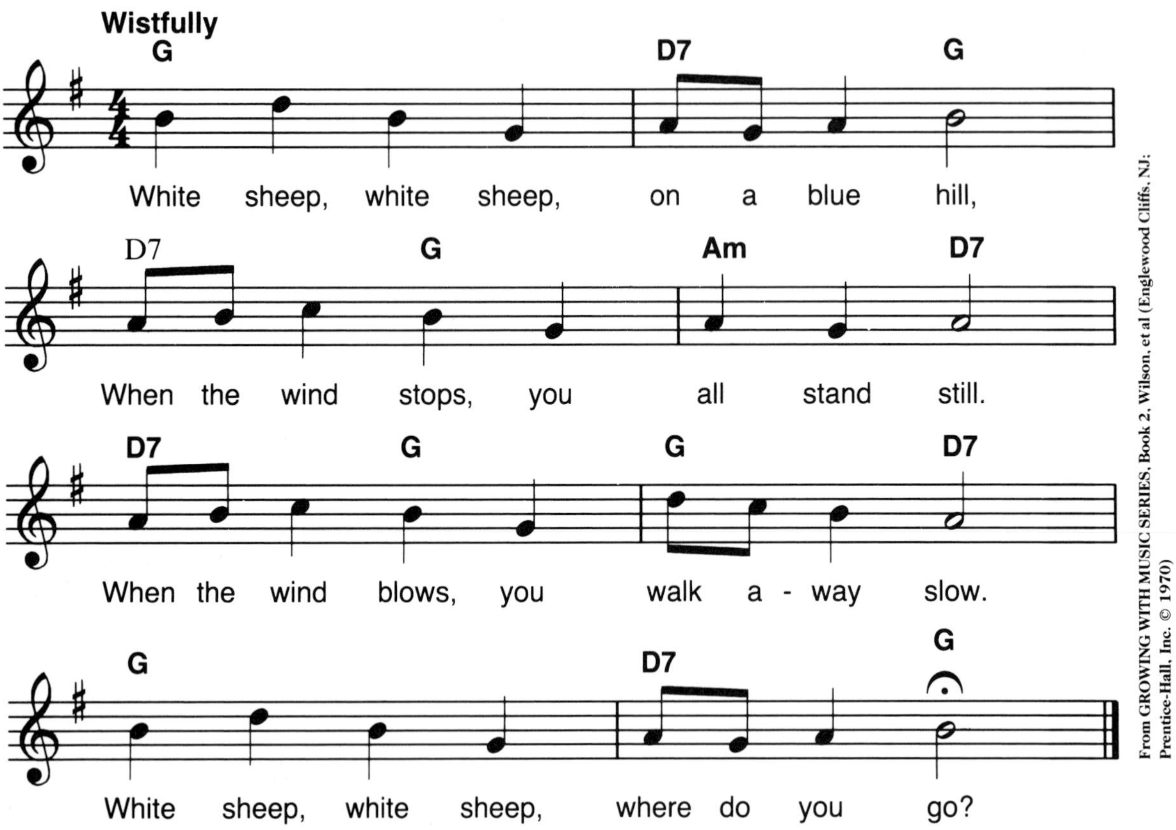

From GROWING WITH MUSIC SERIES, Book 2, Wilson, et al (Englewood Cliffs, NJ: Prentice-Hall, Inc. © 1970)

Clouds

Words by Christina Rossetti

Music by Don Malin

Dreamily

White sheep, white sheep, on a blue hill,

When the wind stops, you all ___ stand still.

When the wind blows, you walk a - way slow.
White sheep, white sheep, where did you go?

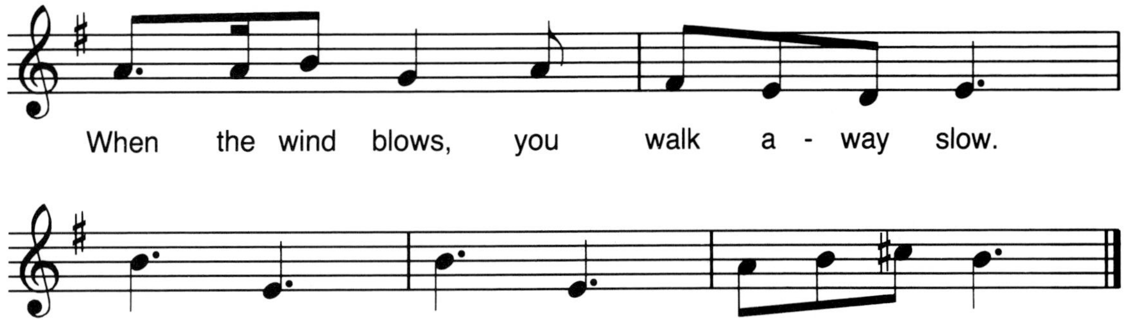

Clouds

Words by Christina Rossetti

Music by Arthur Frackenpohl

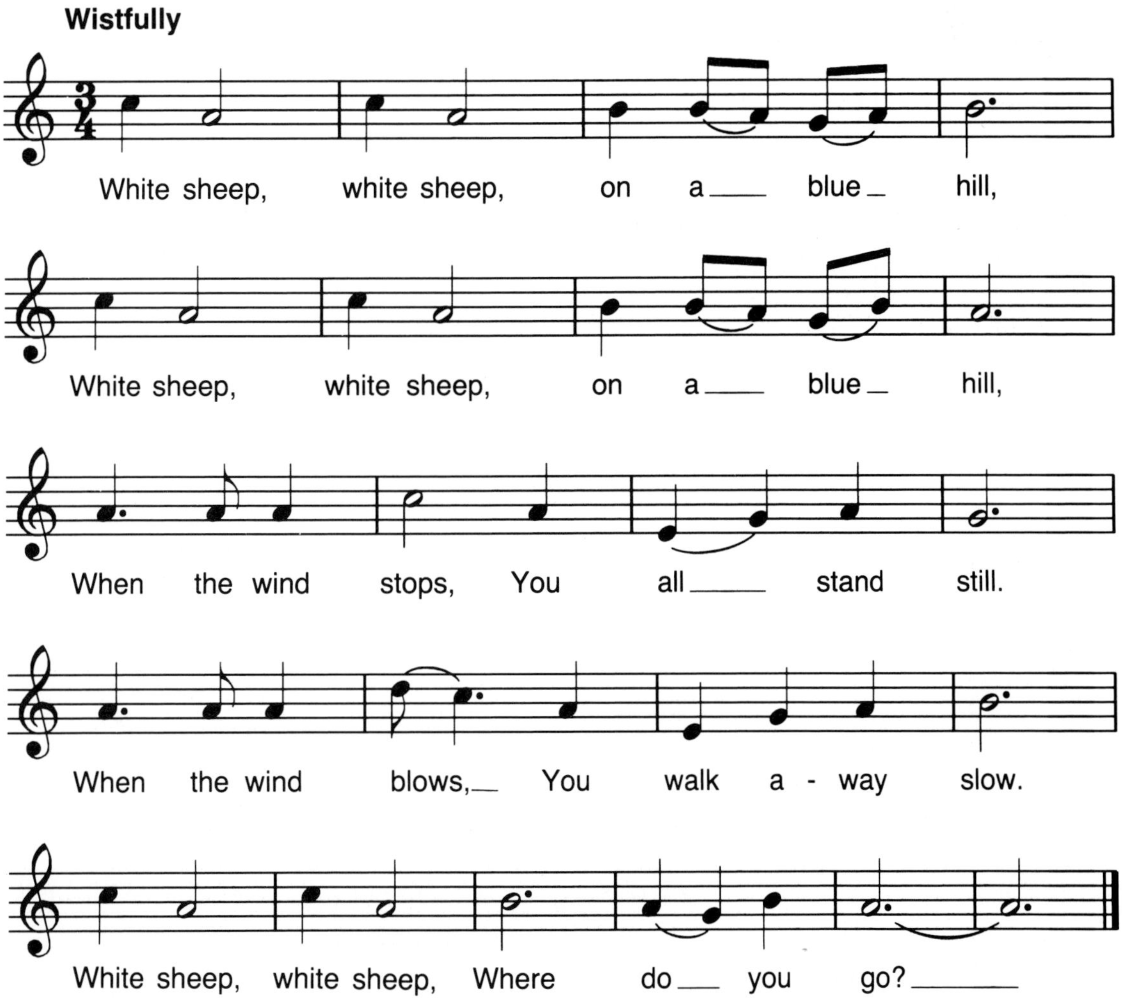

Wistfully
White sheep, white sheep, on a blue hill,
White sheep, white sheep, on a blue hill,
When the wind stops, You all stand still.
When the wind blows, You walk a - way slow.
White sheep, white sheep, Where do you go?

Describe What You Hear

1. Show what you hear:

instruments? mood?

melody? form?

rhythm?

2. Draw what you hear:

melody? form?

rhythm? instruments?

other?

3. Talk about what you hear:

form? rhythm?

instruments? melody?

other?

Me and My Shadow

Words and Music by Billy Rose,
Al Jolson, and Dave Dreyer

Me and my Shadow,
Strolling down the avenue.
Me and my Shadow,
Not a soul to tell our troubles to.
And when it's twelve o'clock,
We climb the stair.
We never knock,
For nobody's there.
Just me and my Shadow,
All alone and feeling blue.

Cantata No. 147 (Excerpt)

by Johann Sebastian Bach

Describe what you hear.
Show the shape of the melodies played by the trumpet.

A

B

How many times did you hear each melody?

Describe what you hear by moving.
Divide into three groups.

Group 1
Follow the melody of the trumpet.

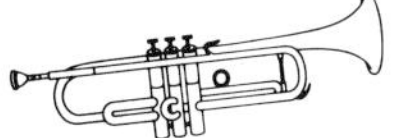

Group 2
Move with the steady rhythm of the low strings.

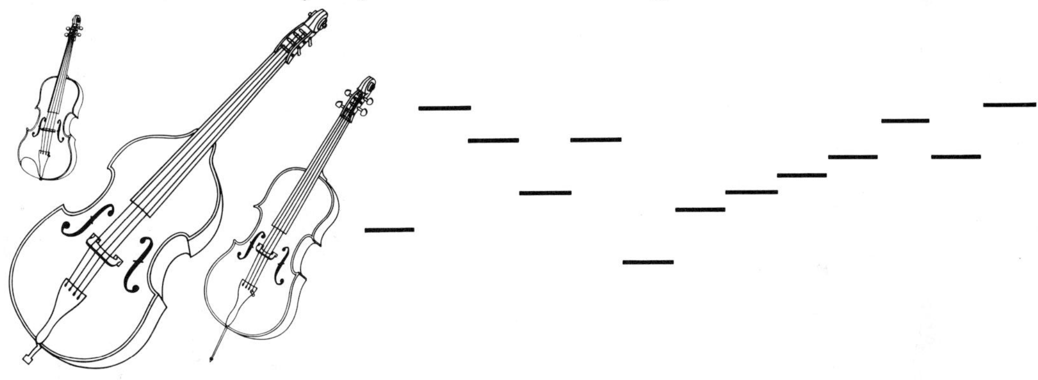

Group 3
Show the constantly moving pattern of the high strings and woodwinds.

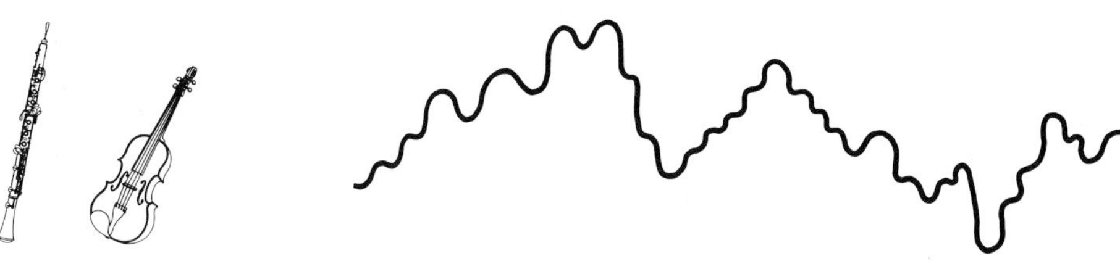

Will all three groups move all of the time?

Six Pieces for Orchestra

Third Piece/First Piece

by Anton Webern

An artist described what she heard by making this design. Listen to the music she heard. What did she do to describe these sounds?

Describe what you hear by drawing.
Listen to another piece of music.
Draw a design to show what you hear.

Describe What You Hear by Talking

Listen to "The Music Is You."

1. Describe what the song is about.
2. Describe how the composer made the music match the words.
3. Describe how the melody moves.
4. Describe how the rhythm moves.
5. Describe the harmony.

Perform "The Music Is You."

Add an accompaniment:

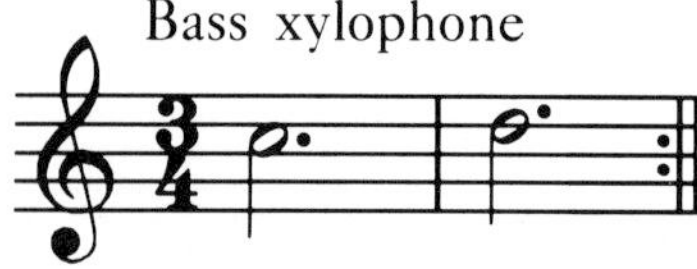

The Music Is You

Words and Music by John Denver

The Unicorn

Find these tempo terms in the song.
Listen to the recording.
Decide what each means.

Words and Music by Shel Silverstein

Allegro

Adagio

Andante

Largo

Accelerando

Ritardando

Allegro Verse 2

But the Lord seen some sinnin' and it caused him pain,
He says, "Stand back, I'm gonna make it rain.
So hey, Brother Noah, I'll tell you what to do.
Go and build me a floating zoo."

Ritardando Refrain

And you take two alligators and a couple of geese,
Two humpback camels and two chimpanzees,
Two cats, two rats, two elephants but sure as you're born,
Noah, don't you forget my unicorns.

Andante Verse 3

Now Noah was there and he answered the callin',
And he finished up the ark as the rain started fallin',
Then he marched in the animals two by two,
And he sung out as they went through.

Largo Refrain

Hey Lord, I got you two alligators and a couple of geese,
Two humpback camels and two chimpanzees,
Two cats, two rats, two elephants but sure as you're born,
I sure don't see your unicorns.

Adagio Verse 4

Well, Noah looked out through the drivin' rain,
But the unicorns was hidin'– playin' silly games.
They were kickin' and a-splashin' while the rain was pourin'
Oh them foolish unicorns.

Accelerando Refrain

And you take two alligators and a couple of geese,
Two humpback camels and two chimpanzees,
Two cats, two rats, two elephants but sure as you're born,
Noah, don't you forget my unicorns.

? Verse 5

Then the ducks started duckin' and the snakes started snakin',
And the elephants started elephantin' and the boat started shakin'.
The mice started squeakin' and the lions started roarin',
And everyone's aboard but them unicorns.

? Refrain

I mean the two alligators and a couple of geese,
The humpback camels and the chimpanzees,
Noah cried, "Close the door 'cause the rain is pourin',
And we just can't wait for them unicorns."

? Verse 6

And then the ark started movin' and it drifted with the tide,
And the unicorns looked up from the rock and cried,
And the water came up and sort of floated them away,
That's why you've never seen a unicorn to this day.

? Refrain

You'll see a lot of alligators and a whole mess of geese,
You'll see humpback camels and chimpanzees,
You'll see cats and rats and elephants but sure as you're born,
You're never gonna see no unicorn.

Once

Israeli Folk Song

Describe what you see by moving.

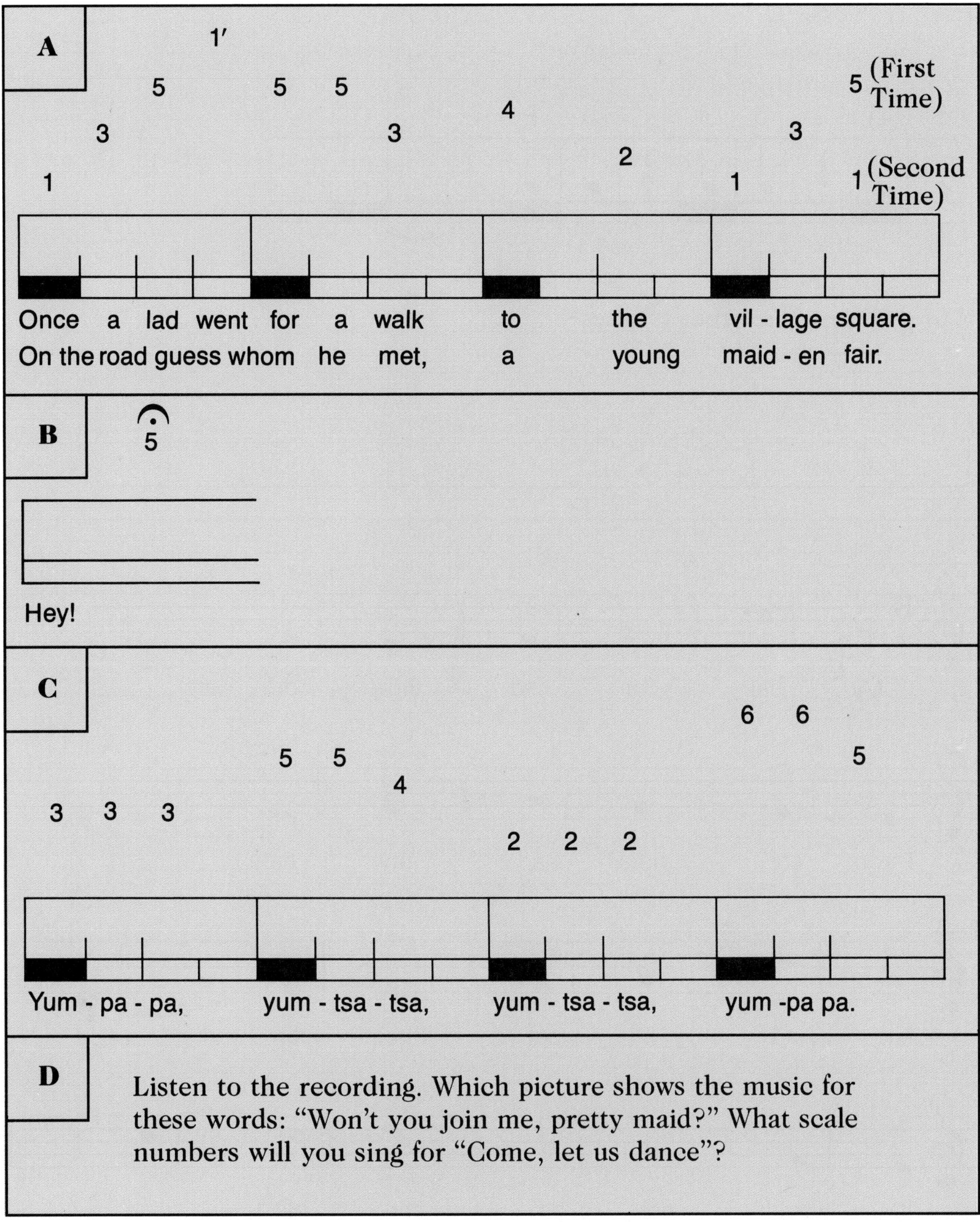

Listen to the recording. Which picture shows the music for these words: "Won't you join me, pretty maid?" What scale numbers will you sing for "Come, let us dance"?

My Hat

German Folk Song

Describe what you see by drawing.

Here is Phrase 1.

5 1′ 5 4 3 4 2

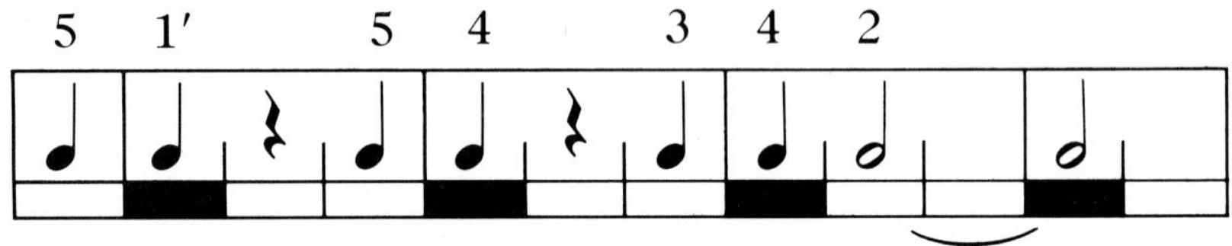

Can you show the other phrases?

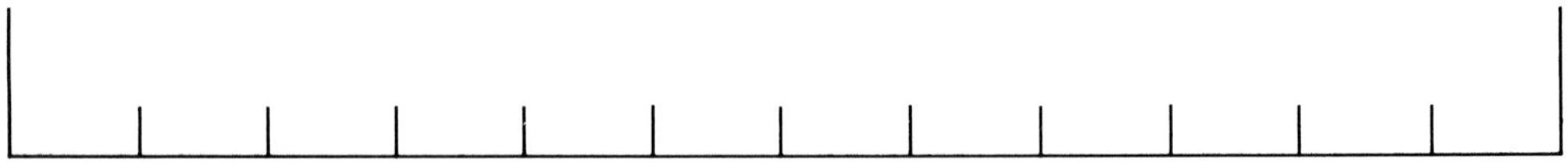

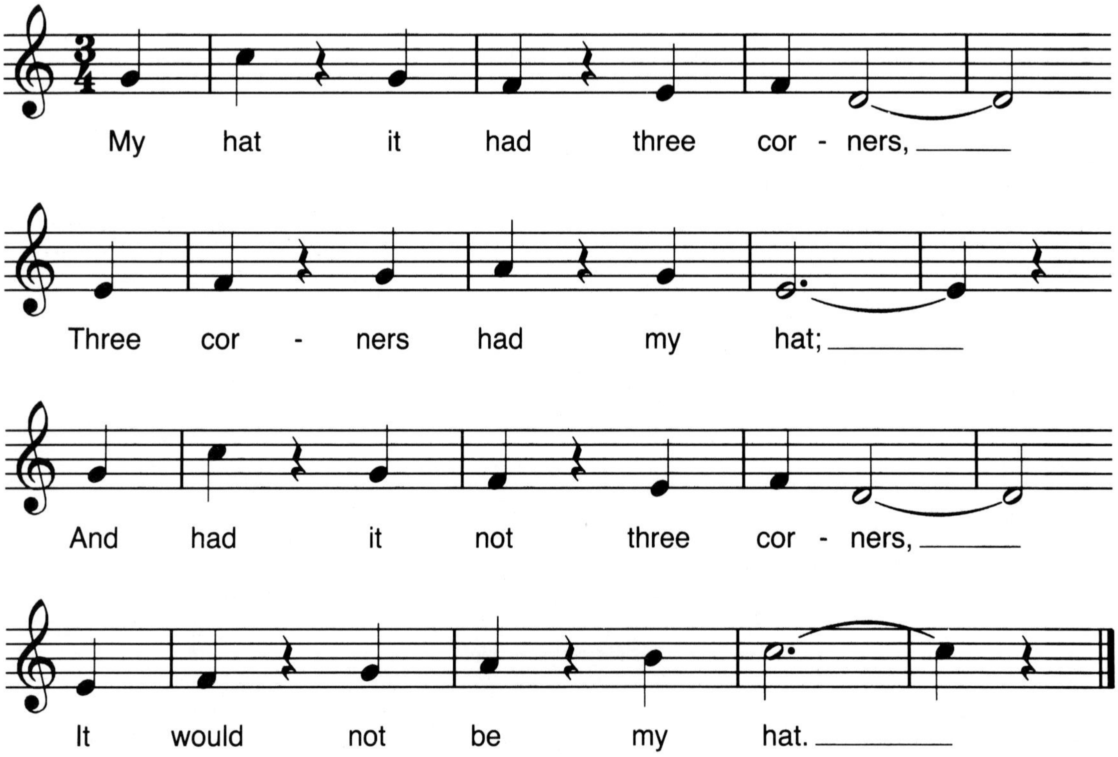

My hat it had three cor - ners,
Three cor - ners had my hat;
And had it not three cor - ners,
It would not be my hat.

The Smoke Went Up the Chimney

American Camp Song

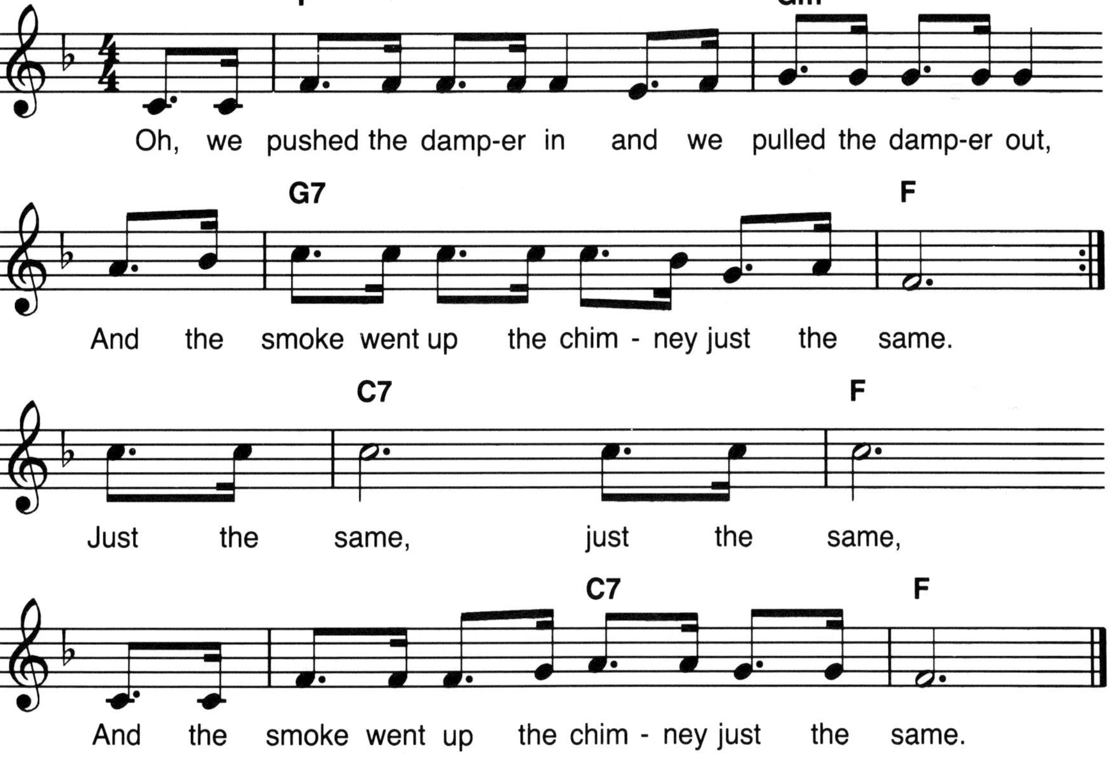

I'm Looking Over a Four-Leaf Clover

Words by Mort Dixon

Music by Harry Woods

- Find the shortest sound in the song.
- Find the sound that will move with the beat.
- Tap the beat. Chant the words.
- Can you find the places where the accents of the words come before the accent of the beat, making a **syncopated** rhythm?

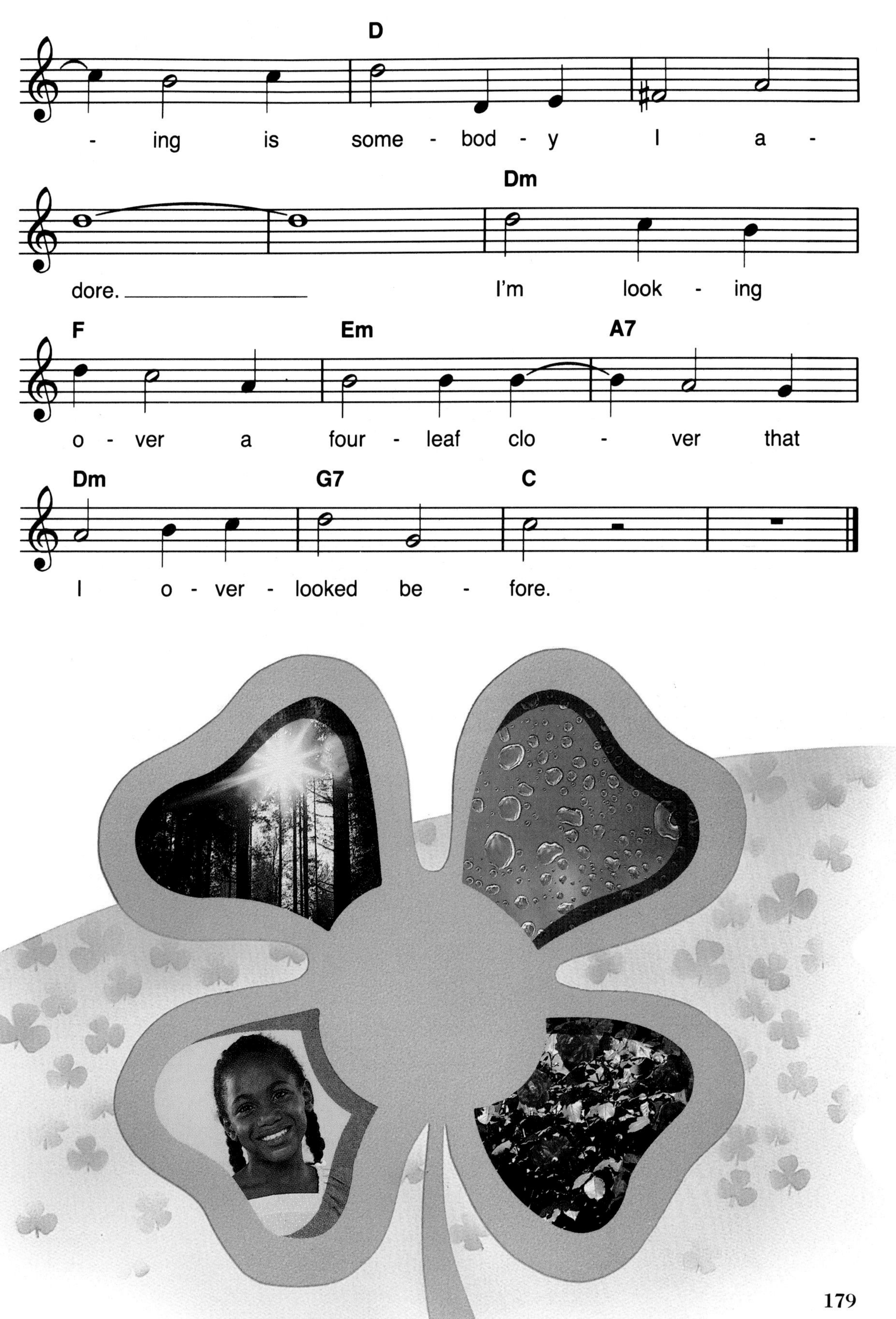
D
- ing is some - bod - y I a -
Dm
dore.
I'm look - ing
F Em A7
o - ver a four - leaf clo - ver that
Dm G7 C
I o - ver - looked be - fore.

One of These Does Not Belong

Listen to the music.

- You will hear four pieces of music in each set.
- Three of the pieces are the same kind of music.
- One is different!
- Can you pick the one that does not belong?

Peach Tree, Peonies and Cranes, Shen Chu'uan (1682-1758), The Metropolitan Museum of Art.

B

C

Music of Different Times and Places

Listen to the musical examples you heard when studying pages 180 and 181.
This time look at the pictures on pages 180, 181, 182, and 183 as you listen.
Can you pick the picture that comes from the same time or place as the music you hear?

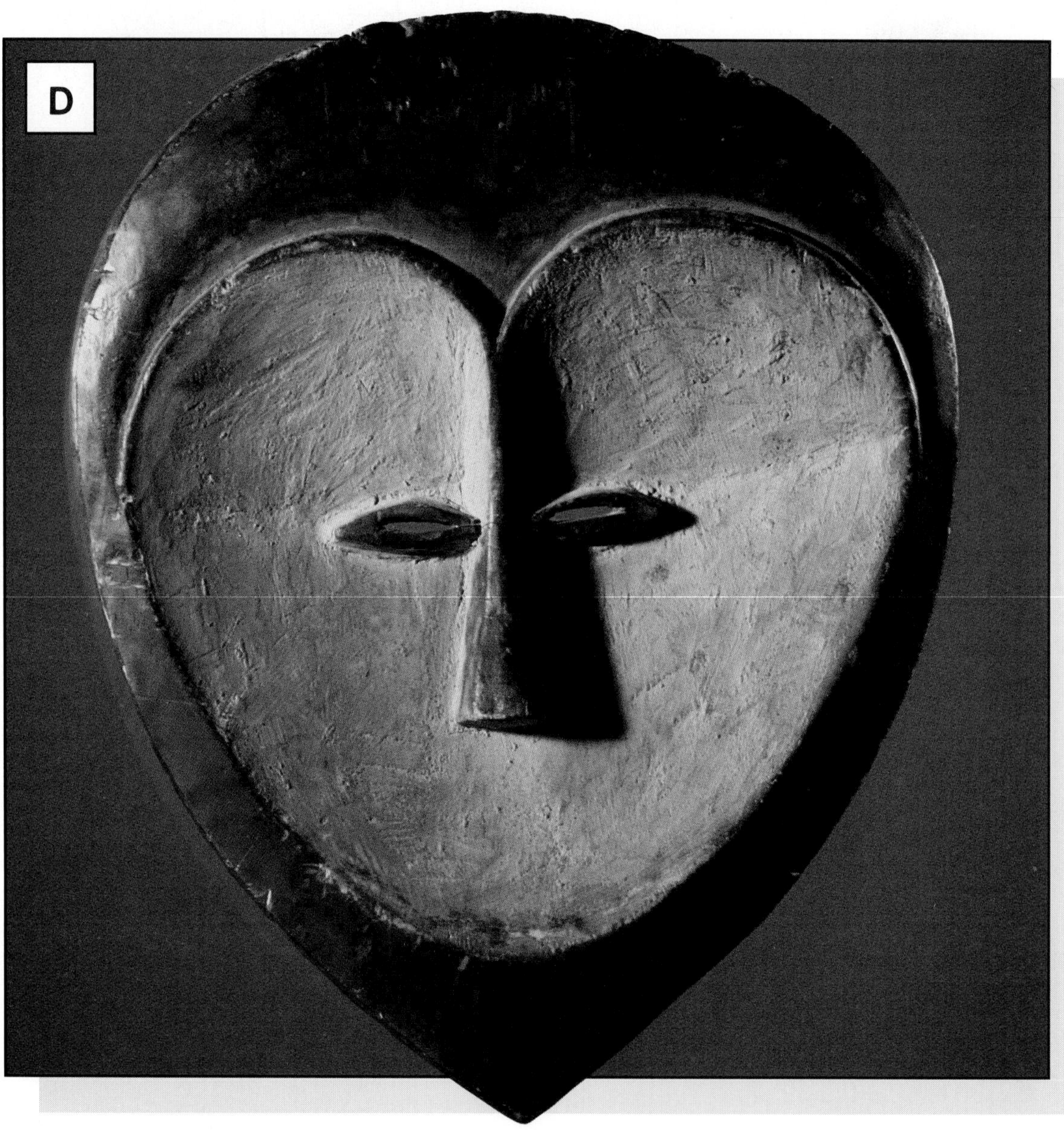

Region of Brooklyn Bridge Fantasy by John Marin, 1932, watercolor on paper, 18 3/4" X 22 1/4", Collection of the Whitney Museum.

La Jesusita

Mexican Folk Song
Brightly
G
D7
Come let us dance where the lan-terns shine bright-ly,
Va-mos al bai - le y ve - rás ¡qué bo - ni - to!
G
Come let us join in the fun, step-ping light - ly,
don - de se a - lum - bran con vein - te lin - ter-nas,
D7
Down in the square where the danc - ers are swing - ing
don - de se bai - lan las dan - zas mo - der - nas,
G
And all the lat - est of steps can be seen. Tra la la
don - de se bai - la de mu-cho va - ci - lón. Ya-ya - ya -
G
3
D7
la! Oh, dance with me, Je - su - si - ta, Oh,
ya! Y quié - re - me, Je - su - si - ta, y
3
G
3
please, won't you dance with me? If you'll be my danc-ing
quié - re - me por fa - vor. Y mi - ra que soy tu a -
D7
3
G
part - ner, Then your faith-ful slave I'll be.
man - te, y se - gu - ro ser - vi - dor.

Add the percussion accompaniments. Someone may improvise a recorder part. Use these pitches: D, E, F♯, A, and B.

The Riddle Song

American Folk Song

Sweet and Low

Words by Alfred Lord Tennyson

Music by Joseph Barnaby

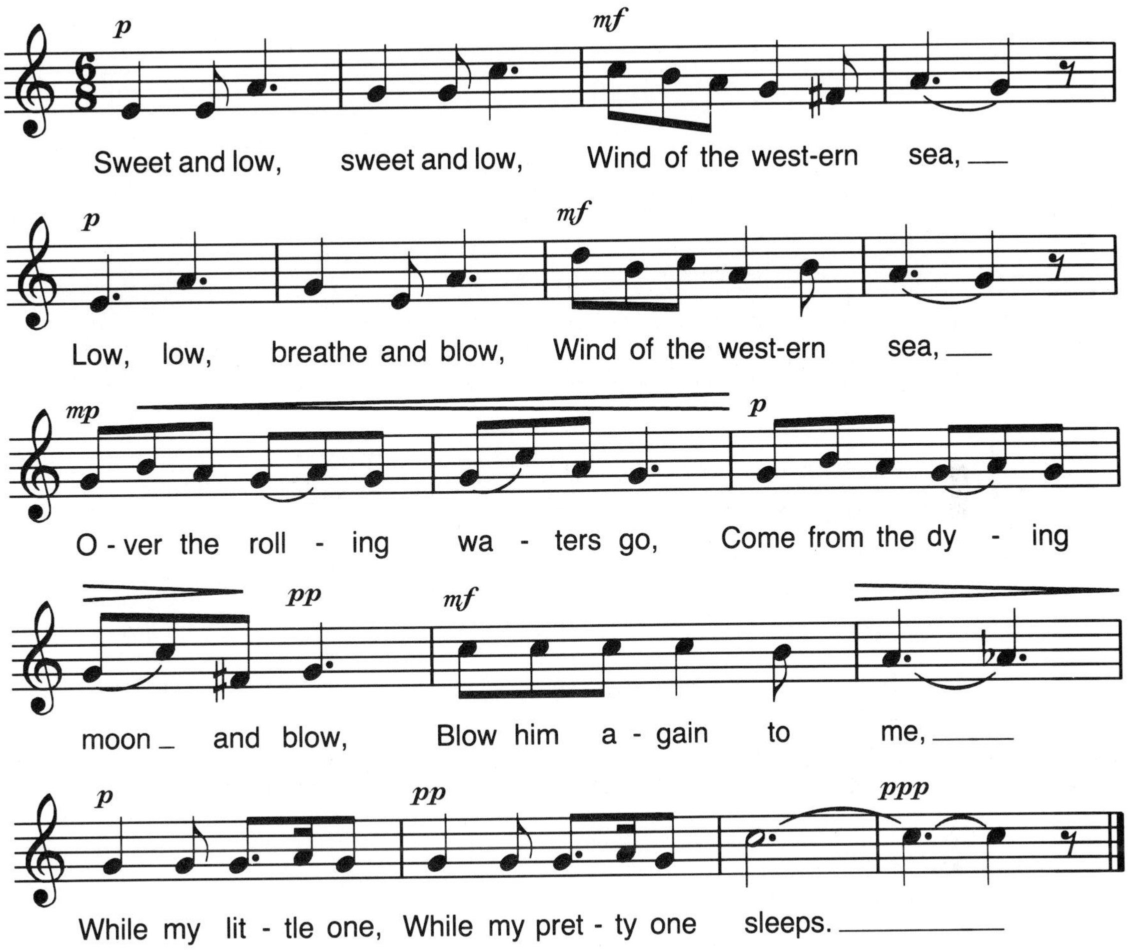

p
mf
Sweet and low, sweet and low, Wind of the west-ern sea, __
p
mf
Low, low, breathe and blow, Wind of the west-ern sea, __
mp
p
O - ver the roll - ing wa - ters go, Come from the dy - ing
pp
mf
moon _ and blow, Blow him a - gain to me, __
p
pp
ppp
While my lit - tle one, While my pret - ty one sleeps. __

After you know the song well, you might want to add this harmonizing part to the last phrase:

While my lit - tle one, While my pret - ty one sleeps. __

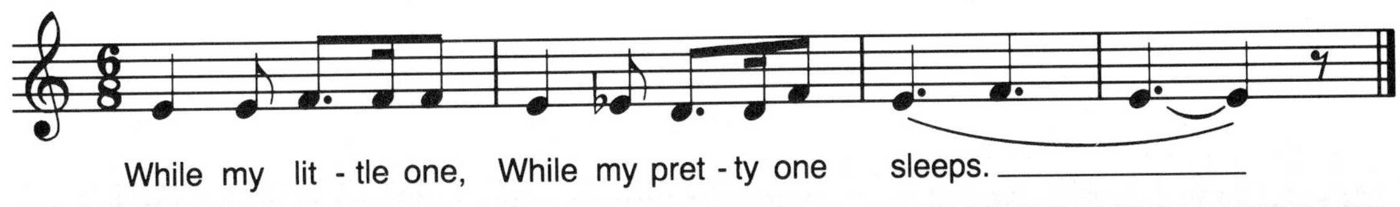

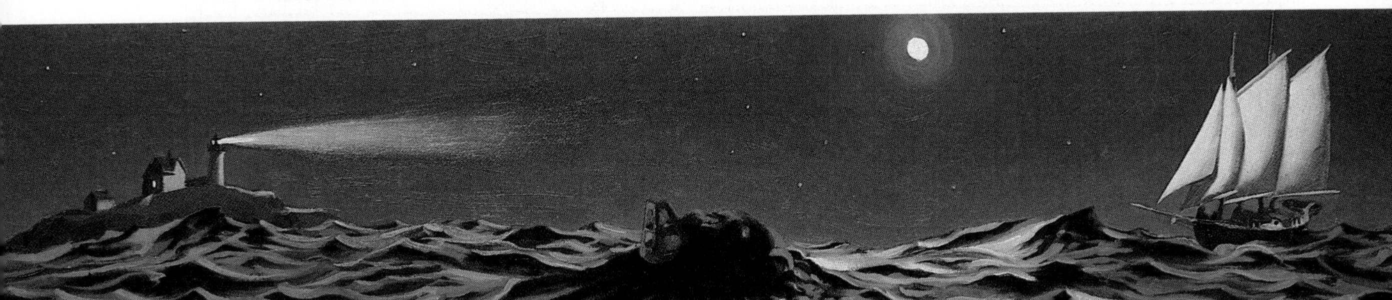

Sir Eglamore
Old English Ballad
Em D G C
1. Sir Eg - la - more, that val - iant knight, Fa la
2. There starts a huge drag - on out of his den, Fa la
G Em
lank - y down dil - ly, He took up his sword and he
lank - y down dil - ly, Which had killed I know not
D G C G
went for to fight; Fa la lank - y down dil - ly.
how man - y men; Fa la lank - y down dil - ly.
C
And as he rode o'er hill and dale, All
But when he saw Sir Eg - la - more, If
D G
arm - èd with a coat of mail,
you'd but heard how the dra-gon did roar!

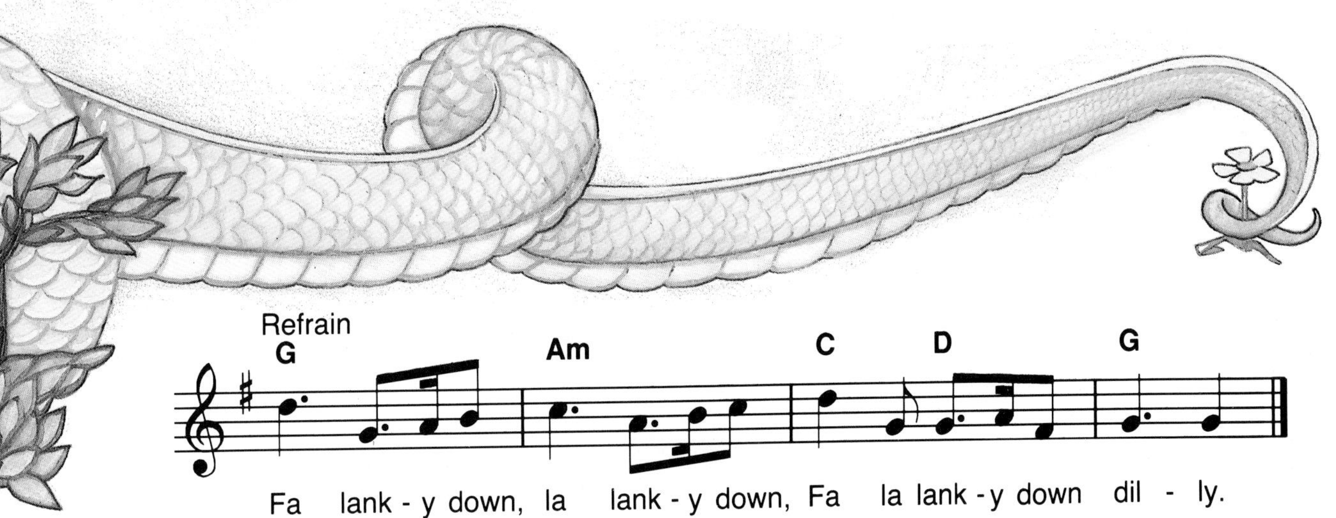

3. This dragon had a plaguey hard hide,
Fa la lanky down dilly,
Which could the strongest steel abide;
Fa la lanky down dilly.
But as the dragon yawning did fall,
He thrust his sword down hilt and all. (*Refrain*)

4. The dragon laid him down and roared,
Fa la lanky down dilly,
The knight was sorry for his sword;
Fa la lanky down dilly.
The sword it was a right good blade,
As ever Turk or Spaniard made. (*Refrain*)

LISTENING

Two Ductiae

Anonymous

Listen to music of long ago.
Then learn to dance as knights and ladies did.

Wedding March

from *Rustic Wedding Symphony*

by Carl Goldmark

Goldmark composed thirteen variations of his wedding march theme. Listen to five of them.

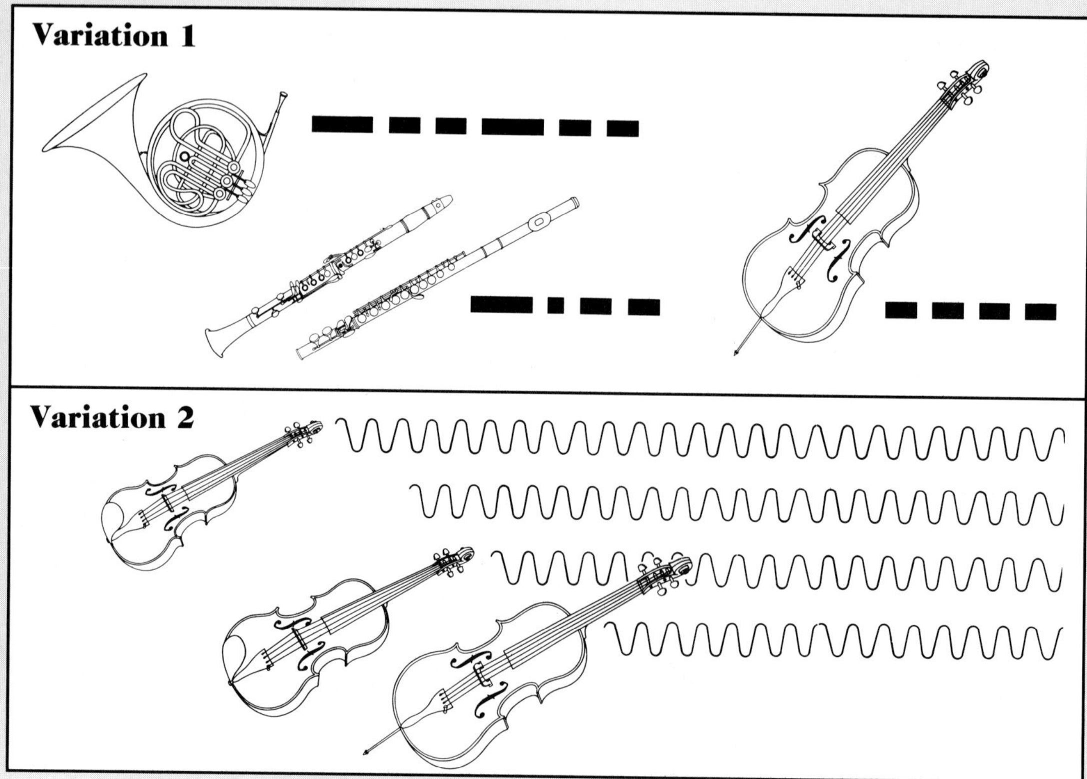

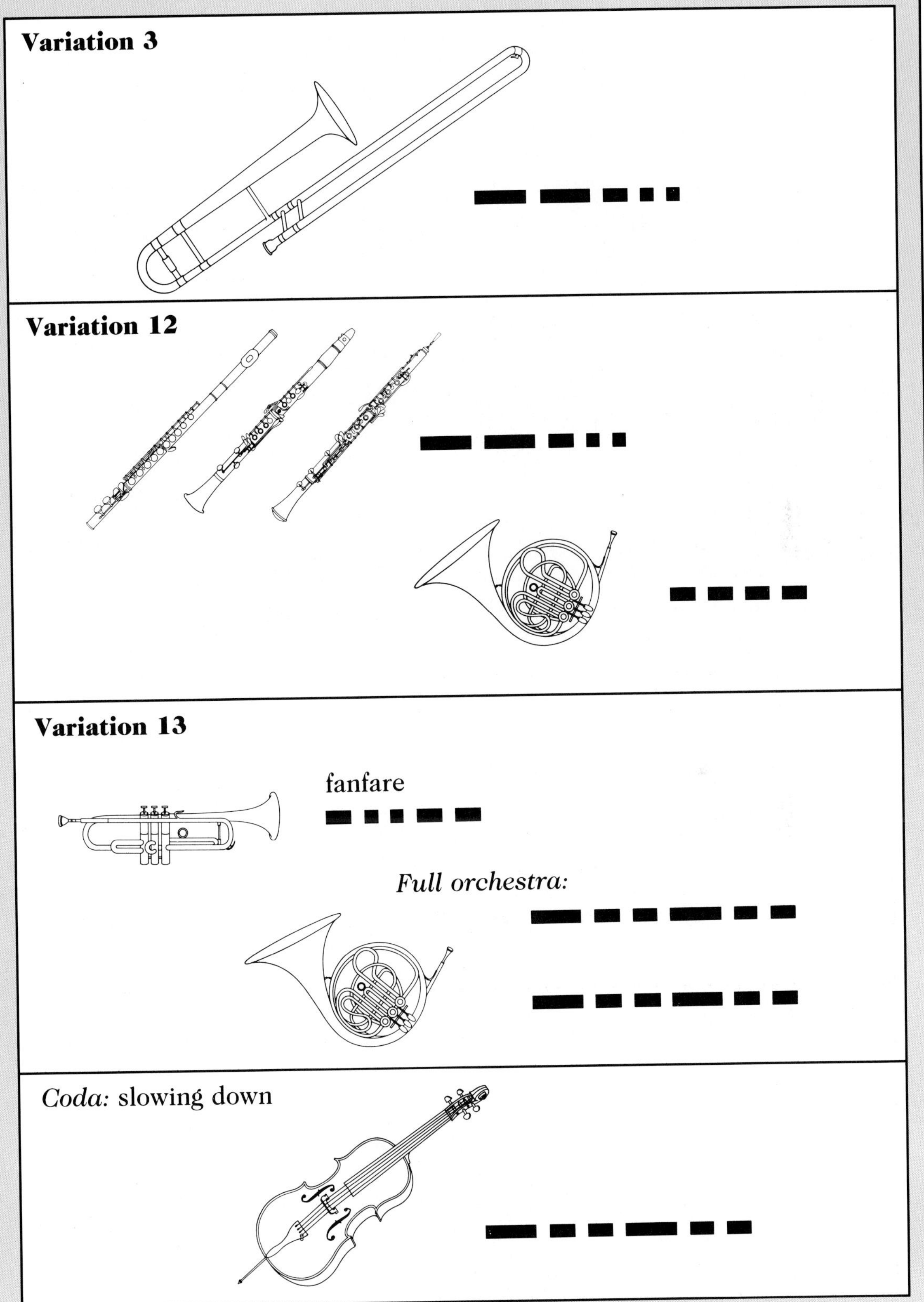
Variation 3
Variation 12
Variation 13
fanfare
Full orchestra:
Coda: slowing down

Create Music

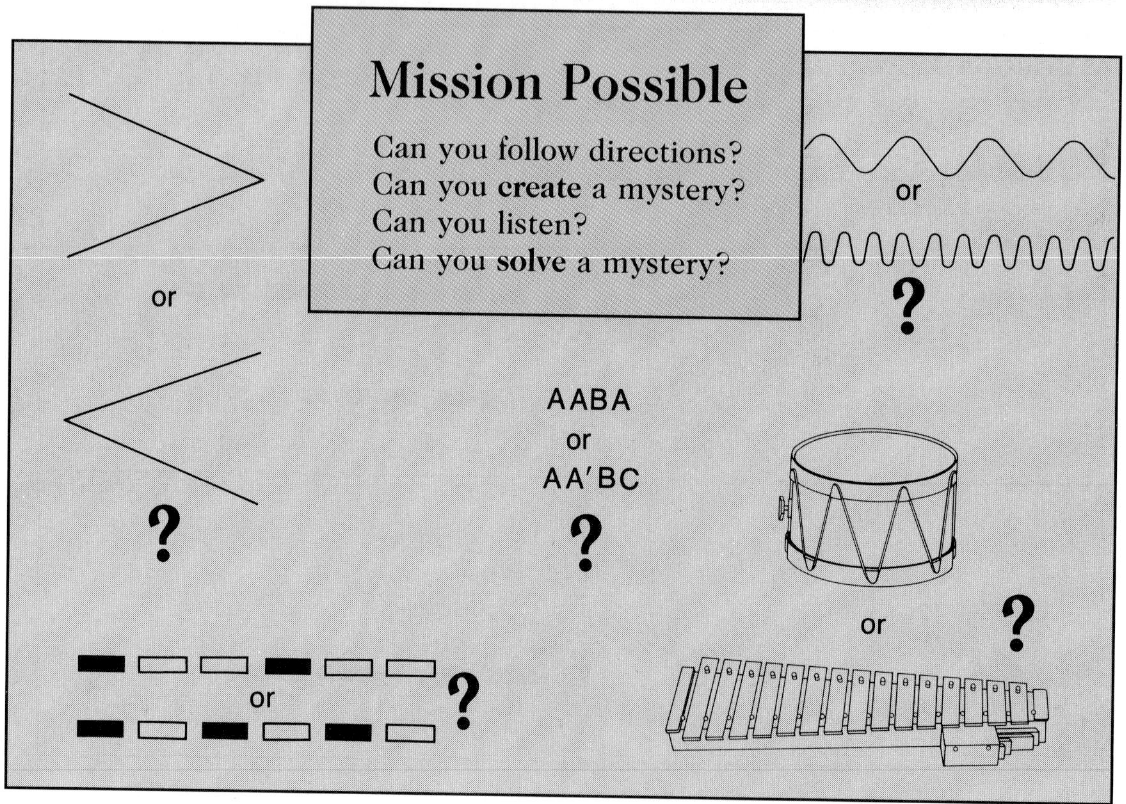

Words and Music

Here are some words made into a poem.
Add rhythm and harmony to make a song.

How I Get Cool

by Richard J. Smith

What a hot and muggy day.
I think I'm going to roast.
What a drippy, sweaty day.
I feel like buttered toast.

These concrete steps are sizzly-hot.
They're cooking my backside.
The heat is coming through my soles.
My toes are almost fried.

On days like this, scorchy days,
Here's how I get cool.
I eat three cherry popsicles
And swim in City Pool.

My Puppy

by Richard J. Smith

My puppy can be my very best
friend.
He'll lick me and play games for
hours on end.
Sometimes he'll kiss me right on the
nose,
And try to snuggle under my clothes.

Sometimes I like my puppy a lot.
Sometimes I do and sometimes not.
I guess with my puppy it's good and
it's bad.
He makes me happy, and he makes
me mad.

Add rhythm and melody to make a song.

Percussion-A-Round

Get ready!

- Draw two circles on a large piece of wrapping paper.
- Divide the inner circle into 16 equal beats. Number them.

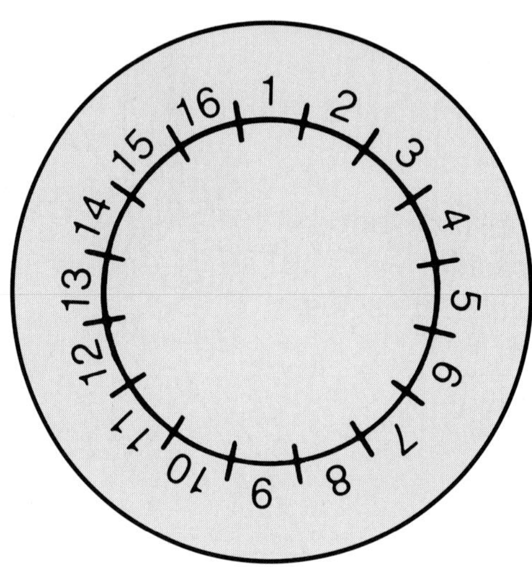

Compose

Make up a 16-count rhythm that sometimes moves

- **with** the shortest sound
- **twice as long** as the shortest sound
- **four times as long** as the shortest sound

Could you use other relationships?
Divide the outer circle into "boxes" of the correct length to show your rhythms. Draw them in.

Perform

Four people may perform this Percussion-A-Round.
Each chooses a different percussion instrument.
Player 1 begins with count 1. When that player reaches 5, **Player 2** begins.
When will **Player 3** begin?
When will **Player 4** begin?

Make Your Own Instrument

Use ideas on these pages or ideas of your own to make new instruments. There is only one rule! You must be able to play at least two different pitches on your instrument.

Clay-Pot Chimes

Floating Timpani

One-String Harp

Bottle Bongos

Other Chimes

Using Your Instruments

1. Work in small groups. Create a **tone row** composition.
   - Stand side by side in a row. Take turns playing two pitches on each instrument you made to create a "tone row."
   - Can you make a "melody" out of this row? To make your melody, you may repeat pitches, use longer sounds, shorter sounds, or sometimes not play at all.
   - How do the different timbres add interest to your piece? What happens when people change places in the row?

2. Work in small groups. Create a piece using **harmony.**
   - Plan a melody.
   - Choose one or more instruments to play an **ostinato** pattern.
   - Use other instruments with the **ostinato.**
   - Will you use one or both pitches of your instrument?
   - Will you repeat any of your patterns?
   - When should certain **timbres** be heard?
   - How can you use expressive ideas, such as **dynamics**, **tempo**, and **articulation**?
   - Select one person to conduct the group. Perform the piece for others in the class.

3. Perform as a large ensemble.

- Group instruments of similar **pitch** and **timbre** together.
  Select a conductor/composer.
- Decide what signals the composer should use to tell the group which sounds to perform.

A specific performer should play.

Stop playing.

Play louder.

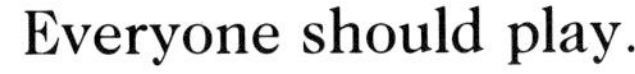

Everyone should play.

Play softer.

What other signals will you need?

- Perform the piece. How do you like your music?
- What in the music made you feel the way you do about the piece?
- What would you suggest to the conductor to improve or change the music?

Sound Together

- Work in small groups.
- Choose one of these ideas.
- One person sets up a steady rhythm that moves in groups of four.
- The other people make up movements to match the rhythm.

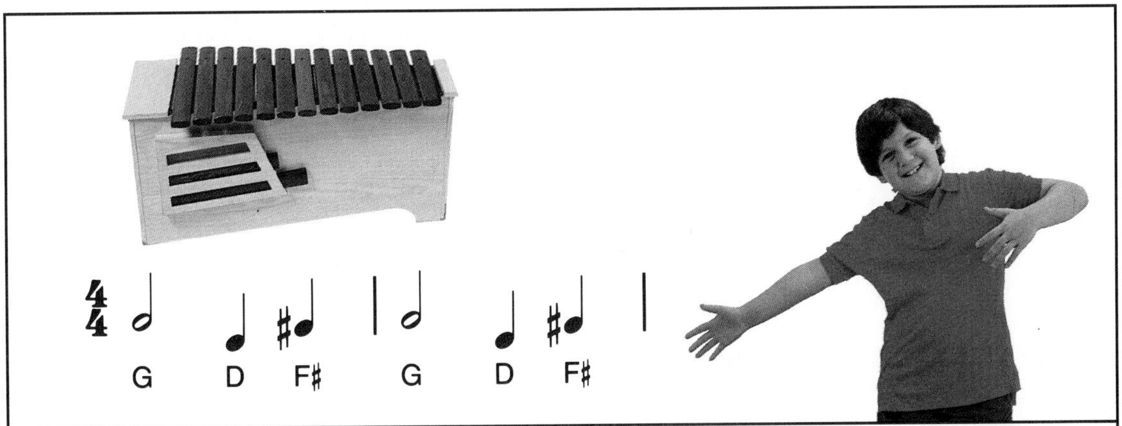

4/4
G D F♯ G D F♯

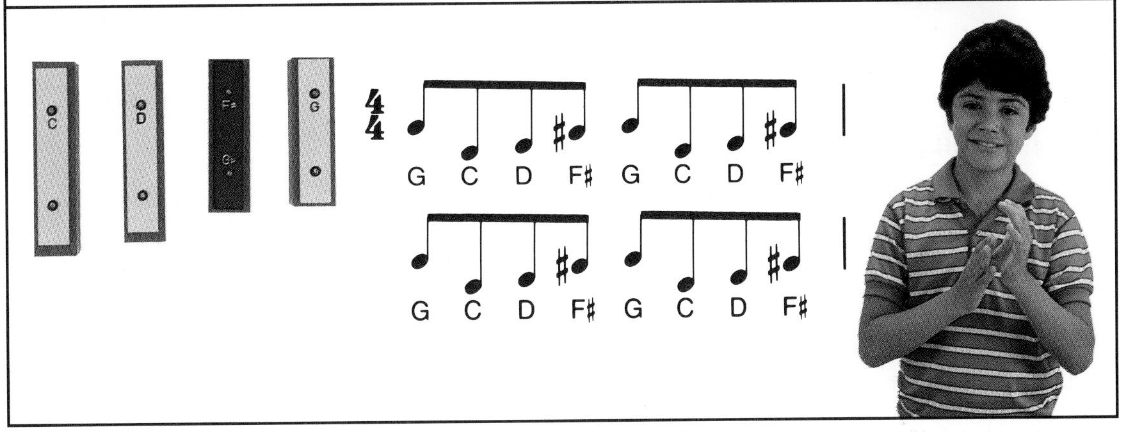

4/4
G C D F♯ G C D F♯
G C D F♯ G C D F♯

When each group has planned its part, put them together as an ensemble.

LISTENING

Tjarabalen

Javanese Folk Melody

Listen! Do you hear any of the patterns you played?

Create Your Own Gamelan Music

Listen to *Tjarabalen* again.
This time follow the score.
After you have listened, create your own gamelan music.

	1	2	3	4	5	6	7	8
Main Pulse	+	+	+	+	+	+	+	+
The Introduction								
Bonang (lower)	●	●	●	●	●	●	●	5/1
Bonang (higher)	●	●	●	●	●	●	●	●
Drum	●	●	●	●	H	H	H H	L H
Kenong	●	●	●	●	●	●	●	K
Gong	●	●	●	●	●	●	●	G

The Main Section is made up of eleven statements of this pattern.

Bonang (lower)	●	5/1	2 4	5/1	2 4	5/1	2 4	5/1
Bonang (higher)	5124	5124	5124	5124	5124	5124	5124	5124
Drum	H H	H H	L H	H H	L H	H L	H H	L H
Kenong	●	K	●	K	●	K	●	K
Gong	●	●	●	●	●	●	●	g

The Ending

Bonang (lower)	●	5/1	2 4	5/1	2 4	5/1	2 4	5/1
Bonang (higher)	5124	5124	5124	5124	5124	5124	5124	5/1
Drum	H H	L H	L H	H L	H H	L	H H	●
Kenong	●	K	●	K	●	K	●	K
Gong	●	●	●	●	●	●	●	G

Key:

+ = main pulse
H = high-pitched drum
L = low-pitched drum

G = large gong
g = small gong
K = kenong

● = rest
1 = A
2 = B

4 = D
5 = E

The Unsweet Suite

Create a **movement** for this suite.
Choose a title.
Make your music suggest the idea of the title.

Theme and Variations on a Handshake

Greet your friend. Shake hands. Try variations on handshakes.

Theme

Variation 1

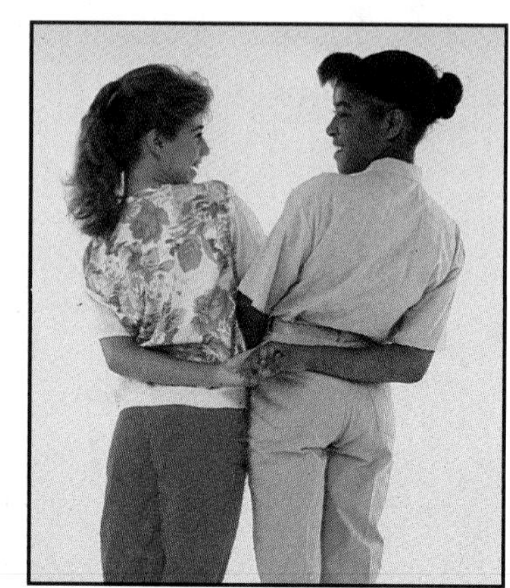

Variation 2

Create a "Theme and Variation on a Handshake for 16 Dancers."

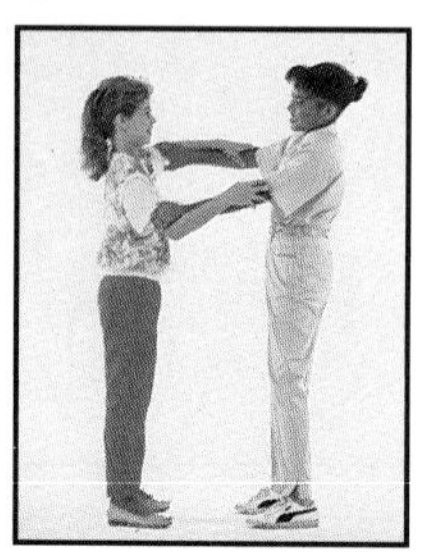

Introduction:	Two people walk toward each other.
Theme:	Greet each other, shaking hands in the usual way.
Interlude:	These two people walk to greet two new people.
Variation 1:	These four people shake hands. Use the first variation pictured above.
Interlude:	These four people greet four new people.
Variation 2:	These eight people shake hands. Use the second variation pictured above.

Create two more variations. Add the interlude between each. Can you think of other ways to shake hands? Can you change the **rhythm** of your handshakes? the **tempo?**

Lovely Evening

Traditional Round

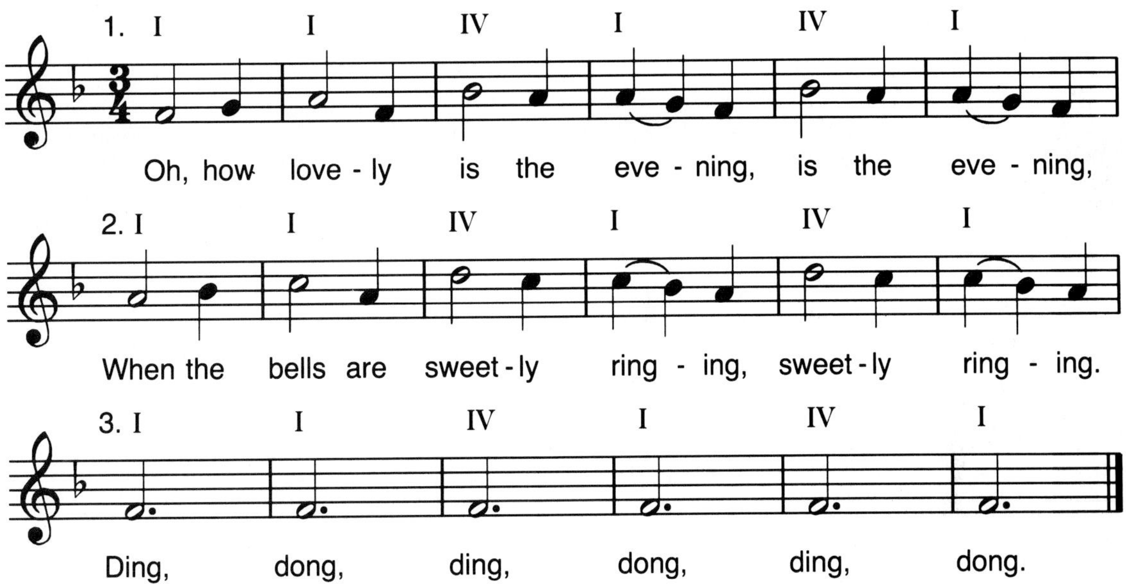

Sing each "ladder." Think the missing steps.

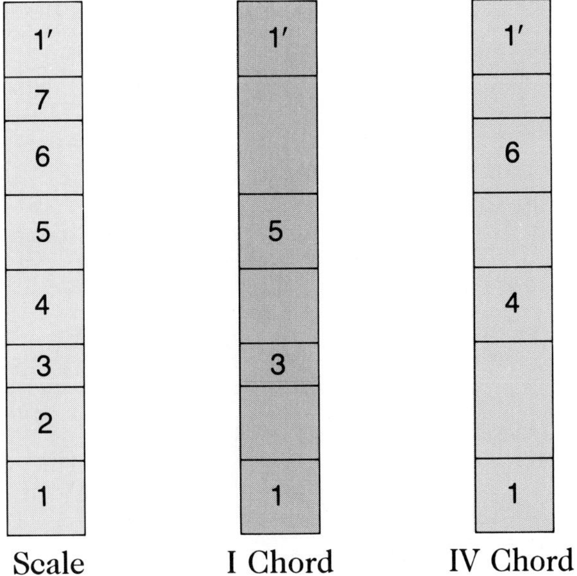

Compose a harmonizing part for "Lovely Evening." When will you use the notes of the I chord? the IV chord?

The Bremen Town Musicians

Traditional Story

Once there was a donkey who lived on a farm. The donkey was getting too old to work anymore, so the farmer thought he would sell the donkey and buy a younger one who could help with the farm work. The old donkey was very sad and decided to run away to Bremen to become a musician. After all, he had a fine voice.

"Listen to my donkey song:
Hee-haw, hee-haw, hee!
I sing it all the whole day long,
Hee-haw, hee-haw, hee!"

As he slowly walked down the road toward Bremen, he met a very sad dog. "What's wrong?" he asked.

"I'm too old to be a watchdog;
I'm too old to hunt;
But I'm not too old to sing a song,
Bow, wow, wow!"

"Why don't you come to Bremen with me? We can sing together." So the dog and the donkey went down the road to Bremen together.

It wasn't long until they met a cat. The cat had a beautiful meow, so the donkey said, "Wouldn't you like to come to Bremen with us to become a musician?"

"I'm too old to catch mice now;
I like to sit in the sun.
I sing with a beautiful meow—
Let's go, we'll all have fun."

As the three new friends continued toward Bremen, they passed a farm. On the fence post sat a rooster. He had such a wonderful voice, they decided to ask him to join them.

"Cock-a-doodle-doo! I'll go with you!
Let's go to Bremen Town,
Cock-a-doodle-doo! We'll sing so well,
We'll bring the house down!"

As they continued down the road, it began to get dark. They found a forest near the road and went into the forest where they could spend the night. The donkey and the dog lay on the ground under a tree; the cat climbed on one of the low branches; and the rooster flew to the very top of the tree.

Before they had gone to sleep for the night, the rooster noticed a light through the trees. The rooster flew down and said, "There must be a house on the other side of the trees; I see a light. Perhaps there will be a barn we can sleep in." The four of them set off toward the light the rooster had seen.

They went closer to the house and the rooster, the cat, and the dog all climbed on the donkey's back so they could see better. Inside the house was a band of robbers. The four friends began to make loud sounds:

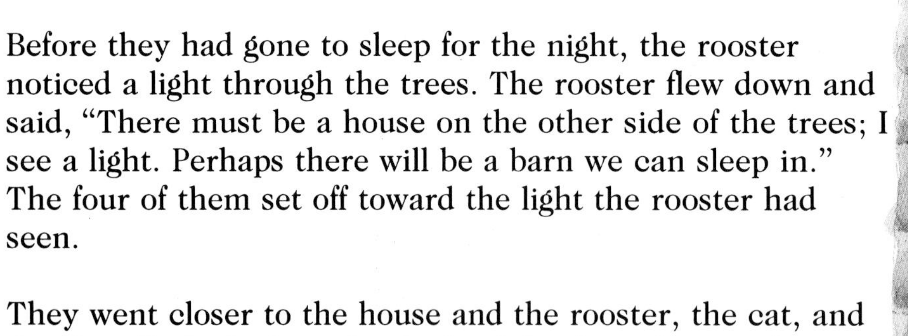

"Hee-haw!"
"Bow-wow!"
"Me-ow!"
"Cock-a-doodle-doo!"

The robbers were so frightened, they ran to the woods to hide. The four friends went inside the house and found a fine dinner that the robbers had not yet eaten, and they ate until they were full. Then they all found comfortable places to sleep. The donkey lay on the floor near the door, the cat on a rug in front of the fireplace, the dog next to the cat, and the rooster on a beam near the ceiling.

After a while, the robbers came back. The donkey began to bray and kick, the dog began to bark, the cat began to hiss, and the rooster angrily flew around their heads. This time, the robbers were so frightened that they ran away and never came back.

The four friends lived in the house and often went to the nearby town of Bremen to give concerts in the park. They sang together in beautiful harmony. First the donkey:

"Listen to my donkey song: Hee-haw, hee-haw, hee!
I sing it all the whole day long, Hee-haw, hee-haw, hee!"
Then the dog: "I'm too old to be a watchdog;
I'm too old to hunt;
But I'm not too old to sing a song, Bow, wow, wow!"
Then the cat:
"I'm too old to catch mice now; I like to sit in the sun.
I sing with a beautiful meow—Let's go, we'll all have fun."
Then the rooster:
"Cock-a-doodle-doo! I'll go with you!
Let's go to Bremen town,
Cock-a-doodle-doo! We'll sing so well,
We'll bring the house down!"

Then they all sang together at the same time.
If you ever visit Bremen, you may be lucky enough to hear them.

Create Your Own Radio Program

On
the Air
Weather Report
Weather Report
Weather Report

Special Times

This Is My Country

Words by Don Raye

Music by Al Jacobs

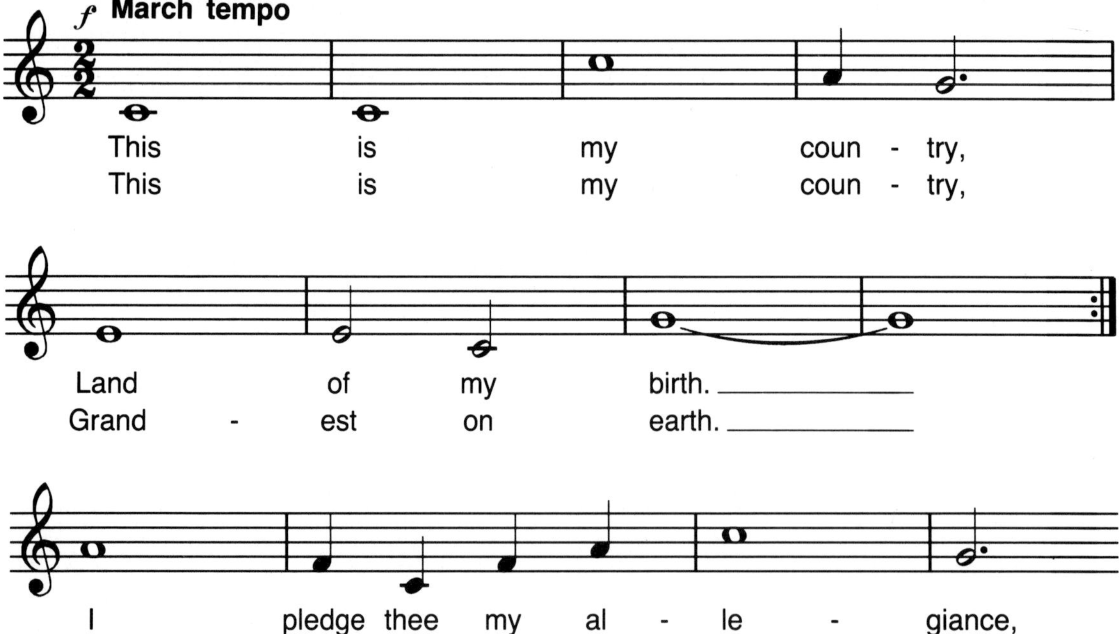

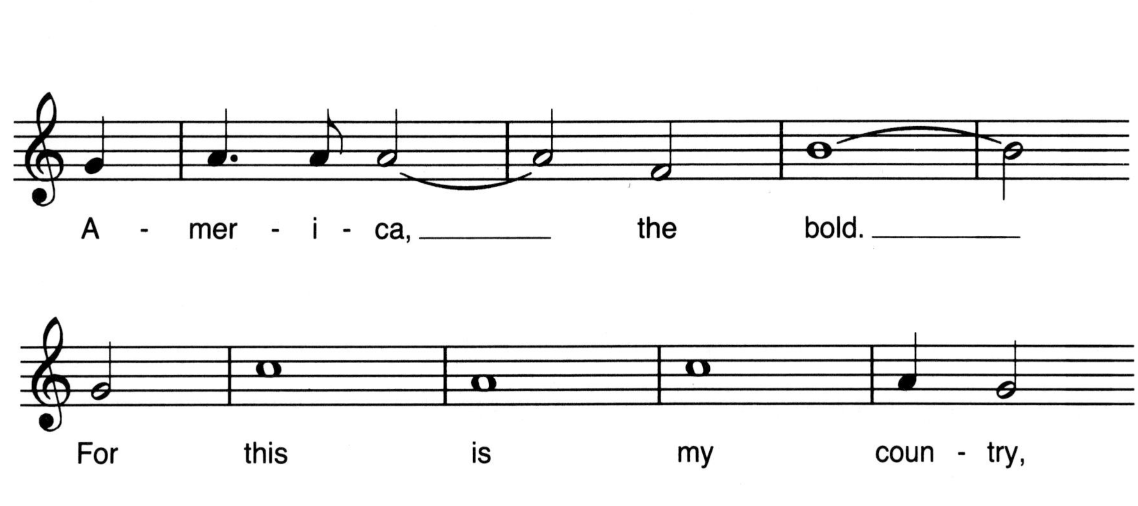
A - mer - i - ca, ___ the bold. ___
For this is my coun - try,
Fine
To have and to hold. ___

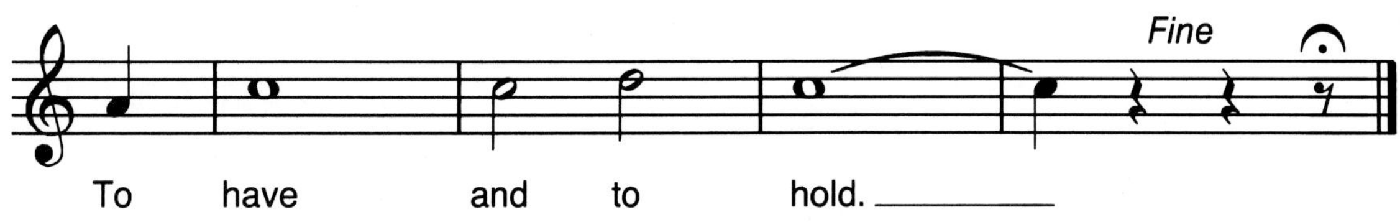
Verse Slower and more freely
p
What dif-f'rence if I hail from North or South, or from the East or West?

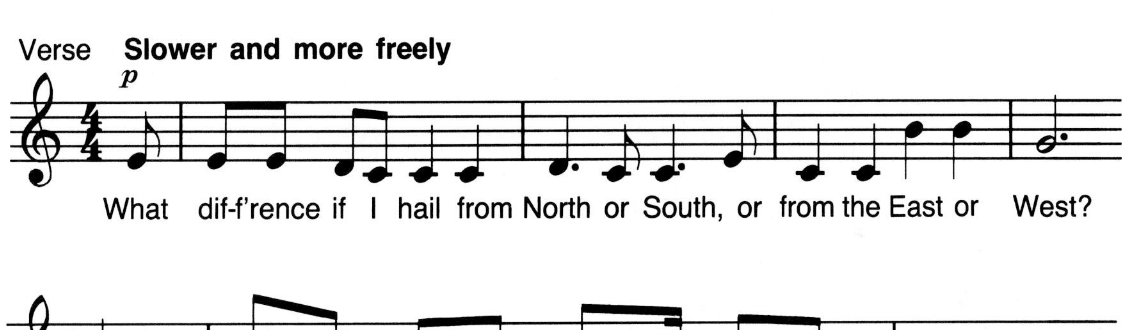
My heart is filled with love for all of these.

I on - ly know I swell with pride and deep with - in my breast,
D.C. al Fine

I thrill to see "Old Glo - ry" paint the breeze. Oh,

I'm Thankful

By Jack Prelutsky

I'm thankful for my baseball bat,
I cracked it yesterday.
I'm thankful for my checker set,
I haven't learned to play.
I'm thankful for my mittens,
One is missing in the snow.
I'm thankful for my hamsters,
They escaped a month ago.

I'm thankful for my basketball,
It's sprung another leak.
I'm thankful for my parakeet,
It bit me twice last week.
I'm thankful for my bicycle,
I crashed into a tree.
I'm thankful for my roller skates,
I fell and scraped my knee.

I'm thankful for my model plane,
It's short a dozen parts.
I'm thankful for my target game,
I'm sure I'll find the darts.
I'm thankful for my bathing suit,
It came off in the river.
I'm thankful for so many things,
Except, of course, for ***liver!***

Birthday Hallelujah

Words and Music by Malvina Reynolds

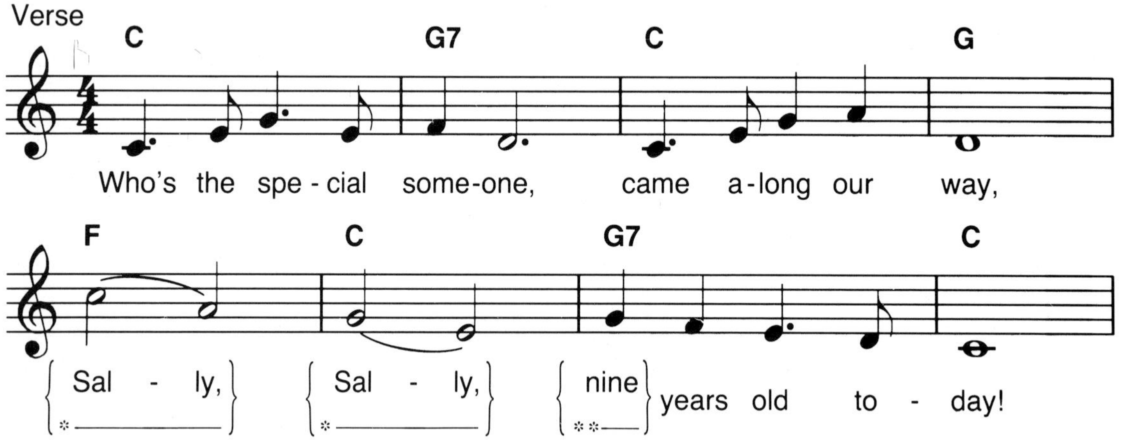

*Insert the name of the person who is celebrating a birthday.
**Insert the age of the person who is celebrating a birthday.

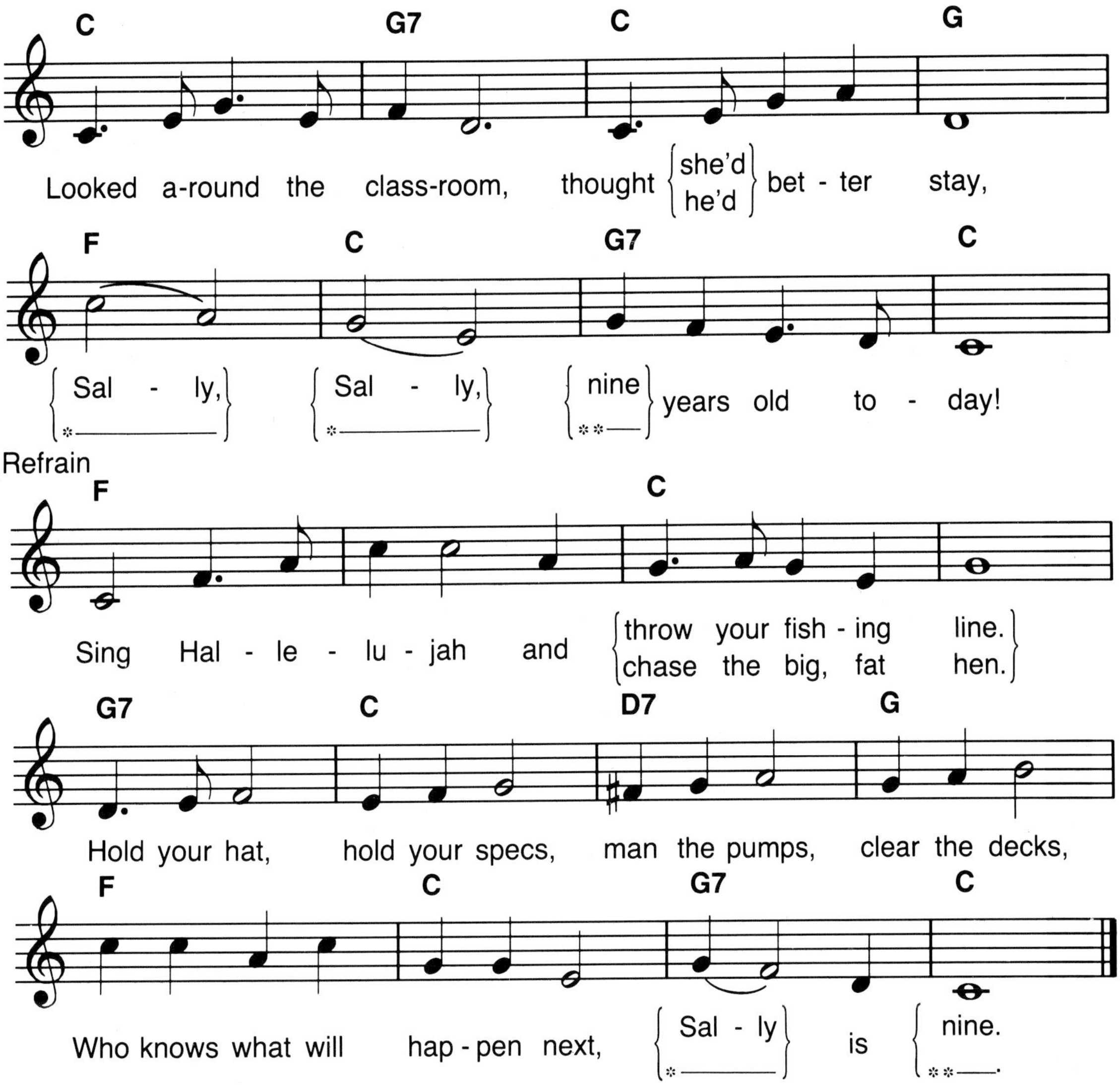

C G7 C G

Looked a-round the class-room, thought {she'd / he'd} bet - ter stay,

F C G7 C

{Sal - ly, / * ______} {Sal - ly, / * ______} {nine / ** ___} years old to - day!

Refrain

F C

Sing Hal - le - lu - jah and {throw your fish - ing line. / chase the big, fat hen.}

G7 C D7 G

Hold your hat, hold your specs, man the pumps, clear the decks,

F C G7 C

Who knows what will hap - pen next, {Sal - ly / * ______} is {nine. / ** ___.}

Sing a Rainbow

Words and Music by Arthur Hamilton

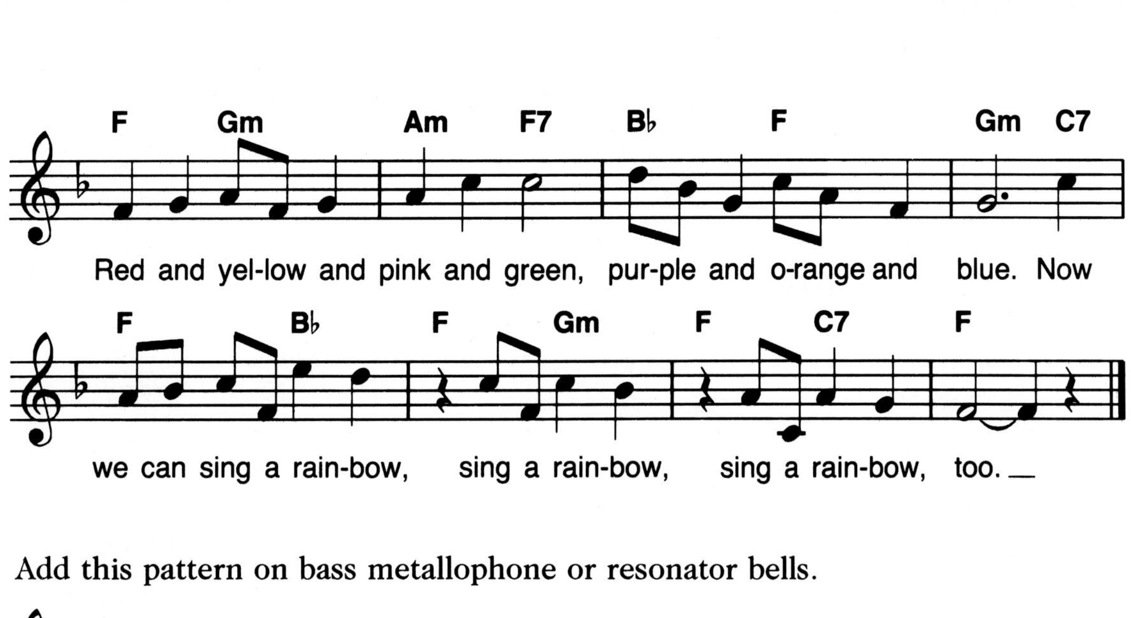

Add this pattern on bass metallophone or resonator bells.

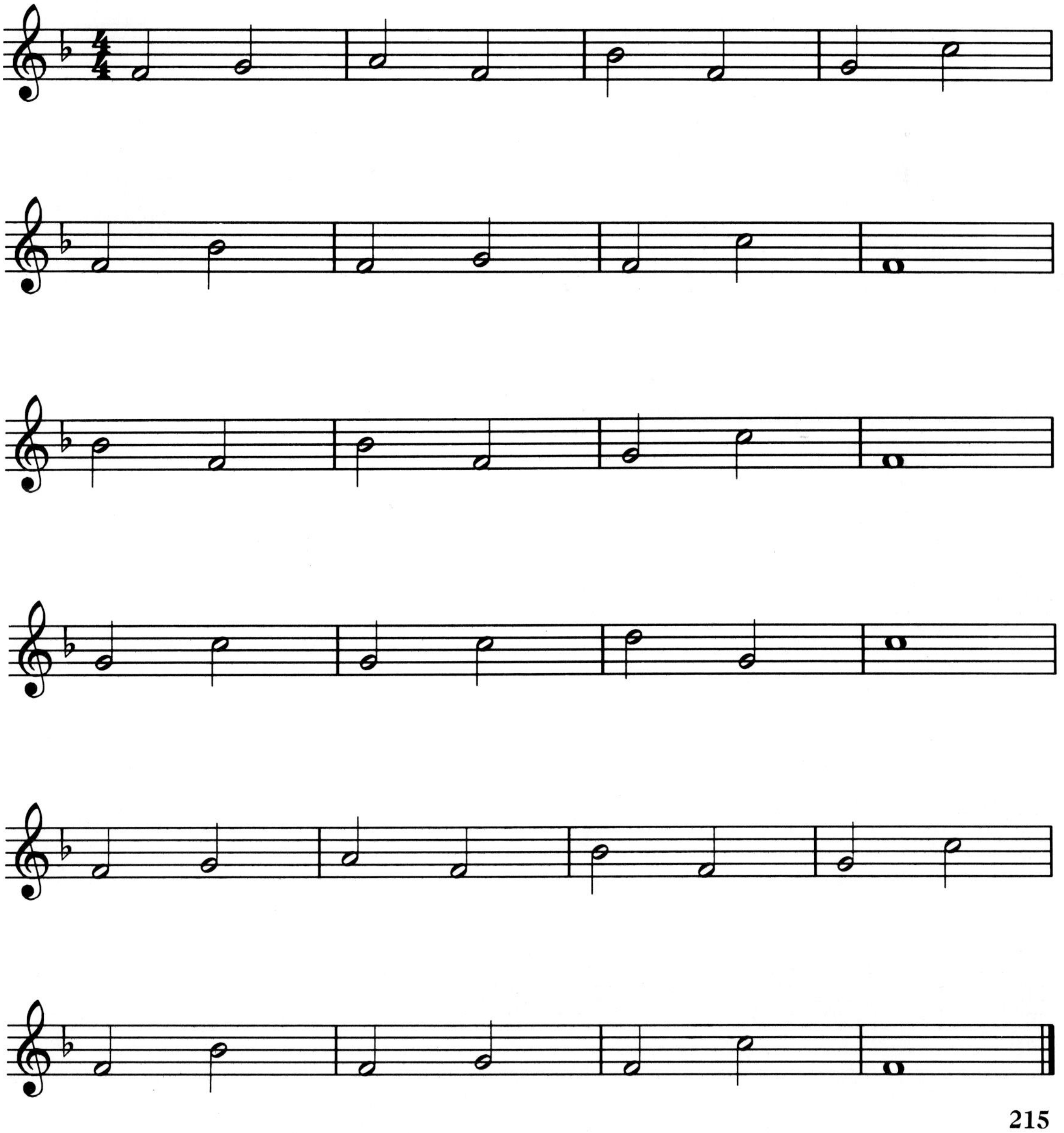

Hallowe'en
Words by Harry Behn
Music by John Wood
Mysteriously
1. To - night is the night when dead leaves fly
2. To - night is the night when leaves do sound
3. To - night is the night when pump-kins stare
Like witch - es on switch-es a - cross the sky,
Like gnomes in their homes far be - neath the ground,
Through brown sheaves and leaves al - most ev - ery - where,
When elf and sprite flit through the night
When spooks and trolls creep out of holes
When ghoul and ghost and gob - lin host
On a moon - y sheen, on a moon - y sheen.
Dark and moss - y green, dark and moss - y green.
Dance a - round their queen, for it's Hal - low - e'en!

Funeral March of a Marionette

by Charles Gounod

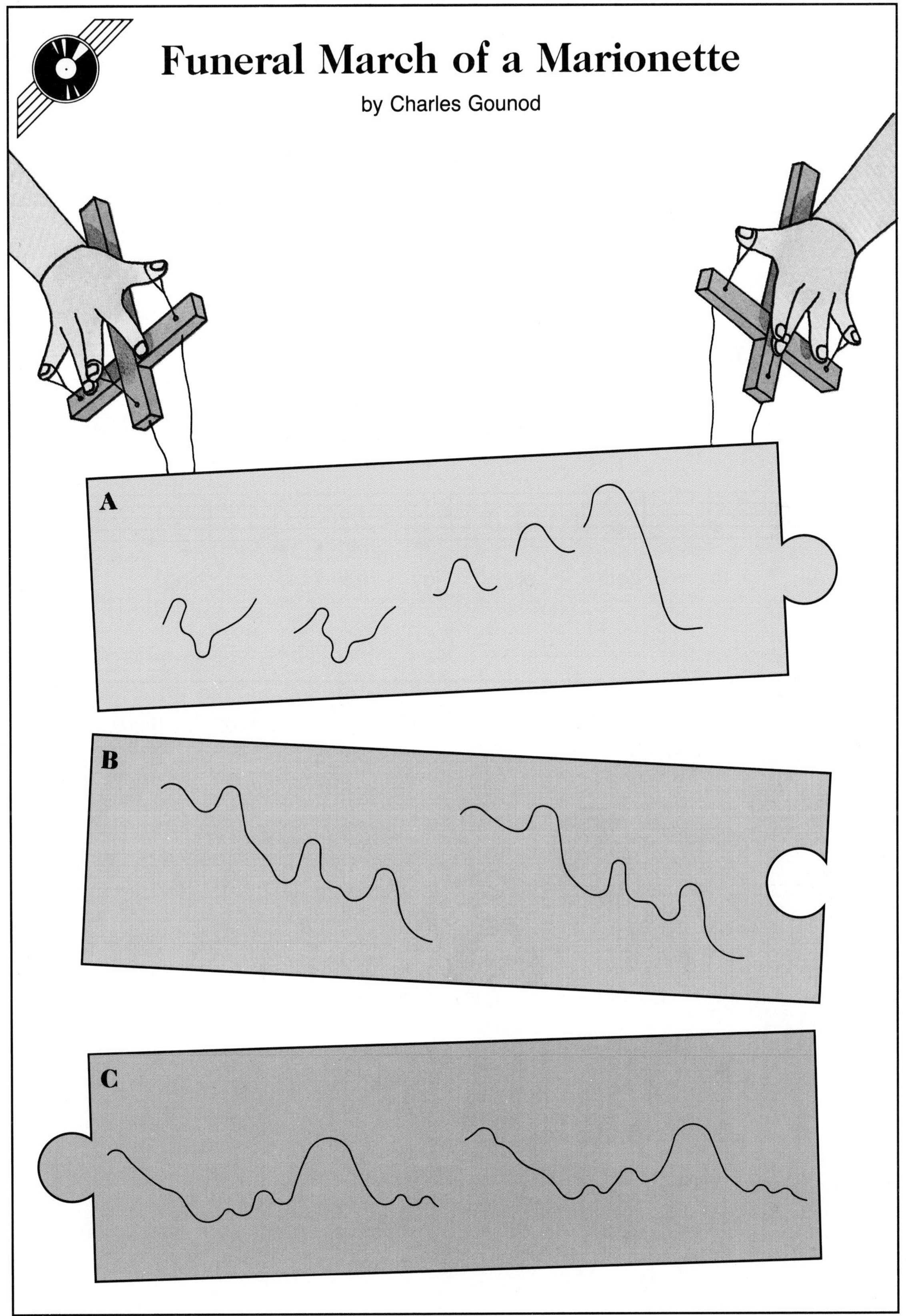

Praise and Thanksgiving

Traditional Round

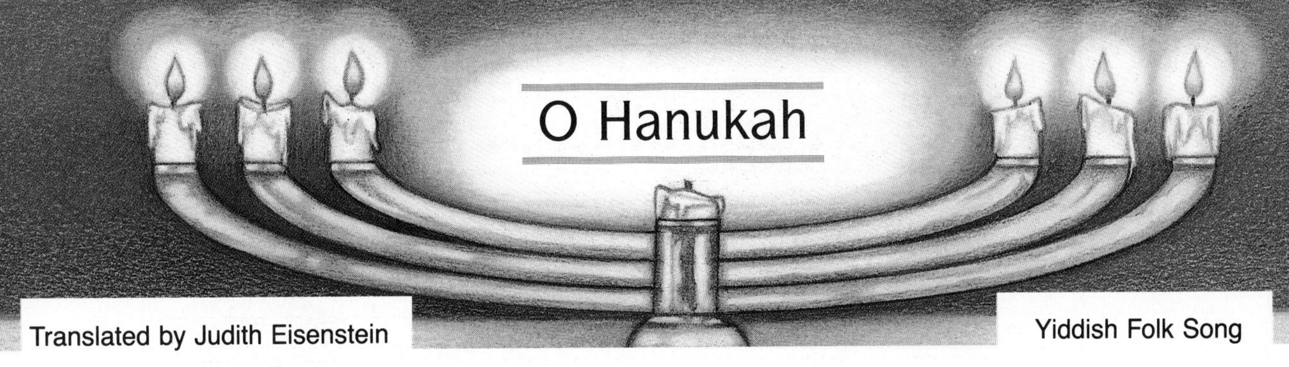

O Hanukah

Translated by Judith Eisenstein

Yiddish Folk Song

Dm A7 Dm
O Ha - nu - kah, O Ha - nu - kah, come light the me - no - rah,

Dm A7 Dm
Let's have a par - ty, we'll all dance the ho - ra.

F C7 F
Gath - er round the ta - ble, we'll give you a treat,

F C7 Dm
Shin - ing tops to play with and pan - cakes to eat;

Dm Dm Dm Gm Dm
And while we are play-ing, the can-dles are burn-ing_ low.

Dm Gm Dm Gm
One for each night, they_ shed a sweet light To re -

1.
Dm A7 Dm
mind us of days long a - go.

2.
Dm A7 Dm
mind us of days long a - go.

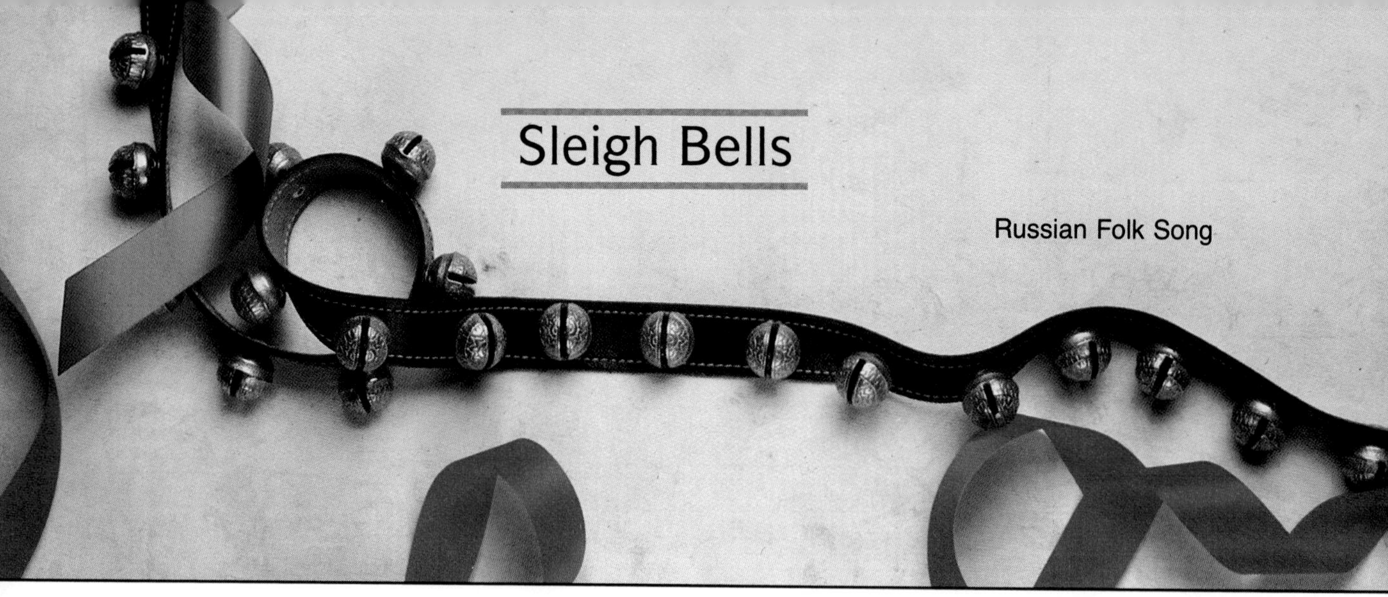

Sleigh Bells

Russian Folk Song

Add this pattern during the introduction, interlude, and coda to imitate the sound of sleigh bells.

Jingle bells

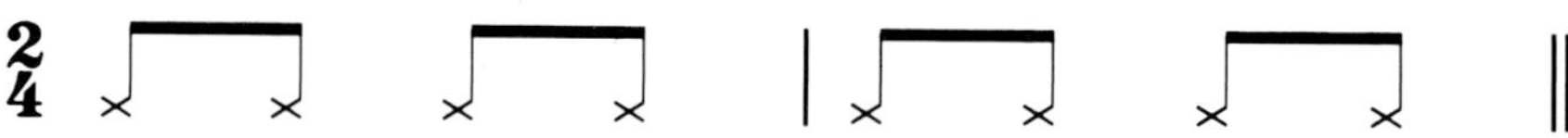

We Wish You a Merry Christmas

Arruru

English Words by Elena Paz

Spanish Folk Melody

O He Did Whistle and She Did Sing

Richard Felciano

(whistle) (whistle)

As I sat on a sun - ny bank, On Christ-mas Day in the morn - ing,

I spied three ships come sail-ing by, On Christ-mas Day in the morn-ing,

And who should be with those three ships but Jo-seph and his fair la - dy.

O he did whis-tle and she did sing And all the bells on earth did ring,

On Christ-mas day in the morn - ing. ___ (whistle)

A'Soalin'

Words and Music by Paul Stookey,
Tracy Batteast and Elena Mezzetti

Refrain

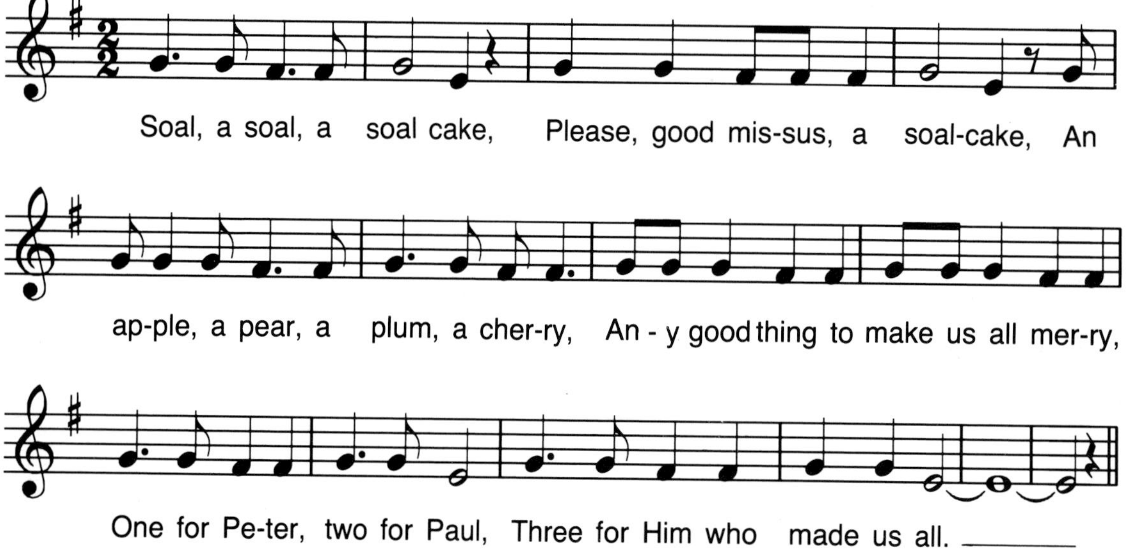

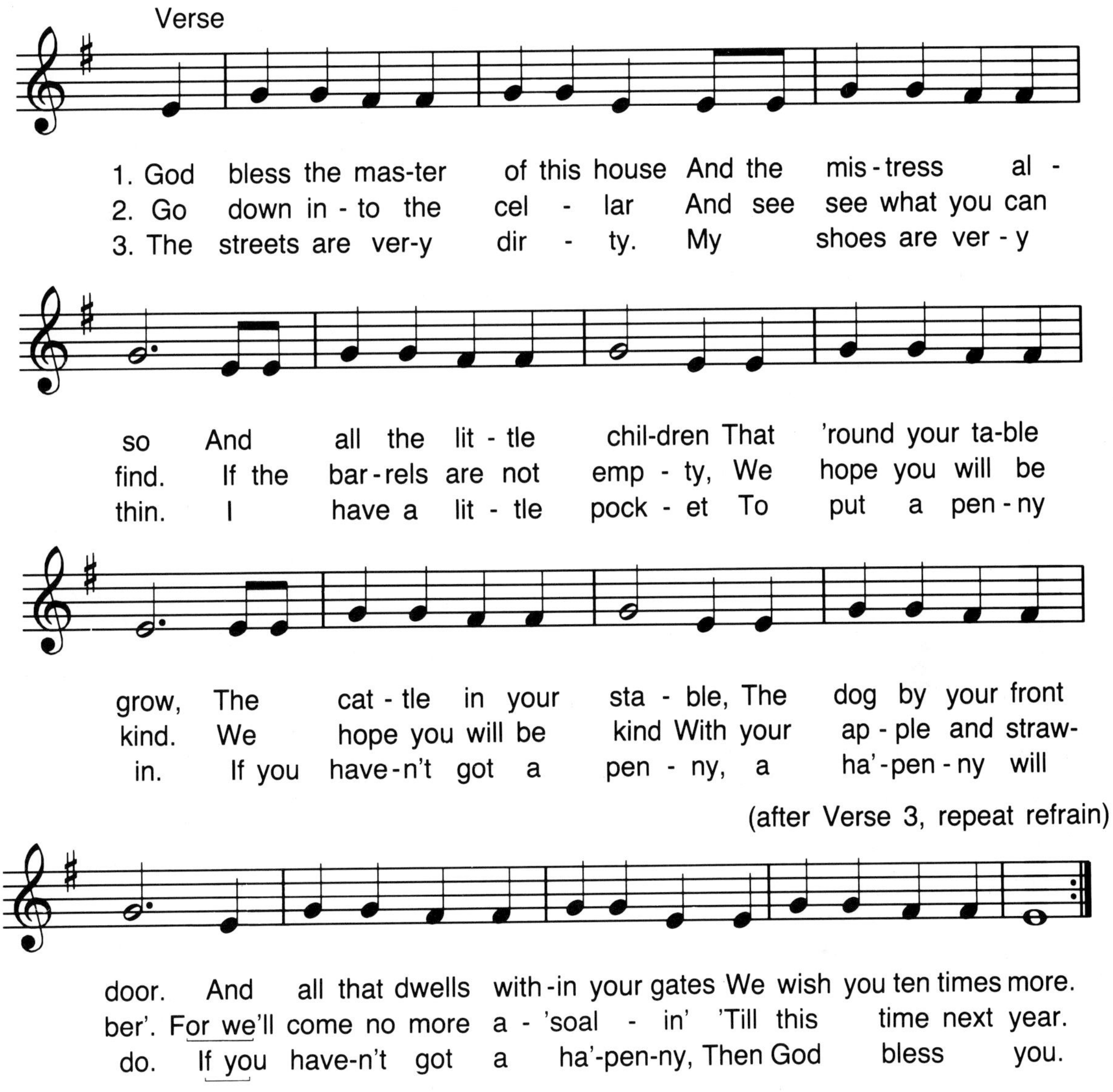

Verse
1. God bless the mas-ter of this house And the mis-tress al -
2. Go down in - to the cel - lar And see see what you can
3. The streets are ver-y dir - ty. My shoes are ver - y
so And all the lit - tle chil-dren That 'round your ta-ble
find. If the bar-rels are not emp - ty, We hope you will be
thin. I have a lit - tle pock - et To put a pen - ny
grow, The cat - tle in your sta - ble, The dog by your front
kind. We hope you will be kind With your ap - ple and straw-
in. If you have-n't got a pen - ny, a ha'-pen - ny will
(after Verse 3, repeat refrain)
door. And all that dwells with-in your gates We wish you ten times more.
ber'. For we'll come no more a - 'soal - in' 'Till this time next year.
do. If you have-n't got a ha'-pen-ny, Then God bless you.

Choose an instrument.
Play one of these ostinato patterns to accompany the song.

Xylophones/Resonator Bells
Bass Xylophone or Piano
(one octave lower)

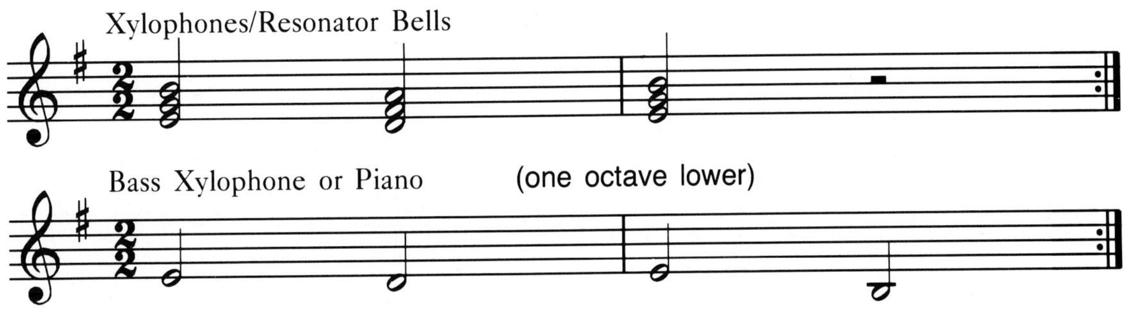

A Valentine Wish

Words and Music by Natalie Sleeth

Part 1
Hope some-one sends me a Val - en-tine
Part 2
I will send you a Val - en-tine
red and white, bold and bright.
bought with care, just to share. Hope some-one sends me a Val-en-tine
trimmed with lace, just a trace.
red and white, bold and bright.
bought with care, just to share. I will send you a Val-en-tine
trimmed with lace, just a trace.
1.
2.
to set my heart a - flame!
and fails to sign his/her name!
and helps me play the
1.
2.
to set your heart a - flame!
and fail to sign my name!
and help you play the

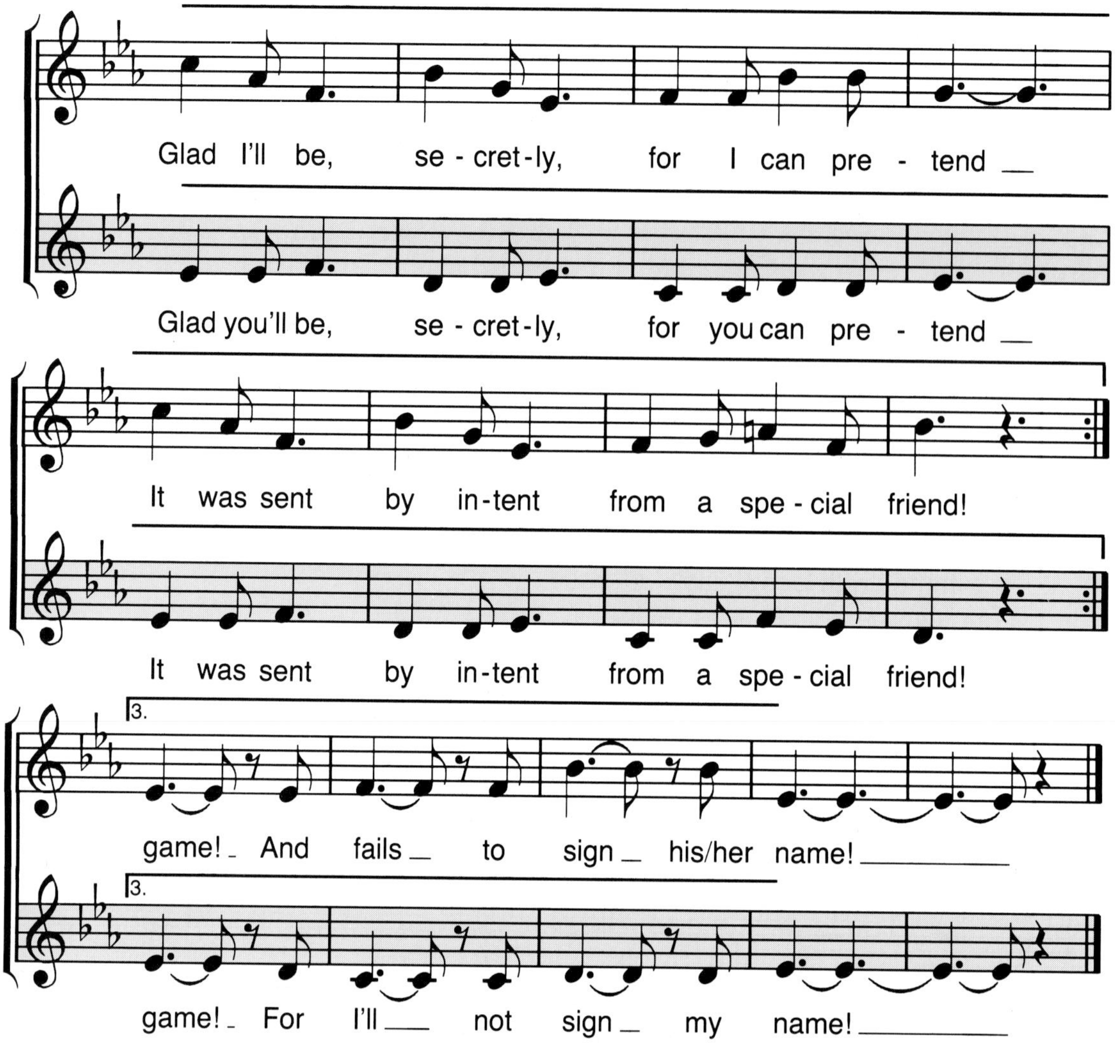
Glad I'll be, se - cret - ly, for I can pre - tend
Glad you'll be, se - cret - ly, for you can pre - tend
It was sent by in - tent from a spe - cial friend!
It was sent by in - tent from a spe - cial friend!
3.
game! And fails to sign his/her name!
3.
game! For I'll not sign my name!

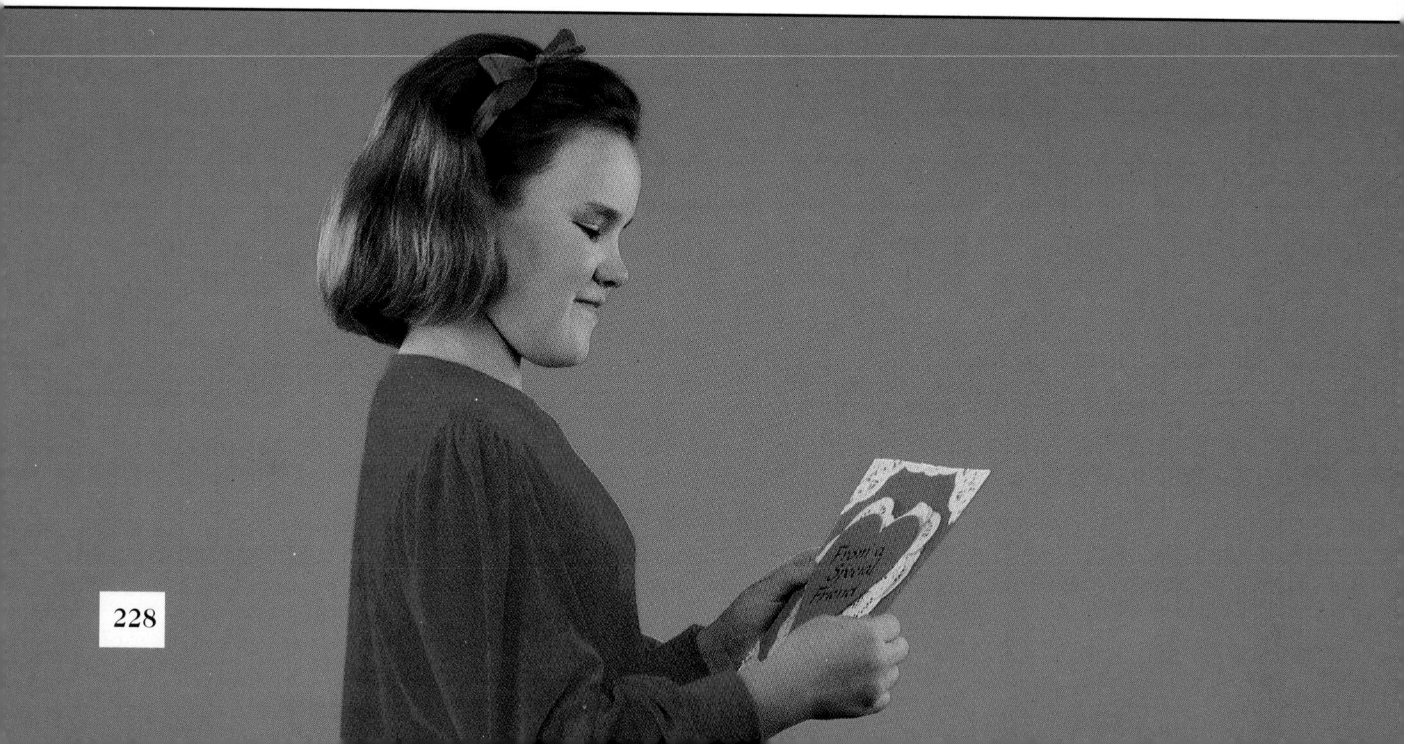
From a Special Friend

Dayenu

Jewish Folk Song

The Seder, watercolor on paper by Michael Pressman, 1950, Art Resource/The Jewish Museum, New York.

Feed My Lambs

Words and Music by Natalie Sleeth

As ye do un - to My flock, thus ye do to Me.
Feed My lambs, Tend My sheep, o - ver all a vig - il keep;
In My name, Lead them forth gen - tly, gen - tly
as a lov - ing shep-herd of the lambs.

America, the Beautiful

Words by Katherine Lee Bates

Music by Samuel A. Ward

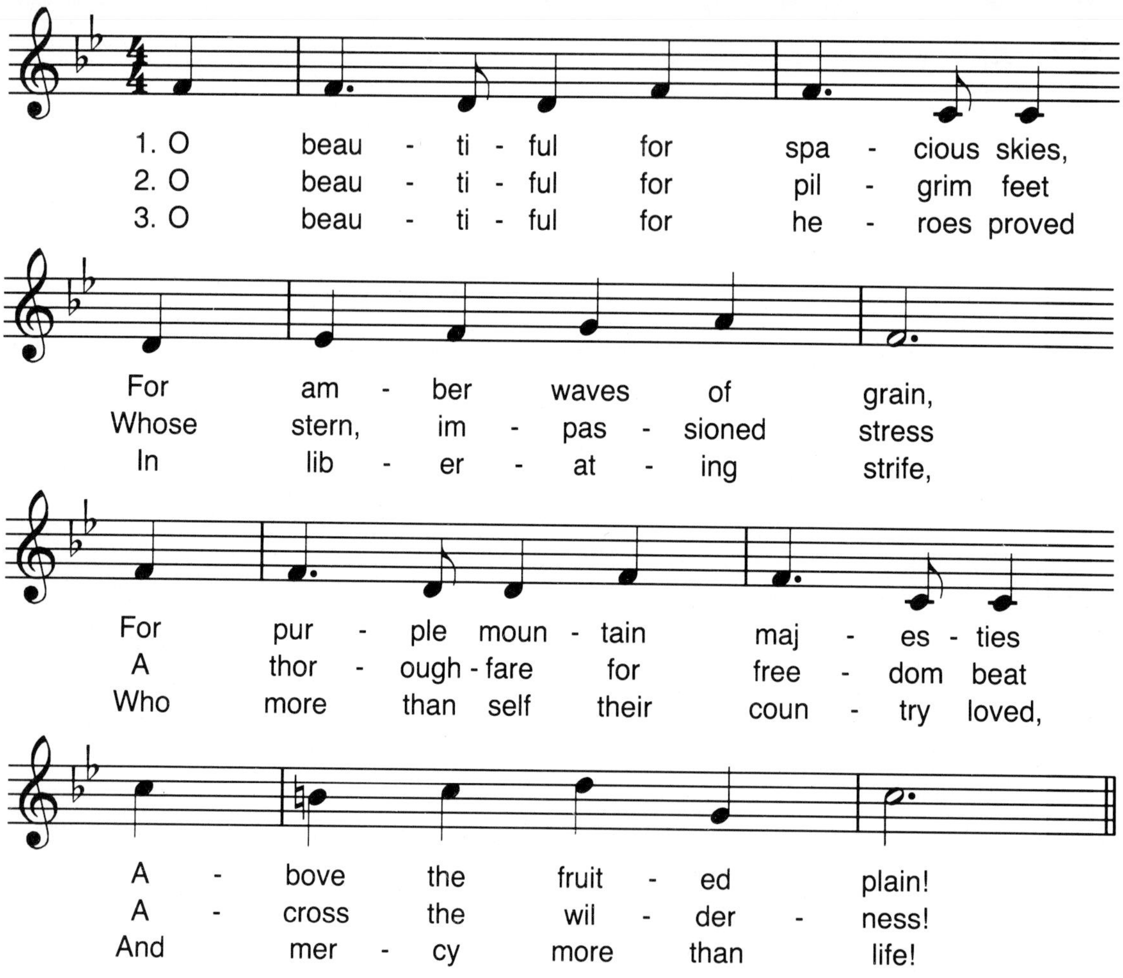

1. O beau - ti - ful for spa - cious skies,
2. O beau - ti - ful for pil - grim feet
3. O beau - ti - ful for he - roes proved

For am - ber waves of grain,
Whose stern, im - pas - sioned stress
In lib - er - at - ing strife,

For pur - ple moun - tain maj - es - ties
A thor - ough - fare for free - dom beat
Who more than self their coun - try loved,

A - bove the fruit - ed plain!
A - cross the wil - der - ness!
And mer - cy more than life!

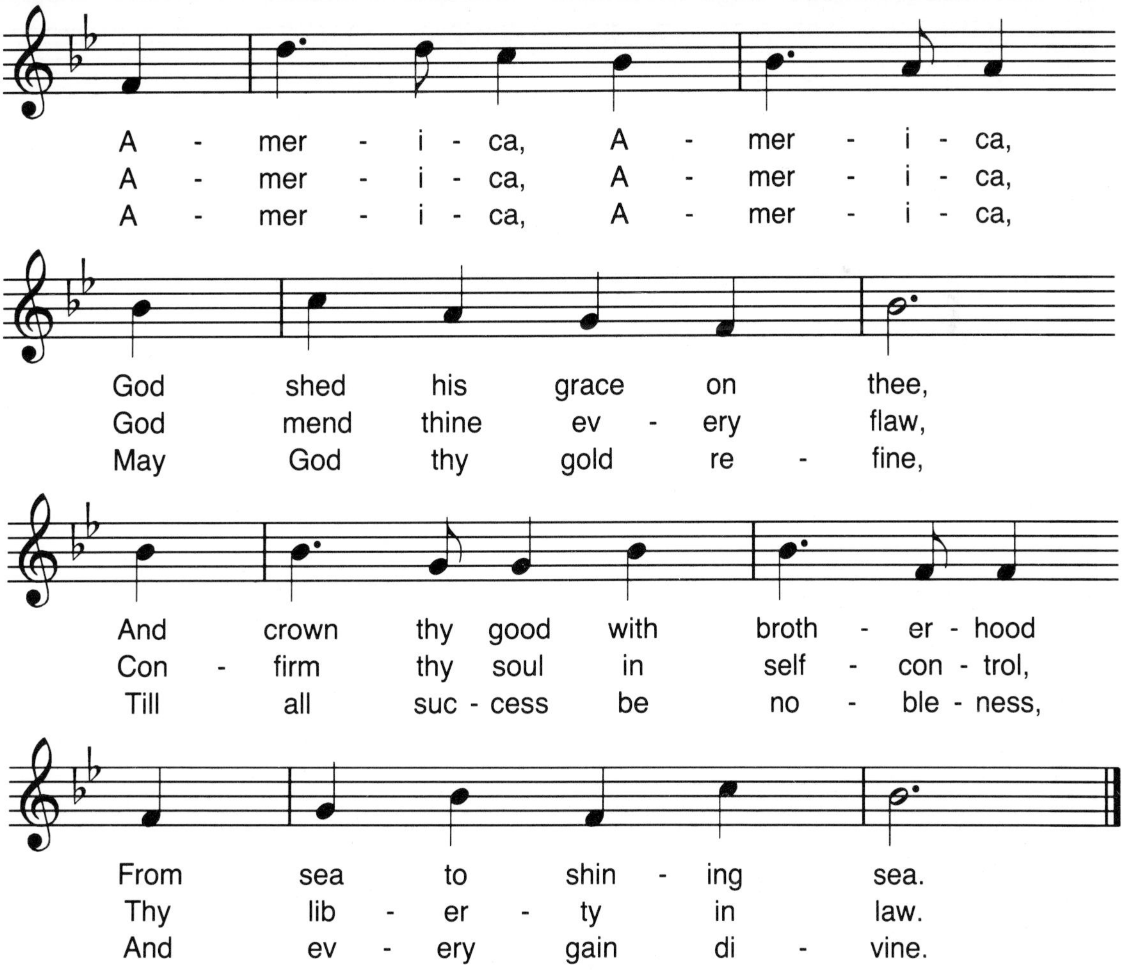

A - mer - i - ca, A - mer - i - ca,
A - mer - i - ca, A - mer - i - ca,
A - mer - i - ca, A - mer - i - ca,

God shed his grace on thee,
God mend thine ev - ery flaw,
May God thy gold re - fine,

And crown thy good with broth - er - hood
Con - firm thy soul in self - con - trol,
Till all suc - cess be no - ble - ness,

From sea to shin - ing sea.
Thy lib - er - ty in law.
And ev - ery gain di - vine.

The Star-Spangled Banner

Words by Francis Scott Key

Composer Unknown

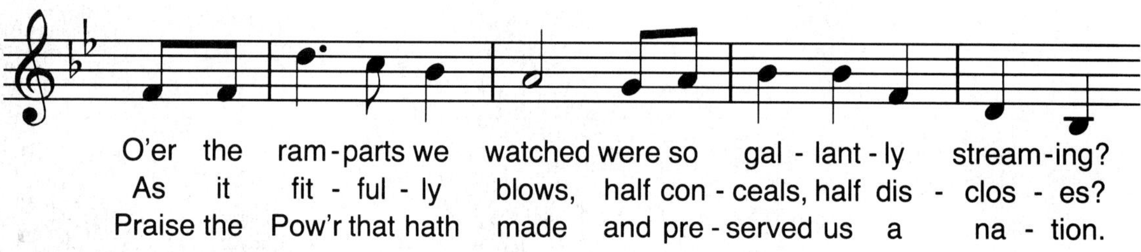

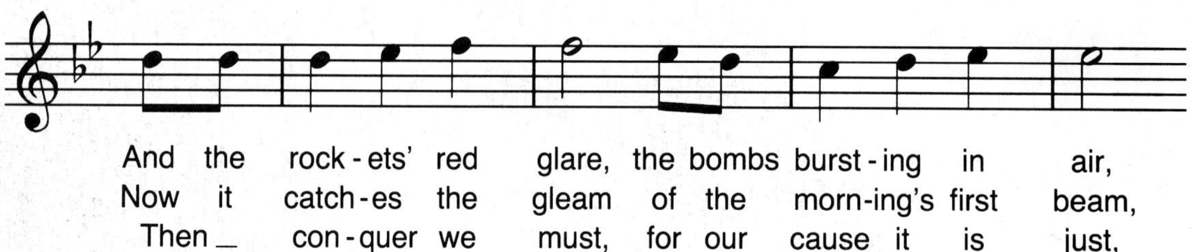

Gave proof through the night that our flag was still there.
In full glo - ry re - flec-ted now_ shines on the stream;
And this be our mot-to: "In ___ God is our trust."
Oh, say, does that_ star-span-gled ban - ner ___ yet ___ wave_
'Tis the star-span-gled_ ban-ner, Oh, long may_ it ___ wave_
And the star-span-gled_ ban-ner in tri - umph_ shall_ wave_
O'er the land ___ of the free and the home of the brave!
O'er the land ___ of the free and the home of the brave!
O'er the land ___ of the free and the home of the brave!

Glossary

Accelerando becoming faster, *172*

Adagio moderately slow, *89*

Allegro fast, *89*

Andante medium speed (a walking tempo), *89*

Articulation how sounds start and stop, *91*

Beat the steady pulse of the music, *72*

Brass Family wind instruments made of brass or other metal, including the trumpet, French horn, trombone, and tuba, *62*

Canon music in which a melody is imitated exactly by another voice or instrument, *117*

Chord three or more pitches occurring at the same time, *45*

Coda a short concluding section of a piece, *27*

Descant a harmony part that is played or sung above the melody, *47*

Dynamics the loud and soft changes in music, *90*

Form the design of a piece of music made up of same, similar, or different parts, *13*

Forte (*f*) loud, *12*

Fortissimo (*ff*) very loud, *90*

Harmony two or more melodies performed at the same time or one melody accompanied by chords, *196*

Interlude a section between two parts of the music, *27*

Introduction a section that comes before the main part of the music, *27*

Key Signature the sharps and flats at the beginning of the music that show where the home tone is located and the kind of scale used, *112*

Largo very slow, *89*

Legato performed in a smooth, connected way, *91*

Marcato tones that are performed heavier and "marked," *91*

Melody a series of tones arranged rhythmically to make a musical idea, *122*

Meter Signature the two numbers at the beginning of a piece of music that tell how the beats are grouped and show the kind of note that moves with the beat, *74*

Mezzo Forte (*mf*) medium loud, *12*

Mezzo Piano (*mp*) medium soft, *12*

Movement(s) the sections of a long composition, *201*

Note a sign that shows the pitch and the length of a tone, *14*

Ostinato an accompaniment pattern repeated over and over, *122*

Percussion Family instruments played by shaking or by striking, including the trap set, celesta, chimes, orchestra bells, and timpani, *63*

Phrase a complete musical idea, *37*

Pianissimo (*pp*) very soft, *90*

Piano (*p*) soft, *34*

Pitch the highness or lowness of a musical sound, *197*

Presto very fast, *89*

Rhythm the pattern of long and short notes and rests, *202*

Ritardando a slowing of the tempo, *172*

Staccato a series of tones that are separated by short silences, *91*

String Family instruments played by plucking or bowing strings, including the violin, viola, cello, and double bass, *60*

Syncopation a type of rhythm that is created when the accents in a melody occur at a different time from the accented beat, *178*

Tempo the speed of the beat, *88*

Theme an important melody, *13*

Tie a musical addition sign used to join two or more notes, *80*

Timbre the distinctive sound made by a particular instrument, *196*

Tonal Center the pitch to which all tones in a song seem to return; the home tone, *22*

Tone Row a series of pitches, *196*

Variation a musical idea that is repeated with some change, *13*

Woodwind Family wind instruments usually made of wood or metal, including the piccolo, flute, oboe, clarinet, and bassoon, *61*

Acknowledgments

Grateful acknowledgement is made to the following copyright owners and agents for their permission to reprint the following copyrighted material. Every effort has been made to locate all copyright owners; any errors or omissions in copyright notice are inadvertent and will be corrected as they are discovered.

"Apusski Dusky," traditional melody,words from *Apusskidu*, edited by B. Harrop. Reprinted and recorded by permission of A & C Black (Publishers) Limited, London. All rights reserved.

"Arruru," Spanish folk song translated into English by Elena Paz. Copyright © 1963 by Elena Paz Travesi. Reprinted and recorded by permission. All rights reserved.

"A Soalin'," words and music by Paul Stookey, Tracy Batteast and Elena Mezzetti, copyright © 1963 by Pepamar Music Corporation. Reprinted by permission of Warner Bros. Music. All Rights Reserved. Recording licensed through the Harry Fox Agency. All rights reserved.

"Birthday Hallelujah," words and music by Malvina Reynolds from *Songs for a New Generation*. Copyright © 1974 Oak Publications. Reprinted and recorded by permission of Schroder Music Co. (ASCAP). All rights reserved.

"Brethren In Peace Together," Jewish folk song paraphrased from Psalm 133:1, text adapted by Vincent Silliman, from *We Sing of Life*, copyright © 1955 by The American Ethical Union. Permission to reprint and record this song was granted by the American Ethical Union. Copyright 1955; The American Ethical Union Library Catalog number 54:11625. All rights reserved.

"Bye-Bye, Blackbird," words by Mort Dixon, music by Ray Henderson. Copyright 1926 (Renewed) WARNER BROS. INC. All Rights Reserved. Reprinted by Permission. Recording licensed through the Harry Fox Agency.

"Bye Bye Blues," words and music by Fred Hamm, Dave Bennett, Bert Lown and Chauncey Gray. Copyright 1930 by Bourne Co., Music Publishers. Reprinted by permission. All rights reserved. Recording licensed through the Harry Fox Agency.

"Chickery Chick," written by Sidney Lippman and Sylvia Dee, copyright © 1945 Sainty-Joy, assigned to Harry Von Tilzer Music Publishing Company (c/o The Welk Music Group, Santa Monica, California, 90401). International Copyright Secured. All Rights Reserved. Used by Permission. Recording licensed through the Harry Fox Agency.

"Clouds," music by Don Malin. From *Birchard Music Series, Book Three*. Copyright © 1962 Birch Tree Group Ltd. All rights reserved. Reprinted by permission. Recording licensed through the Harry Fox Agency.

"Clouds," music by Ruth Bampton, from *Growing with Music, Book 2* by Harry R. Wilson, Walter Ehret, Alice M. Snyder, Edward J. Hermann and Albert A. Renna. Copyright © 1970 by Prentice-Hall, Inc., Englewood Cliffs, NJ. Reprinted and recorded by permission. All rights reserved.

"Ding-Dong! The Witch is Dead," lyric by E.Y. Harburg, music by Harold Arlen. Copyright © 1938 (Renewed 1966) Metro-Goldwyn-Mayer Inc. Copyright © 1939 (Renewed 1967) Leo Feist, Inc. Rights throughout the world controlled by Leo Feist, Inc. Reprinted by permission of Columbia Pictures Publications. Recording licensed through the Harry Fox Agency.

"Down By the Bay," from *Sally Go Round the Sun*, by Edith Fowke. Excerpted and reprinted by permission of The Canadian Publishers, McClelland and Stewart Limited, Toronto. Recording licensed through Edith Fowke.

"Down By the Riverside," arranged by Buryl Red. Copyright © 1971 Generic Music. Reprinted and recorded by permission of the publisher.

"Feed My Lambs," adapted from Scripture by Natalie Sleeth. Copyright © 1972 by Carl Fischer, Inc., New York. This arrangement copyright © 1988 by Carl Fischer, Inc., New York. All Rights Reserved. International Copyright Secured. Reprinted and recorded by permission.

"Gather 'Round," by Margaret Dugard. Copyright © 1984 by Margaret Dugard. Reprinted and recorded by permission. All rights reserved.

"Get Along Little Dogies," originally "Git Along Little Dogies," Copyright © 1975 by Chappell & Co., Inc. International Copyright Secured ALL RIGHTS RESERVED Used by Permission. Recording licensed through the Harry Fox Agency.

"Give a Little Whistle," by Ned Washington and Leigh Harline, copyright 1939 (Renewed) by Bourne Co., Music Publishers. Reprinted by permission. All rights reserved. Recording licensed through the Harry Fox Agency.

"Hallowe'en," words by Harry Behn, music by John Wood, adapted from *The Little Hill*, copyright 1949 by Harry Behn, © renewed 1977 by Alice L. Behn. Adapted, reprinted and recorded by permission of Marian Reiner. All rights reserved.

"Happiness Runs" aka "Pebbles and the Man," words and music by Donovan Leitch, copyright © 1968 by Donovan Music Ltd. Reprinted by permission of Columbia Pictures Publications. All rights reserved. Recording licensed through the Harry Fox Agency.

"The Happy Wanderer," words by Antonia Ridge, music by Friedrich W. Moller. Reprinted in the United States and Canada and recorded by permission of Sam Fox Publishing Company. Reprinted outside the United States and Canada by permission of Bosworth & Co. Ltd., London. All rights reserved.

"Howdido," words and music by Woody Guthrie. TRO - © Copyright 1961 and 1964 Ludlow Music, Inc., New York, NY Reprinted by permission. Recording licensed through the Harry Fox Agency.

"How I Get Cool," reprinted by permission of the publisher from Smith, *Using Poetry to Teach Reading and the Language Arts: A Handbook for Elementary School Teachers* (NY: Teachers College Press © 1985 by Teachers College Columbia University. All rights reserved.) pp. 56 and 78.

"Hurdy Gurdy Man," translated by Merritt Wheeler, music by Franz Schubert, from *Growing with Music, Book 6, Teacher's Edition*, by Harry R. Wilson, Walter Ehret, Alice M. Snyder, Edward J. Hermann and Albert A. Renna. Copyright © 1970 by Prentice-Hall Inc., Englewood Cliffs, NJ. Reprinted and recorded by permission. All rights reserved.

"If I Only Had a Brain (If I Only Had A Heart) (If I Only Had The Nerve)," lyric by E. Y. Harburg, music by Harold Arlen. Copyright © 1938 (Renewed 1966) Metro-Goldwyn-Mayer Inc. Copyright © 1939 (Renewed 1967) Leo Feist, Inc. Rights throughout the world controlled by Leo Feist, Inc. Reprinted by permission of Columbia Pictures Publications. Recording licensed through the Harry Fox Agency.

"I'm Looking Over A Four Leaf Clover," words by Mort Dixon, music by Harry Woods. Copyright © 1927 (Renewed) WARNER BROS. INC. All Rights Reserved. Used by Permission. Recording licensed through the Harry Fox Agency.

"I Ride An Old Paint," Copyright © 1975 by Chappell & Co., Inc. International Copyright Secured ALL RIGHTS RESERVED Used by Permission. Recording licensed through the Harry Fox Agency.

"Kookaburra," Australian round arranged by Sharon Beth Falk. Reprinted and recorded by permission. All rights reserved.

"Lament for a Donkey," Spanish folk tune, words adapted by Martha Harris, from *Growing with Music, Book 4* by Harry R. Wilson, Walter Ehret, Alice M. Snyder, Edward J. Hermann and Albert A. Renna. Copyright © 1966 by Prentice-Hall, Inc., Englewood Cliffs, NJ. Reprinted and recorded by permission. All rights reserved.

"Little Lady From Baltimore," Copyright © 1954 (Renewed) Edward B. Marks Music Company International Copyright Secured ALL RIGHTS RESERVED. Recording licensed through the Harry Fox Agency.

"March Of The Kings," French folk melody, translated by Satis Coleman, from *Christmas Carols from Many Lands*, translated by Satis Coleman. Copyright 1934 by G. Schirmer, Inc. Reprinted by permission of Music Sales Corporation. All Rights Reserved. Recording licensed through the Harry Fox Agency.

"Me and My Shadow," by Billy Rose, Al Jolson and Dave Dreyer. Copyright © 1927 (Renewed) by Bourne Co., Music Publishers. Reprinted by permission. All rights reserved. Recording licensed through the Harry Fox Agency.

"The Merry Old Land of Oz," lyric by E. Y. Harburg, music by Harold Arlen. Copyright © 1938 (Renewed 1966) Metro-Goldwyn-Mayer Inc. Copyright © 1939 (Renewed 1967) Leo Feist, Inc. Rights throughout the world controlled by Leo Feist, Inc. Reprinted by permission of Columbia Pictures Publications. Recording licensed through the Harry Fox Agency.

"The Music is You," by John Denver, © Copyright 1974 CHERRY LANE MUSIC PUBLISHING CO., INC. This Arrangement © Copyright 1986 CHERRY LANE MUSIC PUBLISHING CO., INC. All Rights Reserved. International Copyright Secured. Reprinted by permission. Recording licensed through the Harry Fox Agency.

"My Mama Told Me," song and movement by Margaret Dugard, from *Street Game Trilogy*, copyright © 1979 by Margaret Dugard. Reprinted and recorded by permission. All rights reserved.

"My Puppy," reprinted by permission of the publisher from Smith, *Using Poetry to Teach Reading and the Language Arts: A Handbook for Elementary School Teachers* (NY: Teachers College Press © 1985 by Teachers College-Columbia University. All rights reserved.) pp. 56 and 78.

"O Hanukah," Yiddish folk song translated by Judith Eisenstein, from *Gateway to Jewish Song* by Judith Eisenstein. Copyright 1939 by Judith Eisenstein, published by Behrman House. Reprinted and recorded by permission of Judith Eisenstein. All rights reserved.

"O He Did Whistle and She Did Sing," by Richard Felciano. Copyright © 1972, 1987 by E. C. Schirmer Music Company, Boston. Reprinted and recorded by permission of E. C. Schirmer Music Company, Boston. All rights reserved.

"Old Texas," from *Songs for Swingin' Housemothers*, copyright © 1961, 1963 by James Leisy Music. Reprinted and recorded by permission. All rights reserved.

"Once (Pa'am Akhat)," Israeli folk song, from *Hi Neighbor, Book 2*, published by the United States Committee for UNICEF, United Nations. Reprinted and recorded by permission.

"One Cold and Frosty Morning," Alabama folk song, reprinted and recorded by permission of the publishers from Dorothy Scarborough, ON THE TRAIL OF NEGRO FOLKSONGS, Cambridge, Mass.: Harvard University Press, Copyright 1925 by Harvard University Press; 1953 by Mary McDaniel Parker.

"Over the Rainbow," lyric by E. Y. Harburg, music by Harold Arlen. Copyright © 1938, 1939 (Renewed 1966, 1967) Metro-Goldwyn-Mayer Inc. All rights controlled and administered by Leo Feist, Inc. Reprinted by permission of Columbia Pictures Publications. Recording licensed through the Harry Fox Agency.

"Portland Town," adapted by permission, original words and music by Derroll Adams, From *The Joan Baez Songbook*. Copyright © 1964 by Ryerson Music Publishers, Inc., A Division of Vanguard Records. Reprinted by permission of Big 7 Music Publishers. All rights reserved. Recording licensed through the Harry Fox Agency.

"Praise and Thanksgiving," traditional round, from *The Whole World Singing* by Edith Lovell Thomas. Copyright by Friendship Press, New York. Reprinted and recorded by permission. All rights reserved.

"The Purple Bamboo," from *Folksongs of China*. Copyright by J. Curwen & Sons, Limited, London. Reprinted by permission of G. Schirmer, Inc. Recording licensed through the Harry Fox Agency.

"A Sailor Went To Sea," from *Sally Go Round the Sun*, by Edith Fowke. Reprinted by permission of The Canadian Publishers, McClelland and Stewart Limited, Toronto. Recording licensed through Edith Fowke.

"School Days," words by Will D. Cobb, music by Gus Edwards, from *Growing with Music, Book 4* by Harry R. Wilson, Walter Ehret, Alice M. Snyder, Edward J. Hermann and Albert A. Renna. Copyright © 1966 by Prentice-Hall, Inc., Englewood Cliffs, NJ. Reprinted and recorded by permission. All rights reserved.

"She'll Be Comin' Round the Mountain," from *The Fireside Book of Fun and Game Songs*, collected and edited by Marie Winn, musical arrangements by Allan Miller. Copyright © 1974 by Marie Winn and Allan Miller. Reprinted and recorded by permission of SIMON & SCHUSTER, Inc. All rights reserved.

"The Silver Birch," Russian folk tune, words adapted by Marcella Bannon, from *Growing with Music, Book 4* by Harry R. Wilson, Walter Ehret, Alice M. Snyder, Edward J. Hermann and Albert A. Renna. Copyright © 1966 by Prentice-Hall, Inc., Englewood Cliffs, NJ. Reprinted and recorded by permission.

"Sing Along," from *Song in My Pocket*, songs by Malvina Reynolds, copyright ©1954 by Malvina Reynolds, published by the California Labor School, San Francisco. Reprinted by permission of Music Sales Corporation. Recording licensed through the Harry Fox Agency.

"Sing A Rainbow," words and music by Arthur Hamilton. © 1955 and 1983 by Mark VII Music. Reprinted by permission of Mark VII Music. All rights reserved. Recording licensed through the Harry Fox Agencv.

"Sing Together," from *Music Everywhere* by Theresa Armitage *et al.* Copyright by C. C. Birchard & Co. Reprinted and recorded by permission of The Birch Tree Group, Ltd. All rights reserved.

"So Long Farewell," music by Richard Rodgers, words by Oscar Hammerstein II. Copyright © 1959 by Richard Rodgers and Oscar Hammerstein II. Williamson Music Co., owner of publication and allied rights throughout the Western Hemisphere and Japan. All Rights Administered by Chappell & Co., Inc. International Copyright Secured ALL RIGHTS RESERVED. Used by Permission. Recording licensed through the Harry Fox Agency.

"So Long It's Been Good to Know You," originally "SO LONG It's

Been Good To Know Yuh" ("Dusty Old Dust"), words and music by Woody Guthrie. TRO - © Copyright 1940 (renewed 1968), 1950 (renewed 1978) and 1951 (renewed 1979) Folkways Music Publishers, Inc., New York, NY. Used by Permission. Recording licensed though the Harry Fox Agency.

"Some People," words by Tossi Aaron, music by M. Hauptmann, from *In Canon; Explorations of Familiar Canons for Voices, Recorders and Orff Instruments* by Erling Bisgaard in collaboration with Tossi Aaron. Copyright © 1978 by Magnamusic/Edition Wilhelm Hansen. Reprinted and recorded by permission of MMB Music, Inc. All rights reserved.

"Songmaker," words and music by Fred Willman, written in honor of Malvina Reynolds. Copyright © 1977 by Fred Willman. Reprinted and recorded by permission. All rights reserved.

"Table," a poem from *Sounds* by Wassily Kandinsky, translated and with an introduction by Elizabeth R. Napier. Copyright © 1981 by Yale University Press. All rights reserved. Reprinted by permission.

"Texas Tech Schnitzelbank," German folk tune, chart by Theodor W. Alexander. Chart reprinted by permission of Theodor W. Alexander. All rights reserved.

"This Is My County," words by Don Raye, music by Al Jacobs. © Copyright 1940, Shawnee Press, Inc.; Delaware Water Gap, PA 18327. U. S. Copyright Renewed 1968. Copyright Assigned to Shawnee Press, Inc. All Rights Reserved. Reprinted by permission. Recording licensed through the Harry Fox Agency.

"The Three Fishermen," originally "Three Jolly Fishermen," from *The Fireside Book of Fun and Game Songs*, collected and edited by Marie Winn, musical arrangements by Allan Miller. Copyright © 1974 by Marie Winn and Allan Miller. Reprinted and recorded by permission of SIMON & SCHUSTER, Inc. All rights reserved.

"The Unicorn," words and music by Shel Silverstein. TRO - © copyright 1962 and 1968 Hollis Music, Inc., New York, NY. Used by Permission. Recording licensed through the Harry Fox Agency.

"A Valentine Wish," words and music by Natalie Sleeth, from *Weekday Songbook*, copyright © 1977 by Hinshaw Music, Inc. Reprinted and recorded by permission. All rights reserved.

"Weave Me the Sunshine," words and music by Peter Yarrow, copyright © 1972 by Mary Beth Music. Excerpted, reprinted and recorded by permission.

"We're Off To See The Wizard," lyric by E. Y. Harburg, music by Harold Arlen. Copyright © 1939 (Renewed 1967) Metro-Goldwyn-Mayer Inc. All rights controlled and administered by Leo Feist, Inc. Reprinted by permission of Columbia Pictures Publications. Recording licensed through the Harry Fox Agency.

"The Wells Fargo Wagon" from *The Music Man* by Meredith Willson, © 1957, 1959 FRANK MUSIC CORP. and THE ESTATE OF MEREDITH WILLSON, © Renewed 1985, 1987 FRANK MUSIC CORP. and THE ESTATE OF MEREDITH WILLSON. International Copyright Secured. All Rights Reserved. Reprinted by permission of FRANK MUSIC CORP. Recording licensed through the Harry Fox Agency.

"Woke Up This Morning," copyright © 1975 by Chappell & Co., Inc. International Copyright Secured. ALL RIGHTS RESERVED. Used by Permission. Recording licensed through the Harry Fox Agency.

"You Can't Make A Turtle Come Out," words and music by Malvina Reynolds, from *Little Boxes and Other Handmade Songs* by Malvina Reynolds. © 1963 Schroder Music Co. (ASCAP). Reprinted and recorded by permission. All rights reserved.

Photo Credits

HRW photos by Bruce Buck pp. 104, 134–135, 143, 211; Elizabeth Hathon pp. 18, 92, 160, 179, 186, 197 all, 202 all, 208, 209, 228. Richard Haynes pp. 6, 14, 19, 20, 23 left, 34, 36, 38 all, 40, 41, 52, 67 all, 73, 77, 82, 86, 89, 108, 136, 137, 138, 158, 159 all, 198, 199, 213; Rodney C. Jones p. 70; Ken Karp pp. 60, 61, 62, 63, 76, 137, 195, 196, 198, 220; John Kelly p. 51; Ken Lax pp. 198, 199; John Lei pp. 192, 226, 227; Greg Schaler p. 27; Cliff Watts pp. 68, 69. pp. 4, 5, Nicholas Devore III/Bruce Coleman; p. 8, Culver Pictures; pp. 11, 12, Solomon R. Guggenheim Museum, NY, — Carmelo Guadagno & David Heald; p. 18 (center) Peter Vadnai/The Stock Market; (bottom) Bettmann Archive; p. 23 (center) Peter Krupenye; (right) Eric Levenson/The New York Baroque Dance Co.; p. 28, Lynton Gardner/The Museums at Stony Brook, 1985, Gift of Railway Express Agency, 1951; pp. 32, 33, 46, © Harry Jackson, Artist, © Wyoming Foundry Studios, Inc. 1964; p. 48, Francis Miller/ © Time-Life Inc.; p. 102, Martha Swope; p. 109, The Image Bank/Art Fotopolke; p. 113, Paul Meredith/Click/Chicago; p. 116, Scala/Art Resource; p. 118, Donald Smetzer/Click/Chicago; pp. 122, 123, Tom Hollyman/Photo Researchers; pp. 124, 125, Martin Weaver/ Woodfin Camp; p. 126, © 1982 Michael Furman/The Stock Market; p. 127, Timothy Eagen/Woodfin Camp; p. 128, Memory Shop; p. 145, Balthazar Korab/The Image Bank; p. 170, David Brownell/The Image Bank; p. 171, Bill Warren; p. 177, Dick Smith; p. 181 (top) David Hiser/The Image Bank; (bottom) Guiraudon/Art Resource; p. 182, Marc & Evelyne Bernheim/ Woodfin Camp; p. 183 (top) Margot Granitsas/Photo Researchers; (bottom) Photo by Geoffrey Clements, Collection of the Whitney Museum; p. 199 (bottom) © Kate Bader; p. 214, © 1985 Don King/The Image Bank; p. 223, John Lawlor/The Stock Market; p. 229, Art Resource/The Jewish Museum, NY, — Richard Haynes/HRW from the Jewish Calendar; pp. 230, 231, Susan Leavines/Photo Researchers; pp. 232, 233, Nicholas Devore III/ Bruce Coleman; p. 235, Ted Thai/Time.

Art Credits

pp. 6, 42, 58, 59, 106, 107, 124 Lisa Cypher; pp. 7, 86, 87 Michael Conway; pp. 16, 44, 147 Debbie Dieneman; pp. 24, 25 Nina Winters; pp. 30, 138, 188, 189 Marilyn Janovitz; pp. 40, 100, 101, 149, 193, 217 Sally Springer; pp. 126, 127 Steve Cieslawski; pp. 168, 169 Carolyn Virgil; p. 187 Thomas Thorspecken; pp. 9, 130, 144 Represented by Publisher's Graphics, Inc./ Paul Harvey; pp. 21, 50 Helen Davies; pp. 71, 120, 216 James Watling; pp. 111, 221 Jane Kendall; pp. 136, 140, 141, 142, 143 Eulala Conner; p. 161 Jean Helmer; pp. 179, 201 Patti Boyd; p. 166 Steven Schindler; pp. 15, 67, 81 Represented by Philip M. Veloric/ Lane Yerkes; p. 22 Represented by Mulvey Associates, Inc./ John Killgrew; p. 82 Sally Schaedler; pp. 85, 114, 115 Les Gray; p. 224 Thomas Noonan; pp. 26, 27, 55, 69, 78 Represented by Asciutto Art Representatives/ Jan Pyk; pp. 56, 57, 89, 96, 97, 98, 99, 104, 139 Sal Murdocca; pp. 154, 156, 157, 158, 159 Anthony Accardo; pp. 204, 205, 206, 207 Loretta Lustig; p. 35 Represented by Lou Gullatt/ Guy Kingsbery; pp. 37, 53, 94, 152 Represented by Bookmakers, Inc./ Michele Noiset; p. 113 Carolyn Croll; p. 75 Represented by Carol Bancroft and Friends/ Andrea Eberbach; pp. 164, 165 Jackie Rogers; pp. 172, 174 Susan Dodge; p. 218 Yoshi Miyaki.

All Table of Contents page art for Grades 2 through 8 rendered by Susan Dodge/Represented by Carol Bancroft and Friends.

All technical art prepared by Karen Hoodes, Jimmie Hudson, and Bud Musso. All black and white instrument art prepared by Jimmie Hudson, Brian Molloy, and Bud Musso.

Alphabetical Index of Music

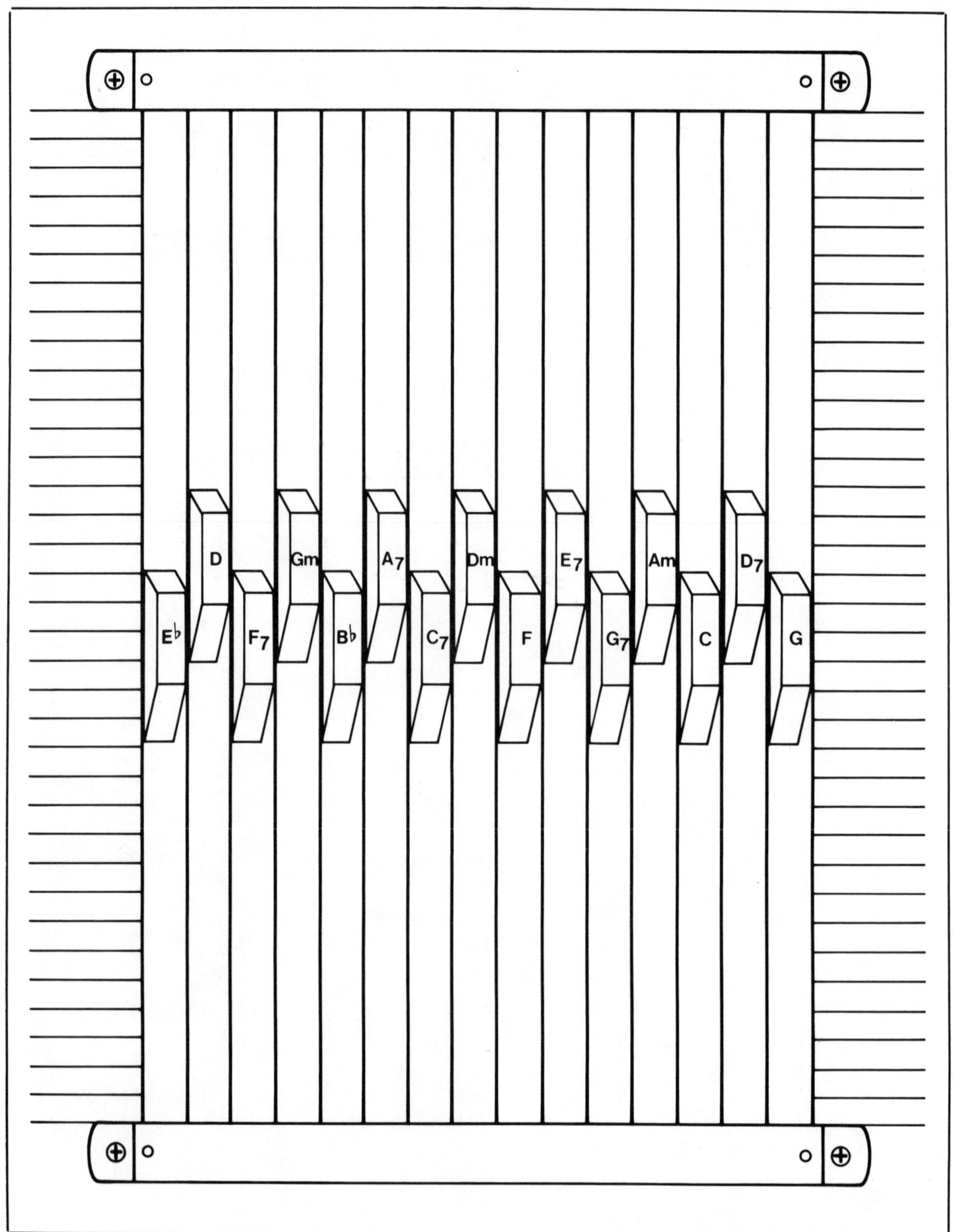

D
Gm
A7
Dm
E7
Am
D7
E♭
F7
B♭
C7
F
G7
C
G